Hague Yearbook of International Law
Annuaire de La Haye de droit international

Hague Yearbook of International Law 2016

Editor-in-Chief

Prof. Jure Vidmar

Vice-Editor-in-Chief

Dr. Ruth A. Bonnevalle-Kok

Editorial Board
Dr. Julian Arato, Dr. Nikos Lavranos, Dr. Daniel Peat, Dr. Daniel Rietiker

Editorial Assistant
Leonor Vulpe Albari

Email address
hagueyearbook@gmail.com

Website
http://hagueyearbook.weebly.com/

Advisory Board
Serge Brammertz (*Prosecutor of the International Criminal Tribunal for the Former Yugoslavia (ICTY)*) – Antônio Cançado Trindade (*Judge at the International Court of Justice (ICJ)*) – Jacomijn J. van Haersolte-van Hof (*Advocate (advocaat) at HaersolteHof and arbitrator (The Netherlands)*) – Peter Hilpold (*University Professor at Innsbruck University (Austria)*) – Bruno Simma ((*former*) *Judge at the International Court of Justice (ICJ)*) – Olivia Swaak-Goldman ((*former*) *Head, International Relations Task Force, Office of the Prosecutor, International Criminal Court (ICC)*)

The titles published in this series are listed at *brill.com/aaaa*

HAGUE YEARBOOK OF INTERNATIONAL LAW

ANNUAIRE DE LA HAYE DE DROIT INTERNATIONAL

VOLUME 29
2016

Edited by

Jure Vidmar, Ruth Bonnevalle-Kok *et al.*

BRILL
NIJHOFF

LEIDEN | BOSTON

Typeface for the Latin, Greek, and Cyrillic scripts: "Brill". See and download: brill.com/brill-typeface.

ISSN 0167-6660
ISBN 978-90-04-39361-5 (hardback)
ISBN 978-90-04-39362-2 (e-book)

Copyright 2018 by Koninklijke Brill NV, Leiden, The Netherlands.
Koninklijke Brill NV incorporates the imprints Brill, Brill Hes & De Graaf, Brill Nijhoff, Brill Rodopi, Brill Sense, Hotei Publishing, mentis Verlag, Verlag Ferdinand Schöningh and Wilhelm Fink Verlag.
All rights reserved. No part of this publication may be reproduced, translated, stored in a retrieval system, or transmitted in any form or by any means, electronic, mechanical, photocopying, recording or otherwise, without prior written permission from the publisher.
Authorization to photocopy items for internal or personal use is granted by Koninklijke Brill NV provided that the appropriate fees are paid directly to The Copyright Clearance Center, 222 Rosewood Drive, Suite 910, Danvers, MA 01923, USA. Fees are subject to change.

This book is printed on acid-free paper and produced in a sustainable manner.

Contents

Editorial
Brexit as an Integration of Legal Orders   VII

1 International Humanitarian Law in the Jurisprudence of African Human Rights Treaty Bodies   1
    Brian Sang YK

2 Against the Law: Turkey's Annexation Efforts in Occupied Cyprus   55
    Ilias Kouskouvelis and Kalliopi Chainoglou

3 Putting the Nail in the Coffin: Isn't it Time to Let the European Consensus Doctrine Put an End to the Use of the Death Penalty in the United States?   103
    Rebecca Huertas

4 The Application of Bilateral Investment Treaties in Annexed Territories: Whose BITs are Applicable in Crimea after its Annexation?   133
    Katharina Wende

5 The Estrada Doctrine and the English Courts: Determining the Legitimate Government of a State in the Absence of Explicit Recognition of Governments   171
    Leonor Vulpe Albari

Editorial
Brexit as an Integration of Legal Orders

The common theme of this volume is the integration of legal orders. Brian Sang discusses how international human rights law is implemented and interpreted by the African Commission on Human and Peoples' Rights, the African Court on Human and Peoples' Rights, and the African Committee of Experts on the Rights and Welfare of the Child. Ilias Kouskouvelis and Kalliopi Chainoglou address the problem of legality and illegality of certain exercises of sovereign powers in an occupied territory.

Katharina Wende addresses another difficult question of occupation: whose bilateral investment treaties (BITs) apply in Crimea, Russia's or Ukraine's? Although the occupation of Crimea is illegal, Russia is in effective control of the territory and has certain rights and duties under international law regarding territorial administration. But where precisely lie the boundaries of such rights and duties when it comes to bilateral treaty obligations? Rebecca Huertas demonstrates how the European Court of Human Rights (ECtHR) has developed the consensus doctrine between the forty-seven states party to the European Convention on Human Rights (ECHR) on difficult societal questions, and analyses, with reference to international and United States (US) constitutional law, and whether this doctrine could be used by the US Supreme Court to determine the legal status of the death penalty in fifty US states.

Leonor Vulpe Albari analyses the United Kingdom's (UK) newest doctrine of recognition of governments. Despite the well-known Estrada doctrine, states may nevertheless need to indicate in some circumstances which competing authority they see as the legitimate representative of a foreign state. A great deal may depend on this determination, including the question of which individuals are entitled to immunities and which authority has access to the assets of a certain state. This somewhat neglected question of international legal doctrine has resurfaced with recent developments in Libya and Syria, among other situations. An explicit or an implicit choice to deal with one competing authority but not another also triggers difficult questions of a relationship between international and domestic law. The original choice of the authority is domestic, while its consequences are both international and domestic.

In 2016, the UK held a referendum on exiting the European Union (EU). The choice to exit won with a roughly 52 percent majority of those who voted. The process which has been wrongly termed as Brexit (it is the whole UK, not only Great Britain that is leaving the EU), is an exemplary question of interaction of legal orders, that of EU law, international (treaty) law and UK public law. This editorial will seek to elucidate this entanglement of legal orders, question the mechanics of Article 50 of the Treaty on European Union (TEU) and argues that the ECHR serves as a safety-net for certain categories of EU citizens should negotiations fail to lead to an agreement between the UK and the EU.

Brexit was legally set in motion on 29 March 2017 when the UK Government triggered Article 50 of TEU. Article 50 gives an EU member state the right to exit the Union. Once it is triggered, a two-year clock starts ticking. In these two years, the future relationship between the EU and the exiting state needs to be negotiated. If no agreement is reached, the exiting state is completely severed from EU treaties after the two-year period expires. For the UK, the guillotine therefore falls on 29 March 2019.

The EU is a complex and constitutionalized legal order. It is established on the basis of international treaties – TEU and the Treaty on the Functioning of the European Union (TFEU) – but these operate differently than ordinary treaties of public international law. EU is a self-contained supranational legal regime and the treaties have both vertical and horizontal effect. This means that unlike other international treaties – including those regulating international human rights law – EU treaties do not merely apply in relations between states. An individual can derive their rights directly from TEU and TFEU, and an individual or other non-state actors can also have obligations directly under EU law, not via attribution to states as is the case in public international law.

The UK's EU exit thus also means that many rights enjoyed by certain EU citizens will be extinguished. It is true that EU law is not a human rights treaty regime, but prima facie an economic and political association. Yet, the EU and its member states are committed to the respect of human rights and democracy, all member states are parties to the ECHR, and the termination of certain rights stemming from EU law could well lead to violations of the European Convention. Furthermore, it is questionable whether the process of Brexit as such does not lead to certain violations of ECHR and fundamental democratic principles on which post-WWII Europe has been built.

Article 50 and 'democratic' decision-making

The Brexit referendum held on 23 June 2016 was formally not legally binding and did not have any self-executing effects. It was a political decision rather than a legal obligation that the UK triggered Article 50 TEU. But was the majoritarian method of decision-making the correct way of ascertaining the will of the people at the Brexit referendum? Notably, the choice to exit was supported by 52 percent of all votes cast, at a turnout of 71.8 percent. In absolute figures, this means that Brexit was supported by around 37.3 percent of all those eligible to vote in the referendum. Even in terms of relative majorities, the exit choice was prominently supported in England (53.4 percent) and Wales (52.5 percent), while exit was determinedly rejected in Scotland (62 percent) and Northern Ireland (55.8 percent). Scotland and Northern Ireland were thus outvoted by England and Wales which together represent nearly 90 percent of the UK's population.

Prior to the Brexit referendum, the Scottish National Party (SNP) put forward a proposal that a decision on exiting the EU should not only be a matter of a UK-wide majoritarian vote but ought to require support in all four constitutive countries: England, Wales, Scotland and Northern Ireland. If such a solution were implemented, Brexit would have been rejected. The vote for Brexit was thus based on majoritarian decision-making whereby two devolved units – Scotland and Northern Ireland – were simply outvoted.

Quite differently, in the *Quebec case*, the Supreme Court of Canada took a stance against majoritarian decision-making at territorial referenda. The Court declared that a successful vote for independence would not create a legal entitlement to independence, neither under Canadian constitutional law nor under international law. At the same time, the Canadian constitutional principle of democracy requires, said the Court, that the will of the people cannot be ignored. An affirmative vote should thus lead to negotiations on the future legal status of a territory where several options are possible, including a wider autonomy without independence. Furthermore, the Supreme Court of Canada noted that many groups within Quebec vociferously opposed secession, including the indigenous peoples and most English-speakers in the province. According to the Court, Quebec's path to independence would not have been just and legitimate in the circumstances of majoritarian outvoting.

The reasoning of the Supreme Court of Canada clearly adopts the position that a democratic will of the people on territorial matters should not be expressed by a simple majority of all votes cast and by outvoting the opponents. Rather, a territorial referendum is a mechanism of deliberative democracy. If a majority of all votes cast decides in favour of a change in territorial status, negotiations need to take place without a pre-determined outcome, and it needs to be ensured that the will of the people is not mistaken for simple majority rule.

Pursuant to the Quebec deliberative model, the Brexit referendum gave the UK government the mandate to negotiate its future relationship with the EU, but in so doing the UK would need to take into account the interests of Scotland, Northern Ireland, non-UK EU citizens residing in the UK, and UK citizens residing in other EU member states. But is this really compatible with Article 50 TEU?

Article 50 in principle supports the deliberative model, as it specifies that within two years the EU and the UK (in this case) need to negotiate their future relationship. The problem is, however, that Article 50 requires the negotiations to begin only after the notification has been given, and then sets a two-year guillotine. The exiting state is thus pushed into an unequal position which is hardly compatible with the deliberative model of the *Quebec case*. If the UK does not manage to secure sufficient guarantees for Scotland, Northern Ireland and its own nationals residing in other EU member states, the UK nevertheless needs to exit. At the same time, Article 50 does not foresee negotiations before giving a withdrawal notification at which moment the clock starts ticking. The outcome of the Article 50 mechanics is that the deliberative model for a change in territorial legal status is severely disadvantaged and majoritarian principles effectively favoured.

So, we can criticize UK government for triggering Article 50 on the basis of a pure majoritarian vote, and overriding the will of the people in two constitutionally devolved units: Northern Ireland and Scotland. But at the same time, it is questionable whether the Article 50 mechanics actually support any other solutions. Once triggered, it sets off the two-year guillotine, regardless of the outcome of the negotiations. This may make the process of withdrawal efficient, but efficiency does not always yield comprehensive results. Article 50 was simply designed to be in the TEU as a formalistic safety valve; it was not designed to be used.

Extinguishing the rights stemming from EU citizenship

The standstill in negotiations and the two-year-guillotine mechanics of Article 50 TEU make the no deal option a realistic possibility. In this case, the body of EU law would no longer be opposable between the UK and the remaining EU member states. This would, *inter alia*, lead to the loss of EU citizenship rights and have adverse effects on current non-UK EU citizens resident in the UK and UK citizens currently resident in other EU member states.

Article 20(1) of TFEU provides: "Citizenship of the Union is hereby established. Every person holding the nationality of a Member State shall be a citizen of the Union. Citizenship of the Union shall be additional to and not replace national citizenship." EU citizenship, among other things, underpins the free movement of persons within the EU, including the right to take up residency and work in another member state.

The combined number of non-UK EU citizens in the UK and UK citizens in other EU member states is 4.5 million. The figure does not include those non-EU citizens who are family members of EU citizens presently exercising their free movement rights to whom such benefits of EU citizenship are also extended. The loss of EU citizenship could thus have adverse effects for a great number of people and it may also affect their right to family life under the ECHR.

As Article 20 TFEU specifies, Union citizenship depends on citizenship of a member state. After Brexit, UK citizenship will no longer 'carry' EU citizenship and the rights stemming from EU citizenship will be lost to UK nationals. This means, inter alia, that UK nationals will no longer exercise free movement rights in the EU and vice versa, EU citizenship will no longer generate any rights in the UK.

Pursuant to Article 50 TEU the exact terms of withdrawal of a member state from the EU ought to be negotiated. The status of persons presently exercising free movement rights will inevitably become one of the most important questions to tackle in the course of negotiations. Even if negotiations failed, the ECHR would kick in and afford protection to those UK citizens who are already resident in other EU member states and those non-UK EU citizens who are already resident in the EU. Analogies could be drawn to the case of *Kurić v Slovenia* before the European Court of Human Rights (ECtHR).

Upon achieving independence, Slovenia denied the continued right to residency to a number of citizens of other states emerging in the territory of the former Socialist Federal Republic of Yugoslavia (SFRY) who had, at the time of the former federation, established their permanent residency in Slovenia. According to the ECtHR withdrawing the right to permanent residency to these foreign citizens upon independence was, *inter alia*, a violation of the Convention right to private and family life.

The Court recalled that the ECHR did not give a citizen of a party to the Convention a right of residence in another party state. However, under some circumstances, restrictions on the right to residence can interfere with the Convention right to private and family life. As the Court put it in the case of Slovenia: "[P]rior to Slovenia's declaration of independence, [the applicants] had been lawfully residing in Slovenia for several years, and? had, as former SFRY citizens, enjoyed a wide range of social and political rights." (*Kurić v Slovenia*, para 356). The Court then continued:

> [A]n alien lawfully residing in a country may wish to continue living in that country without necessarily acquiring its citizenship. As shown by the difficulties faced by the applicants, for many years, in obtaining a valid residence permit, the Slovenian legislature failed to enact provisions aimed at permitting former SFRY citizens holding the citizenship of one of the other republics to regularise their residence status if they had chosen not to become Slovenian citizens or had failed to do so. Such provisions would not have undermined the legitimate aims of controlling the residence of aliens or creating a corpus of Slovenian citizens, or both. (*Kurić v Slovenia*, para 357).

Following this logic, once you have legally established permanent residency, you keep the right of residence, even if the legal status of either your home or your host state changes and, as a result of this change, your new citizenship status alone would no longer give you a right to residence. What matters is that you have acquired the right before the change in territorial status. It is notable that the Court established that non-citizen residents enjoy this guarantee under the Convention right to private and family life *in their own right*; it does not depend on, for example, family relationship with a citizen of the host state.

Following the *Kurić* doctrine, it appears that regardless of the outcome of the EU-UK negotiations, UK nationals residing in other EU member states and non-UK EU citizens residing in the UK will retain their right to residence. The ECHR steps in and protects the right of residence of those lawfully residing in the territories covered by EU law on the critical date. Importantly, this effect only 'cements' the existing residence rights but does not extend the applicability of EU law to the UK after Brexit, nor does it give UK citizens a post-Brexit EU citizenship. It only means that the already acquired residency rights could not be lost. It is important to note the ECHR remains directly effective in UK domestic law even after Brexit. The Human Rights Act, which incorporates the Convention and makes it a body of UK public law, will remain unaffected in this process, although it may well be challenged in the future.

In order to establish eligibility of those entitled to benefit from the *Kurić* doctrine, a critical date will need to be set. Since the Brexit referendum is formally not legally binding, nothing had been modified in law until a formal notice of withdrawal had been given. Pursuant to Article 50, the notice itself somewhat modifies the legal status of the exiting state within the EU, but the UK is currently nevertheless still an EU member state. Two critical dates are now possible for establishing the residency status: 29 March 2017 or 29 March 2019. Since the UK retains the status of an EU member state until the moment of exit, the latter date is more plausible. The critical date for determining residency status of non-UK EU citizens in the UK and of UK citizens in other EU member states will be 29 March 2019. Those exercising their free-movement rights under EU law on that date will be able to retain those rights to the extent applicable at the moment of exit. But this will no longer be free movement under EU law; rather, it is merely a continuation of pre-established residency status. As an effect of the ECHR, certain aspects of EU citizenship will merely remain frozen in time, with continued effectiveness in domestic law of the UK and member states of EU-27. For some categories of people, EU law governing Union citizenship will thus continue to live within the domestic legal systems of 28 states as intertemporal law as of 29 March 2019, but only with the status of national law.

An interaction of legal orders, indeed. It reminds us that EU law, while a self-contained legal regime, is at the end of the day based on international treaty law, that the ECHR, which is not a part of EU law, nevertheless interferes with EU law, and that the effects of international law are both international and domestic.

    Prof Jure Vidmar
    Chair of Public International Law, Maastricht University
    Editor-in-Chief, the Hague Yearbook of International Law

1 International Humanitarian Law in the Jurisprudence of African Human Rights Treaty Bodies

Brian Sang YK*

Abstract

Questions concerning the legal status, role, and effect of international humanitarian law (IHL) in the jurisprudence of African human rights treaty bodies remain little examined. They have not received as much, as detailed, or as sustained attention as that given to the same questions in the practice of other human rights treaty mechanisms. This article seeks to fill this gap by assessing how African human rights treaty bodies have interacted with IHL in their practice, and how they can be used to induce compliance with IHL. It analyses trends in the use of IHL by the African Commission on Human and Peoples' Rights, the African Court on Human and Peoples' Rights, and the African Committee of Experts on the Rights and Welfare of the Child. Also explored is the relevant prospective role of the African Court of Justice and Human Rights as the African Union's principal judicial organ. This article demonstrates that, though offering an enabling basis for the co-application of IHL and human rights law, the African human rights system's protective potential is yet to have full scope due to an acute lack of systematic analysis of the nature and effect of IHL-human rights law relations. Nonetheless, recent developments like the African Commission's General Comment No. 3 on the right to life indicate a systemic turn towards greater recognition of the utility of IHL for the African human rights system.

1 Introduction

Most, if not all, human rights treaties have established bodies that are mandated to monitor and supervise the implementation of the respec-

---

* Lecturer, Faculty of Law, Egerton University.

Jure Vidmar, Ruth Kok, *et al.* (eds.), *Hague Yearbook of International Law 2016*.
© 2018 Koninklijke Brill NV. ISBN 978-90-04-39361-5. pp. 1-53.

tive treaty obligations by States parties thereto.[1] In the execution of their roles, these treaty bodies have frequently adopted outward-looking approaches by having regard to sources of law beyond the scope of the relevant human rights instrument.[2] International humanitarian law ('IHL') is one of the sources of international law that has featured in the work of various human rights treaty bodies, particularly in relation to situations of armed conflict in which human rights violations occur.[3] This has given rise to a substantial amount of scholarly interest in and debate about the conceptual and normative relations between IHL and human rights law. A voluminous body of work has emerged on the interplay between these two sets of laws and their respective norms, with a key focus on how they have shaped one another's content and how they have been applied by judicial and quasi-judicial bodies.[4]

However, there is a critical gap in this debate and the related discourse: the status, role and effect of IHL in the jurisprudence of African human rights bodies have not been the subject of as frequent or detailed attention as that given to similar inquiries in the practice of other human rights treaty mechanisms.[5] Only very recently has there been an effort to systematically analyse how the African human rights system interacts with IHL.[6] It has rightly been observed that, at a conceptual as well as ac-

---

1   H. Keller and G. Ulfstein (eds.), *UN Human Rights Treaty Bodies: Law and Legitimacy* (Cambridge University Press, Cambridge, 2012); C.M. Cerna (ed.), *Regional Human Rights Systems* (Routledge, New York, 2014).

2   M. Killander, 'Interpreting Regional Human Rights Treaties', 7 *SUR - International Journal on Human Rights* (2010) p. 145.

3   See B. Sang-YK, 'International Humanitarian Law in the Work of Regional Human Rights Courts: African and Comparative Trends', 4 *Journal of Comparative Law in Africa* (2017) pp. 1-33; L. van den Herik and H. Duffy, 'Human Rights Bodies and International Humanitarian Law: Common but Differentiated Approaches', in C.M. Buckley, A. Donald and P. Leach (eds.), *Towards Convergence in International Human Rights Law: Approaches of Regional and International Systems* (Brill, Leiden, 2016) pp. 366-406.

4   G. Oberleitner, *Human Rights in Armed Conflict* (Cambridge University Press, Cambridge, 2015) pp. 2-3; D. Jinks et al. (eds.), *Applying International Humanitarian Law in Judicial and Quasi-Judicial Bodies: International and Domestic Aspects* (Springer, The Hague, 2014) pp. 219-287.

5   Sang-YK, *supra* note 3, p. 2; Oberleitner, *supra* note 4, p. 312.

6   B. Sang-YK, 'The Approach of African Human Rights Treaty Bodies to International Humanitarian Law: Normative Basis and Institutional Practice', *African Yearbook on International Humanitarian Law* (2017) pp. 1-36; F. Viljoen, 'The Relationship between International Human Rights and Humanitarian Law in the African Human Rights System: An Institutional Approach', in E. de Wet and J. Kleffner (eds.), *Convergence and Conflicts of Human Rights and International Humanitarian Law in*

ademic level, Africa "maintains a very low profile in the global debate on [IHL]."[7] As a result, many important questions concerning IHL-human rights law relations in the African regional context remain less clear or unanswered. What is the legal status of IHL in the African human rights system? What is the precise nature of the relationship between IHL and the African Charter on Human and Peoples' Rights[8] (hereafter 'African Charter') as well as other African human rights treaties, and how have the relevant treaty bodies sought to elaborate it? How and to what effect has IHL been applied in the practice of African human rights treaty bodies? Cumulatively, these questions seek to inquire about the legal status, role and effect of IHL in the jurisprudence of African human rights treaty bodies.

This article examines the conceptual and practical aspects of the application of IHL in the jurisprudence of African human rights treaty bodies. Its objective is two-fold: (a) to contribute towards filling the knowledge gap by clarifying the status, role, and effect of IHL in the African human rights system; and (b) to promote a nuanced understanding of how African human rights treaty bodies have been or can better be utilised to induce compliance with IHL. In pursuit of these ends, this article systematically analyses the practice of the African Commission on Human and Peoples' Rights (hereafter 'African Commission'), the African Court of Human and Peoples' Rights (hereafter 'African Court') and, to a lesser extent, the African Committee of Experts on the Rights and Welfare of the Child (hereafter 'African Children's Rights Committee'). It also explores the future role of the African Court of Justice and Human Rights, which is expected to be the principal judicial organ of the African Union ('AU'), in implementing IHL.

In order to achieve its two-fold object, the content of this article will be structured as follows. After this introduction, part 2 provides a concise overview of the present state of the debate on the complex relationship between IHL and human rights law. This informs the thesis, developed in the part 3, that the African human rights system has a unique capacity to

---

    Military Operations (Pretoria University Law Press, Pretoria, 2014) pp. 303-332; M. Hailbronner, 'Laws in Conflict: The Relationship between Human Rights and International Humanitarian Law under the African Charter on Human and Peoples' Rights', 16 *African Human Rights Law Journal* (2016) pp. 339-364.

7   G. Waschefort, 'Africa and International Humanitarian Law: The More Things Change, the More They Stay the Same', 92 *International Review of the Red Cross* (2016) p. 593.

8   21 I.L.M. 58 (27 June 1981).

promote fundamental standards of humanity during armed conflict and other violence situations. In part 4, the article surveys the African Commission's IHL-related practice, with a focus on questions relating to: (a) the legal basis for and approach to applying IHL; (b) the co-application of IHL and human rights law; and (c) the advance from co-application to concurrent violations of IHL and human rights law. This is followed, in part 5, by a review of IHL in the work of the African Court, with an emphasis on its jurisdiction and practice. Attention is also given, in part 6, to the future role of the African Court of Justice and Human Rights in applying IHL. In part 7, the article critically analyses the status, role and effect of IHL in the jurisprudence of African human rights treaty bodies by focusing on thematic issues drawn from their cumulative practice. These are then summarised in the concluding remarks in part 8.

2   Conceptual and Normative Interactions between IHL and Human Rights Law

In order to understand the status and effect of IHL in the jurisprudence of African human rights treaty bodies, it is necessary to first consider the conceptual and normative interactions between IHL and human rights law. Being both complex and contested, the relationships and interactions between these two sets of law are best analysed at the legal and operational levels. Accordingly, this section provides a concise overview of the development and current status of the principal notions in which the interplay of IHL and human rights law is often contextualised: *lex specialis*, complementarity and systemic integration.[9] How these understandings of the IHL-human rights law interactions have been elaborated by international and regional (quasi-)judicial bodies offer an instructive background for assessing the related practice of the African human rights system.

2.1   *A Brief History of a Normative Relationship*
IHL and human rights law are two systems of law that have different doctrinal origins, derive from disparate normative sources and arose

---

[9] S. McCosker, 'The "Interoperability" of International Humanitarian Law and Human Rights Law: Evaluating the Legal Tools Available to Navigate their Relationship', in A. Byrnes, M. Hayashi and C. Michaelsen (eds.), *International Law in the New Age of Globalization* (Nijhoff, Leiden, 2013) pp. 145-177.

from distinctive historical particularities.[10] The two sets of law developed on parallel tracks of conceptual evolution and were informed by discrete institutional praxis.[11] While human rights law in its current form gained prominence in the post-Second World War period, IHL has more ancient roots as it is the normative progeny of the laws of war which developed from the customs and usages of war.[12] IHL and human rights law also discharge their protective functions in dissimilar ways.[13] Yet despite these differences, both sets of law evolved with the aim of protecting individuals and groups by preventing or reducing the impact of threats to human life or dignity.[14] Given this common purpose, the separate paths on which IHL and human rights law developed have gradually begun to converge.

Starting in the 1960s, there was a strategic move towards recognising the common objectives of and close normative link between IHL and human rights law as a basis for strengthening the protection of victims of armed conflict.[15] It was in this period that the continued application of the most fundamental human rights during armed conflict was emphasised and promoted. As a result of the increasing interest of State and non-State actors in better securing the protection of human rights in armed conflict, a crucial resolution was adopted in 1968 during the International Conference on Human Rights in Tehran.[16] This resolution was

10   T. Meron, 'On the Inadequate Reach of Humanitarian and Human Rights Law and the Need for a New Instrument', 77 *American Journal of International Law* (1983) p. 594.
11   R. Kolb, 'Human Rights Law and International Humanitarian Law between 1945 and the Aftermath of the Tehran Conference in 1968', in R. Kolb and G. Gaggioli (eds.), *Research Handbook on Human Rights and Humanitarian Law* (Edward Elgar, Cheltenham, 2013) pp. 35-52.
12   D. Schindler and J. Toman, *The Laws of Armed Conflicts* (Nijhoff, Leiden, 2004) p. 365.
13   C. Droege, 'Elective Affinities? Human Rights and Humanitarian Law', 90 *International Review of the Red Cross* (2008) p. 521.
14   *Decision on Precautionary Measures (Detainees at Guantanamo Bay, Cuba)*, 12 March 2002, IACtHR, Precautionary Measures, 2002 41 I.L.M. p. 432; D. Schindler, 'The International Committee of the Red Cross and Human Rights', 208 *International Review of the Red Cross* (1979) p. 9.
15   R. Kolb, 'The Main Epochs of Modern International Humanitarian Law Since 1864 and their Related Dominant Legal Constructions', in K.M. Larsen, C.G. Cooper and G. Nystuen (eds.), *Searching for a 'Principle of Humanity' in International Humanitarian Law* (Cambridge University Press, Cambridge, 2015) p. 51.
16   International Conference on Human Rights, Resolution XXIII, 'Human Rights in Armed Conflicts', adopted by the International Conference on Human Rights, Tehran, 12 May 1968.

subsequently reaffirmed by the UN General Assembly in a Resolution entitled 'Respect for Human Rights in Armed Conflict'.[17] Coupled with the work of influential activists and scholars, the Tehran Resolution and the General Assembly Resolution had significant impact on the drafting of the Additional Protocols to the 1949 Geneva Conventions, which integrate human rights norms that have "influenced, in ways both subtle and profound, the application of IHL."[18]

The mutual influence and gradual move towards convergence of IHL and human rights law is most clearly illustrated by the tendency of human rights instruments to express "concepts typical of humanitarian law and vice versa".[19] This development has been welcomed by some and regarded with suspicion by others. For the most part, however, IHL and human rights law are considered to be complementary and mutually supportive, rather than incompatible and mutually exclusive,[20] a position that owes much to the jurisprudence of the International Court of Justice (hereafter 'ICJ'). In its *Wall* advisory opinion, the ICJ explained that some matters may fall to be determined by IHL, others by human rights, and others by both sets of law.[21] This has informed the view that rules belonging to both IHL and human rights law "can indeed be applied and interpreted in light of one another when they provide rules in areas that are common to both."[22] Even so, while this co-application is supported by the practice of international courts and tribunals as well as human rights treaty bodies, the articulation of how the two sets of law interact has been contentious.[23] The most controversial aspect of the interrelation-

---

17   UN General Assembly, Resolution 2444 of 1968 (19 December 1968).
18   J.D. Ohlin, 'The Inescapable Collision', in J.D. Ohlin (ed.), *Theoretical Boundaries of Armed Conflict and Human Rights* (Cambridge University Press, Cambridge, 2016) p. 16.
19   R. Iguyovwe, 'The Inter-play between International Humanitarian Law and International Human Rights Law', in A.Z. Borda (ed.), *International Humanitarian Law and the International Red Cross and Red Crescent Movement* (Routledge, New York, 2012) p. 22.
20   UN Human Rights Council, *Fundamental Standards of Humanity, Report of the Secretary-General*, UN Doc. A/HRC/8/14 (2008).
21   *Legal Consequences of the Construction of a Wall in the Occupied Palestinian Territory*, 9 July 2004, ICJ, Advisory Opinion, I.C.J. Reports 2004, p. 178, para. 106.
22   G. Giacca, *Economic, Social and Cultural Rights in Armed Conflict* (Oxford University Press, Oxford, 2014) p. 165.
23   A. Clapham, 'The Complex Relationship between the Geneva Conventions and International Human Rights Law', in A. Clapham, P. Gaeta and M. Sassòli (eds.), *The 1949 Geneva Conventions: A Commentary* (Oxford University Press, Oxford, 2016) pp. 701-735.

ship between IHL and human rights law concerns how conflicts between their respective competing norms should be resolved.[24]

2.2 Complex and Contextual Interactions: Competing Claims of Priority, Contested Visions of Complementarity

The *Nuclear Weapons* advisory opinion of the ICJ is arguably the most influential judicial decision in which the question of the interaction between IHL and human rights law was considered by an international court.[25] While affirming that "the right not arbitrarily to be deprived of one's life" enshrined in Article 6 of the International Covenant on Civil and Political Rights (hereafter 'ICCPR') also applies in armed conflict, the ICJ enunciated the *lex specialis* concept as determinative of what would constitute an arbitrary deprivation of life in that context.[26] In the sense used by the ICJ, the relationship between IHL and human rights law is one of general law to special law in which IHL, as the special law "which is designed to regulate the conduct of hostilities", takes normative precedence over human rights law.[27] Thus the ICJ used *lex specialis* to assert the primacy of the IHL-specific norm relating to permissible killing over the analogous and more restrictive human rights norm.

These two opinions of the ICJ reflect competing visions of the role and use of *lex specialis* to navigate IHL-human rights law relations; one seeks partial modification, the other wholesale exclusion of the general norm. Hence, the precise implication of the use to which *lex specialis* was deployed by the ICJ has been a matter of much debate. The matter is further complicated by the ICJ's avoidance of *lex specialis* to clarify the interplay of IHL and human rights law in its subsequent *Armed Activities* judgment.[28] Save for the Inter-American Commission on Human Rights

---

24 M. Milanović, 'Norm Conflicts, International Humanitarian Law, and Human Rights Law', in O. Ben-Naftali (ed.), *International Humanitarian Law and International Human Rights Law* (Oxford University Press, Oxford, 2011) pp. 95-128.
25 *Legality of the Threat or Use of Nuclear Weapons*, 8 July 1996, ICJ, Advisory Opinion, I.C.J. Reports 1996, p. 240.
26 *Ibid.*, para. 25.
27 M. Milanovic, 'The Lost Origins of *Lex Specialis*: Rethinking the Relationship between Human Rights and International Humanitarian Law', in J.D. Ohlin (ed.), *Theoretical Boundaries of Armed Conflict and Human Rights* (Cambridge University Press, Cambridge, 2016) pp. 83-84.
28 *Armed Activities on the Territory of the Congo (Democratic Republic of the Congo* v. *Uganda)*, 19 December 2005, ICJ, Judgement, I.C.J. Reports 2005, pp. 242-3, para. 216.

in two isolated decisions,[29] none of the international or regional courts and tribunals have used *lex specialis* to analyse and elaborate how and to what extent IHL interacts with human rights law. Academic commentary has therefore sought to fill the void left by the lack of judicial guidance. A large body of work has since emerged in which the use of *lex specialis*, in the context of IHL and human rights law, is extensively debated and critiqued.[30]

In sum, three broad theories, albeit conceptualised in diverse and overlapping ways, are used to explain the interaction between IHL and human rights law: separation, complementarity, and integration.[31] Drawing on the historical and operational dissimilarities between IHL and human rights law, separationists have invoked *lex specialis* to assert that IHL is always the more specific law in armed conflict and thus overrides human rights law.[32] In contrast, complementarity theory posits the co-application of IHL and human rights law by holding that *lex specialis* is a context-specific tool and so, depending on the circumstances, either IHL or human rights law can offer the appropriate norm for optimal protection.[33] For its part, integration theory posits that, given the extensive integration of IHL and human rights norms, it is possible to identify and elaborate a normative core common to both IHL and human rights law that has been referred to as fundamental standards of humanity.[34]

The broad description of these three theories obscures the contested visions about, and sub-theories within, them.[35] The theoretical and func-

---

29   *Gregoria Herminia Contreras et al v. El Salvador*, 23 February 2005, IACtHR, Report No. 11/2005, para. 20; *Coard et al.* v. *United States*, 29 September, IACtHR, Report No. 109/99, para. 42.

30   R. Kolb and G. Gaggioli, *supra* note 11; R. Arnold and N. Quénivet (eds.), *International Humanitarian Law and Human Rights Law: Towards a New Merger in International Law* (Martinus Nijhoff, Leiden, 2008).

31   H.J. Heintze, 'Theories on the Relationship between International Humanitarian Law and Human Rights Law', in Kolb and Gaggioli, *supra* note 11, pp. 53-64.

32   N.K. Modirzadeh, 'The Dark Side of Convergence: A Pro-Civilian Critique of the Extraterritorial Application of Human Rights Law in Armed Conflict', 86 *US Naval War College International Law Studies* (2010) p. 353.

33   Droege, *supra* note 13, p. 524.

34   B. Sang-YK, 'Contemporary Conflicts and Protection Gaps in International Humanitarian Law: The Necessity and Practical Utility of Fundamental Standards of Humanity', *African Yearbook on International Humanitarian Law* (2015) p. 24.

35   W. Schabas, '*Lex Specialis*? Belt and Suspenders? The Parallel Operation of Human Rights Law and the Law of Armed Conflict, and the Conundrum of *Jus ad Bellum*', 40 *Israel Law Review* (2007) p. 593; R. Kolb and R. Hyde, *An Introduction to the International Law of Armed Conflict* (Hart Publishing, Oxford, 2008) pp. 270-274.

tional role of *lex specialis*, and its effect on IHL-human rights law interactions have been the subject of much contention.[36] It is not settled whether *lex specialis* means that IHL is always the source of specialised norms in armed conflict situations thus displacing human rights law, or whether determination of the best suited rule must be made on a case-by-case basis.[37] The methodology for identifying the specialised rules or norms is debateable,[38] and *lex specialis'* role (as a tool for resolving conflicts or for treaty interpretation) and effect is disputable.[39] A review of the jurisprudence of regional and international adjudicatory bodies shows two problems arising from this legal uncertainty: (a) an institutional aspect where the competence of human rights adjudicatory bodies to apply IHL is challenged; and (b) a normative aspect where it is not clear whether IHL or human rights law should prevail when both apply to a common situation but "pull in different directions".[40]

Institutional aspects of the interaction between IHL and human rights law are relevant to the present study of the IHL-related jurisprudence of African human rights treaty bodies. Challenges to the institutional competence of the African Commission or Court to apply IHL have not been explicitly raised but, as will be detailed further below, how these bodies have engaged with IHL in their respective work indicates a considerable measure restraint. In some cases where there was scope to apply IHL, the Commission or Court elected not to apply it.[41] The normative aspects of the IHL-human rights law relations are also useful for this study as they offer insights into how African human rights treaty bodies have or can meaningfully apply IHL in their work.

---

36 M. Koskenniemi, *Study on the Function and Scope of the Lex Specialis Rule and the Question of 'Self-Contained Regimes'*, 4-7 May 2004, (ILC(LVI)/SG/FIL/CRD.1 and Add. 1, p. 4.
37 Droege, *supra* note 13, p. 523.
38 H. Duffy, 'Harmony or Conflict? The Interplay between Human Rights and Humanitarian Law', in L. van den Herik and N. Schrijver (eds.), *Counter-Terrorism Strategies in a Fragmented International Legal Order* (Cambridge University Press, Cambridge, 2013) pp. 507-508.
39 J. D'Aspremont, 'Articulating International Human Rights and International Humanitarian Law: Conciliatory Interpretation under the Guise of Conflict of Norms Resolution', in M. Fitzmaurice and P. Merkouris (eds.), *The Interpretation and Application of the European Convention on Human Rights: Legal and Practical Implications* (Brill, Leiden, 2013) pp. 1-31.
40 J.D. Ohlin, *The Assault on International Law* (Oxford University Press, Oxford, 2015) p. 180.
41 See Sections 4.1, 4.2 and 4.3 below.

3 Integration of IHL in African Human Rights Treaties

There is a growing tendency towards the convergence of IHL and human rights norms. This can be seen in the interpretation of treaty obligations as well as in the jurisprudence of international courts and tribunals.[42] This convergence is also evident by the fact that human rights law instruments incorporate IHL norms to specify obligations or protections that apply in armed conflict or other situations of violence.[43] The use of IHL in African human rights treaties is varied and complex. It ranges from the explicit use language drawn from the 1949 Geneva Conventions and their Additional Protocols to application of IHL standards as the yardstick for interpreting human rights. The most beneficial result of the integration of IHL and human rights norms would be to create a normative basis that African human rights treaty bodies could utilise to evaluate and induce compliance with both African human rights treaty law and IHL.[44] Three distinct treaty regimes in the African human rights system – namely children's rights, women's rights, and the rights of internally displaced persons (IDPs)[45] – best illustrate this trend and are discussed below.

3.1 *Children's Rights Regime*

Children have long borne the disproportionate brunt of collective violence and are recognised as a category in need of special protection in armed conflict and other situations of violence.[46] First articulated in the Convention on the Rights of the Child, international human rights law

---

42 F.J. Hampson, 'The Relationship between International Humanitarian Law and Human Rights Law from the Perspective of a Human Rights Treaty Body', 90 *International Review of the Red Cross* (2008) pp. 549-572.

43 Article 11, Convention on the Rights of Persons with Disabilities; Article 16, International Convention for the Protection of All Persons from Enforced Disappearance; Article 4, Optional Protocol on the Involvement of Children in Armed Conflict.

44 F.Z. Ntoubandi, 'Comment - Enforcement of International Humanitarian Law through the Human Rights Organs of the African Union', in H. Krieger (ed.), *Inducing Compliance with International Humanitarian Law: Lessons from the African Great Lakes Region* (Cambridge University Press, Cambridge, 2015) pp. 300-312.

45 *See* J. Fowkes, 'Armed Conflicts and the *Lex Specialis* Debate in Africa: Implications of the Emerging Women's and Children's Rights Regimes', 41 *South African Yearbook of International Law* (2016) pp. 73-96.

46 K. Månson, 'The Principle of Humanity in the Development of "Special Protection" for Children in Armed Conflict: 60 Years beyond the Geneva Conventions and 20 Years beyond the Convention on the Rights of the Child', in K.M. Larsen, C.G. Cooper and G. Nystuen (eds.), *Searching for a 'Principle of Humanity' in International Humanitarian Law* (Cambridge University Press, Cambridge, 2015) p. 149.

has progressively developed a treaty regime for the protection of children involved in or affected by armed conflict.[47] The African human rights system also has a dedicated treaty law framework for children caught up in armed conflict: the African Charter on the Rights and Welfare of the Child (African Children's Charter).[48] This Charter makes clear provisions for the co-application of IHL and human rights law in two ways: (a) by outlining the protection children have against participating in or suffering the consequences of armed conflict; and (b) by detailing specific obligations all parties to armed conflict have in relation to the internal displacement of children.

Article 22 of the African Children's Charter expressly makes IHL a key source of the legal obligations relative to the human rights of children. It clarifies States Parties' obligation "to respect and ensure respect for rules of [IHL] applicable in armed conflicts affecting the child".[49] This has resulted in the description of the Charter as an instrument of both IHL and human rights law,[50] in part because the text of Article 22(1) mirrors Article 1 of the 1949 Geneva Conventions. Recognising the particular vulnerability of children in armed conflict, Article 22 further obliges States to "take all necessary measures to ensure that no child shall take a direct part in hostilities and refrain in particular from recruiting any child".[51] The wording of this provision indicates that States are not only prohibited from conscripting children into the ranks of their armed forces or otherwise using them to actively participate in hostilities; they are also under an obligation to ensure that non-State armed groups do not use children in similar ways.[52]

Even clearer proof of the incorporation of IHL into the African Children's Charter and the high degree of convergence of IHL and human rights law is the legal protection accorded to children as a particularly vulnerable constituency of the civilian population. Aware of the grave risks to which children are exposed in armed conflict and other situations

---

47 Article 38, Convention on the Rights of the Child (1989), 1577 UNTS, p. 3.
48 *African Charter on the Rights and Welfare of the Child*, OAU Doc. CAB/LEG/24.9/49 (1990); A. Lloyd, 'A Theoretical Analysis of the Reality of Children's Rights in Africa: An Introduction to the African Charter on the Rights and Welfare of the Child', 2 *African Human Rights Law Journal* (2002) pp. 11-32.
49 African Children's Charter, *supra* note 48, Article 22(1).
50 V. Popovski, 'Protection of Children in International Humanitarian Law and Human Rights Law', in Arnold and Quénivet (eds.), *supra* note 30, p. 384.
51 African Children's Charter, *supra* note 48, Article 22(2).
52 Viljoen, *supra* note 6, p. 322.

of violence, the Charter makes it mandatory for States Parties to provide them with appropriate protection throughout an armed violence:

> [States Parties] shall, in accordance with their obligations under [IHL], protect the civilian population in armed conflicts and shall take all feasible measures to ensure the protection and care of children who are affected by armed conflicts. Such rules shall also apply to children in situations of internal armed conflicts, tension and strife.[53]

Displacement of populations is an inevitable consequence of armed violence; adults and children will flee from their places of habitual residence or countries of origin.[54] In such circumstances children are often separated from their families and may be entirely unaccompanied, thereby heightening their exposure to risk.[55] Article 23 of the African Children's Charter therefore offers special protection to refugee and unaccompanied minor children in situations of armed conflict and internal disturbances or tensions. It establishes an obligation on the part of States Parties to take all appropriate measures to ensure that refugee children or those seeking refugee status "receive appropriate protection and humanitarian assistance in the enjoyment of the rights set out in [the] Charter and other *international human rights and humanitarian* instruments to which the States are Parties."[56] The protection of the African Children's Charter, generally, applies to children accompanied by parents, legal guardians or close relatives, as well as to those who are not accompanied.

IHL treaty law imposes an obligation on States to provide special care and protection to refugee children or unaccompanied minors, and to ensure that they are reunited with their close relatives.[57] This obligation is reiterated in Article 23(2) of the African Children's Charter which requires States Parties to cooperate with international organisations that protect and assist such refugees in their efforts to "trace the parents or

---

53   African Children's Charter, *supra* note 48, Article 22(3).
54   M. Jacques, *Armed Conflict and Displacement: The Protection of Refugees and Displaced Persons under International Humanitarian Law* (Cambridge University Press, Cambridge, 2015) p. 2.
55   African Committee of Experts on the Rights and Welfare of Children (ACERWC), *Concept Note for the Commemoration of the Day of the African Child* (2016) para. 27.
56   African Children's Charter, *supra* note 48, Article 23.
57   Articles 24(1) and 50, Geneva Convention Relative to the Protection of Civilian Persons in Time of War (Fourth Geneva Convention), 12 August 1949, 75 UNTS 287.

other close relatives of an unaccompanied refugee child in order to obtain information necessary for reunification with the family." To add, the protections relating to refugee children apply similarly to children who are internally displaced "whether through natural disaster, armed conflict, civil strife, breakdown of economic and social order or howsoever caused."[58] By expanding the scope of causes of displacement, the African Children's Charter adopts a comprehensive approach to protecting and assisting displaced children.[59] It also, importantly, prevents States from denying the existence of an armed conflict in an attempt to argue that IHL protections do not apply.

Apart from providing a basis for the co-application of IHL and human rights law, the African Children's Charter also establishes a monitoring and supervisory mechanism through which IHL can be used to secure the protection of children involved in or affected by armed conflict. Article 32 establishes the African Committee of Experts on the Rights and Welfare of the Child, which promotes and protects the rights and welfare of children. Its mandate includes: monitoring the implementation of children's rights; ensuring the protection of children's rights; and interpreting the provisions of the African Children's Charter at the request of a State Party, or AU institution, or any other person or institution recognised by the AU. In the discharge of this broad mandate, the African Children's Rights Committee is authorised to receive and examine reports on the measures that States Parties have adopted at the national level to give effect to the Charter's provisions, and on the progress made in the protection of children's rights.[60] The Committee is also competent to receive communications relating to alleged breaches of Charter rights from any person, group, or governmental organisation recognised by the AU, a Member State of the AU, or the United Nations ('UN').[61] Given its expansive mandate, the Committee holds much promise for the implementation of children's rights in Africa.[62]

---

58   African Children's Charter, *supra* note 48, Article 23.
59   T. Kaime, 'Protection of Refugee Children under the African Human Rights System', in J.S. Nielsen (ed), *Children's Rights in Africa: A Legal Perspective* (Ashgate Publishing, Farnham, 2008) p. 184.
60   African Children's Charter, *supra* note 48, Article 43.
61   Rules of Procedure of the Committee of Experts on the Rights and Welfare of the Child, Doc. Cmtee/ACRWC/II.Rev.2, rule 74.
62   A. Lloyd, 'Evolution of the African Charter on the Rights and Welfare of the Child and the African Committee of Experts: Raising the Gauntlet', 10 *International Journal of Children's Rights* (2002) pp. 179-98.

IHL has featured in the work of the African Children's Rights Committee and in particular when children are involved in or affected by armed conflict.[63] Pursuant to Article 45 of the African Children's Charter which authorises the Committee to "resort to any appropriate method of investigating any matter" falling within its jurisdictional remit, it has undertaken advocacy missions to South Sudan and Central African Republic to assess how the respective armed conflicts in those countries have affected children's rights.[64] The reports of both missions make indirect references to IHL in the context of assessing serious violations of children's rights, including their arbitrary killings, subjection to sexual violence, and forcible recruitment by belligerents to take a direct part in hostilities.[65]

A more overt use of IHL in the work of the African Children's Rights Committee is to be found in its comprehensive assessment of the impact of armed conflict and other situations of armed violence on children in Africa.[66] In its report, the Committee explicitly situates IHL within the AU legal framework for the protection of children: "[t]he obligation of States to protect children in armed conflict is drawn from a range of international and regional human rights instruments and humanitarian law."[67] It also expounds the obligation to protect children in Article 18 of the African Children's Charter, expressly stating that it "implies that States Parties are enjoined not only to fulfil their duties but to conform to the standards under international human rights and humanitarian law to protect children in armed conflicts."[68] In addition, the Committee assessed the extent to which national legislation in selected States, namely South Sudan and Mali, protects children in armed conflict in accordance with the provisions of the African Children's Charter read together with IHL.[69] This indicates increasing relevance of IHL in the work of the African Children's Rights Committee.

---

63 Sang-YK, *supra* note 6, p. 17-18.
64 ACERWC, *Report on the Advocacy Mission to Assess the Situation of Children in South Sudan* (2014) pp. 5-8 and 10-13; ACERWC, *Mission Report of the ACERWC to Assess the Situation of Children Affected by the Conflict in Central African Republic* (2014) pp. 15-18.
65 *Ibid.*
66 ACERWC, *Comprehensive Study on the Impact of Conflicts and Crisis on Children in Africa* (AU, Addis Ababa, 2016).
67 *Ibid.*, p. 15.
68 *Ibid.*, p. 17.
69 *Ibid.*, p. 22 (South Sudan) and p. 25 (Mali).

3.2 Women's Rights Regime

During armed conflicts women are exposed to the risk of death, torture, sexual violence and slavery, trafficking, and forced evictions, among other forms of physical and psychological trauma.[70] As a vulnerable group, therefore, women need special measures of protection in armed conflict and other situations of violence. This fact is recognised in the African human rights system which offers a distinct treaty regime for the protection of women against all forms of discrimination and violence: the Protocol to the African Charter on Human and Peoples' Rights on the Rights of Women in Africa (hereafter 'African Women's Protocol').[71]

Article 11 of this Protocol provides normative human rights standards for protecting women in armed conflict situations that explicitly integrate IHL norms.[72] It thus offers a clear basis for the co-application of IHL and human rights law by obliging States Parties to "undertake to respect and ensure respect for the rules of IHL applicable to armed conflict situations which affect the population, particularly women." As already stated, this wording derives from Article 1 common to the 1949 Geneva Conventions and imposes a general obligation on States Parties to comply with the specified rules of IHL, as well as to induce non-State armed groups to similar compliance.

Women are also protected by the African Women's Protocol as part of the civilian population to the extent that they do not take a direct part in hostilities: "States Parties shall, in accordance with the obligations incumbent upon them under the international humanitarian law, protect civilians including women, irrespective of the population to which they belong, in the event of armed conflict."[73] Specific provision is also made for the protection of women who are uprooted and in flight as a result of armed conflict or other situations of violence. This class includes women who are asylum seekers, refugees, returnees, or internally displaced. Article 11 obliges States Parties to protect these women "against all forms of violence, rape and other forms of sexual exploitation".[74] A further duty

---

70   C. Chinkin, 'Gender and Armed Conflict', in A. Clapham and P. Gaeta (eds.), *The Oxford Handbook of International Law in Armed Conflict* (Oxford University Press, Oxford, 2014) pp. 675-699.
71   AU Doc. CAB/LEG/66.6, entered into force 25 November 2005.
72   F. Banda, 'Protocol to the African Charter on the Rights of Women in Africa', in M. Evans and R. Murray (eds.), *The African Charter on Human and Peoples' Rights: The System in Practice 1986-2006* (Cambridge University Press, Cambridge, 2006) p. 455.
73   African Women's Protocol, *supra* note 71, Article 11(2).
74   *Ibid.*, Article 11(3).

is imposed on States: they must criminalise these forms of sexual and gender-based violence and impose criminal sanctions in their domestic legal system to eliminate impunity.[75] In this regard, States Parties are obliged to "ensure that such acts are considered war crimes, genocide and/or crimes against humanity and that their perpetrators are brought to justice before a competent criminal jurisdiction."[76]

All children, particularly girls under 18 years of age, are expressly protected from direct participation in hostilities and recruitment as child soldiers under the African Women's Protocol. States Parties are accordingly obliged to "take all necessary measures to ensure that no child, especially girls under 18 years of age, take active part in hostilities or is recruited as a soldier."[77] States Parties to the African Children's Charter are obligated to report on the specific steps they have taken towards implementing the obligations to criminalise and punish sexual or gender-based violence, and to prevent the recruitment of girls as soldiers.

3.3   *Internally Displaced Persons' Regime*

A number of provisions in the AU Convention for the Protection and Assistance of Internally Displaced Persons in Africa (hereafter 'Kampala Convention')[78] clearly and extensively integrate IHL norms with human rights standards for prevention of internal displacement and the amelioration of conditions of those already displaced. In its preamble, the States Parties recognise the "inherent rights of IDPs as provided for and protected in international human rights and humanitarian law and as set out in the 1998 Guiding Principles on Internal Displacement."[79] It is significant that the Kampala Convention is the only binding, multilateral treaty that specifies legal obligations for the prevention of internal displacement and the protection and assistance of IDPs.[80] It therefore offers a legal basis for the crystallisation of the 'soft law' in the UN Guiding Principles – a normative forerunner in the integration of IHL and human

---

75   African Women's Protocol, *supra* note 71, Article 11(3).
76   *Ibid.*, Article 11(3).
77   *Ibid.*, Article 11(4).
78   (2009) 49 I.L.M. 86 adopted 23 October 2009 (entered into force 6 December 2012).
79   *Ibid.*, Preamble, Articles 6, 7, and 9.
80   F.Z. Guistiniani, 'New Hopes and Challenges for the Protection of IDPs in Africa: The Kampala Convention for the Protection and Assistance of Internally Displaced Persons in Africa', 39 *Denver Journal of International Law and Policy* (2011) p. 347.

rights norms to advance IDP protection – and avails an avenue for enforcing 'hard' treaty law obligations towards IDPs in Africa.[81]

As for its content, the Kampala Convention leaves little doubt that IHL influenced its drafting. By using language directly drawn from the 1949 Geneva Conventions and incorporating obligations of a distinctly IHL character, the provisions of the Kampala Convention offer an explicit basis for the implementation of IHL norms.[82] International human rights norms also form a crucial part of the rights and corresponding duties that are articulated in the Kampala Convention.[83] But what is perhaps the most remarkable aspect of the Kampala Convention is the high degree of convergence of IHL and human rights norms; it has even been noted that the Kampala Convention is "both a human rights convention as well as a humanitarian law instrument."[84] This observation is supported by a close examination of general obligations undertaken by States Parties, including:

> c. Respect and ensure respect for the principles of humanity and human dignity of internally displaced persons; ... e. *Respect and ensure respect for international humanitarian law* regarding the protection of internally displaced persons; f. *Respect and ensure respect for the humanitarian and civilian character* of the protection of and assistance to internally displaced persons, including ensuring that such persons do not engage in subversive activities; g. Ensure individual responsibility for acts of arbitrary displacement, in accordance with applicable domestic and international criminal law; h. Ensure the accountability of non-State actors concerned, including multinational companies and private military or security companies, for acts of arbitrary displacement or complicity in such acts.[85]

---

81   D.J. Cantor, *Returns of Internally Displaced Persons in Armed Conflict: International Law and Its Application in Colombia* (Brill Nijhoff, Leiden, 2018) p. 5; L. Groth, 'Engendering Protection: An Analysis of the 2009 Kampala Convention and Its Provisions for Internally Displaced Women', 23 *International Journal of Refugee Law* (2011) p. 222.

82   W. Kidane, 'Managing Forced Displacement Law in Africa: The Role of the New African Union IDPs Convention', 44 *Vanderbilt Journal of Transnational Law* (2011) p. 1.

83   Kampala Convention, *supra* note 78, Articles 11-13.

84   B. Kioko and L. Wambugu, 'The African Union and the Protection of Civilians', in H. Willmot *et al.* (eds.), *Protection of Civilians* (Oxford University Press, Oxford, 2016) p. 283.

85   Kampala Convention, *supra* note 78, Article 3.

What then is the practical implication of the integration of IHL and human rights norms in the Kampala Convention? The most relevant result for present purpose is that IHL is expressly recognised as one of the sources of law applicable to IDPs in the African human rights system.[86] This, in turn, provides a legal basis for African human rights treaty bodies to use IHL in their respective work.[87] As well as providing an avenue for African human rights treaty bodies to give effect to IHL, the incorporation of IHL standards in the Kampala Convention establishes positive and negative obligations on States Parties to implement IHL. Negative obligations require States Parties to refrain from conduct that interferes with the benefit of treaty rights, while positive obligations place a duty on States Parties to take proactive measures to secure the enjoyment of such rights. Article 4(1) of the Kampala Convention, concerning protection against internal displacement, imposes a broad duty on States Parties to "respect and ensure respect for their obligations under international law, so as to prevent and avoid conditions that might lead to arbitrary displacement of persons."

Like Common Article 1 to the 1949 Geneva Conventions under which States Parties must "respect and ensure respect" of the Convention, Article 4(1) of the Kampala Convention obliges States Parties to make every effort to respect the Convention and prevent and avoid situations that may trigger arbitrary displacement of civilians by members of its security forces.[88] It also requires them to ensure that non-State armed groups do not cause such displacement. Even though this obligation may seem onerous, it is only an elaboration of obligations already accepted by States Parties to the Kampala Convention: they are obliged to enact and enforce laws that prohibit forced displacement, and declare as punishable by law acts of arbitrary displacement that amount to genocide, war crimes, or crimes against humanity.[89] By enacting robust criminal laws and prosecuting its soldiers as well as members of non-State armed groups who violate such laws, States Parties play a crucial part in fulfilling this obligation.

---

86   D.L. Tehindrazanarivelo, 'The African Union and International Humanitarian Law', in Kolb and Gaggioli, *supra* note 11, pp. 503-530.

87   Van den Herik and Duffy, *supra* note 2, p. 398.

88   ICRC, *Commentary on the First Geneva Convention: Volume 1: Convention (I) for the Amelioration of the Condition of the Wounded and Sick in Armed Forces in the Field* (Cambridge University Press, Cambridge, 2016).

89   Kampala Convention, *supra* note 78, Article 4(6).

That States Parties bear the primary legal burden of ensuring that the Kampala Convention is respected, including by non-State armed groups, is corroborated by the content of other positive obligations.[90] Article 7 prohibits, on pain of individual criminal responsibility, members of non-State armed groups from violating the rights of IDPs under domestic and international law, and further states that the relevant protection and assistance of IDPs "shall be governed by" IHL. This provision creates a mandatory positive duty on States Parties to take measures to ensure that armed groups comply with all the obligations set out in Article 7.

Besides the positive obligations to protect individuals against arbitrary displacement, the Kampala Convention also specifies negative obligations in the form of a non-exhaustive list of prohibited forms of displacement. This list, which makes explicit reference to IHL, prohibits the following:

> b. Individual or mass displacement of civilians in situations of armed conflict, unless the security of the civilians involved or *imperative military reasons so demand, in accordance with* [*IHL*]; c. Displacement intentionally used *as a method of warfare or due to other violations of* [*IHL*] in situations of armed conflict; ... g. Displacement used as a *collective punishment*; h. Displacement caused by any act, event, factor, or phenomenon of comparable gravity to all of the above and which is not justified under international law, including human rights and [IHL].[91]

Another important function of the Kampala Convention is its reinforcement of the obligation on States Parties to prevent the participation of children in armed conflict, as stated in the African Children's Charter.[92] Article 7 of the Kampala Convention prohibits the armed forces of the States Parties as well as members of non-State armed groups from recruiting children or requiring or permitting them to take part in hostilities under any circumstances.[93] This explicit prohibition establishes a positive obligation on States Parties to ensure that neither its armed forces nor other armed groups recruit children as soldiers or abuse them.[94]

---

90   Tehindrazanarivelo, *supra* note 86, p. 504.
91   Kampala Convention, *supra* note 78, Article 4(4).
92   Groth, *supra* note 81, p. 222.
93   Kampala Convention, *supra* note 78, Article 7(5)(e).
94   *Ibid.*, Article 9(1)(d).

In sum, the extensive integration of IHL provisions into the Kampala Convention has beneficial consequences for African human rights treaty bodies who wish to rely on IHL in their judgments. First, by incorporating IHL norms into African human rights treaty law, it supplies a principled basis for a finding by the relevant treaty monitoring bodies of concurrent violations of IHL and human rights norms. Secondly, some provisions such as Article 7 of the Kampala Convention indicate that IHL is the better suited law which offers greater protection in governing matters of internal displacement in times of armed conflict; this in turn requires relevant human rights treaty bodies to have regard to IHL as a matter of law. Thirdly, even in relation to the provisions where no express mention is made of the priority of IHL norms, the incorporation of IHL makes it necessary for African human rights treaty bodies to interpret human rights norms in light of IHL.

4   IHL in the Jurisprudence of the African Commission on Human and Peoples' Rights

The African Commission is arguably the most important African human rights treaty body in relation to the review of the role and contribution of IHL in jurisprudence of the African human rights system. Established by Article 30 of the African Charter, the Commission is the oldest and longest-serving treaty supervisory body or compliance mechanism in the African human rights system.[95] This in turn means that it has the most extensive jurisprudence.[96] More crucially, it has dealt with the most complaints of alleged human rights violations occurring in the context of armed conflict where IHL presumably applies. Hence, any analysis of the status and effect of IHL in the jurisprudence of African human rights treaty bodies is incomplete if it does not address the practice of the African Commission. To understand fully and systematically how the Commission has engaged with IHL, it is necessary to first examine its mandate and material jurisdiction before turning to analyse its protective and non-adjudicatory practice.

---

95   D. Abebe, 'Does International Human Rights Law in African Courts Make a Difference?', 56 *Virginia Journal of International Law* (2017) p. 540.

96   R. Murray and D. Long, *The Implementation of Findings of the African Commission on Human and Peoples' Rights* (Cambridge University Press, Cambridge, 2015) p. 5.

4.1 Mandate and Material Jurisdiction of the African Commission

Article 45 of the African Charter stipulates the functions of the African Commission in pursuit of its mandate to protect and promote human rights, and to interpret African human rights treaties as well as its own mandate. Article 45 specifies the mandate of the Commission by outlining four functions that it must discharge. These include the promotion of human rights; the protection of human rights; interpretating - the Charter, including its own mandate; and performing any other tasks that may be assigned to it by the AU Assembly. These functions have been categorised into a three-part mandate: promotional mandate, protective mandate, and interpretive mandate.

In discharging its promotional mandate, the African Commission is required to make the provisions of the African Charter as widely known as possible so as to enhance their respect and implementation.[97] Thus the Commission is authorised to: collect and analyse any information relating to African human rights problems and, where appropriate, to publicise its findings and make recommendations to concerned governments; formulate and draft principles and rules that may serve as legislative guidance for national laws; and cooperate with African or international institutions concerned with the promotion or protection of human rights.[98] Worthy of mention is the fact that, under its promotional mandate, the Commission has adopted thematic resolutions advocating the domestication, dissemination, and implementation of IHL in Africa.[99]

The protective mandate of the African Commission is not precisely defined in Article 45(2), which states that it must ensure the protection of human and peoples' rights "under conditions laid down by the present Charter." Nonetheless, the Commission has interpreted its related function as determining inter-State and individual communications.[100] The communications procedure has given rise to a robust body of jurisprudence, including that relating to human rights in armed conflict.[101] As

---

97 African Charter, *supra* note 8, Article 45(1); R. Murray, *African Commission on Human and Peoples' Rights and International Law* (Hart Publishing, Oxford, 2000) pp. 15-16.
98 Ntoubandi, *supra* note 44, p. 302.
99 Resolution on the Promotion and Respect of International Humanitarian Law and Human and Peoples' Rights, 14th Ordinary Session, 1-10 December 1993.
100 M.K. Mbondenyi, 'Institutional Mainstreaming and Rationalisation', in M. Ssenyonjo (ed.), *The African Regional Human Rights System: 30 Years after the African Charter on Human and Peoples' Rights* (Martinus Nijhoff, Leiden, 2012) p. 437.
101 F. Viljoen, *International Human Rights Law in Africa* (Oxford University Press, Oxford, 2012) p. 339.

will be shown in greater detail below, IHL has featured in a number of decisions in which alleged violations of human rights law overlap with breaches of IHL.[102] Equally important to the effective discharge of the protective mandate is the State reporting procedure, whereby the Commission supervises compliance by States Parties with legal obligations under the African Charter.[103] Where there are contested facts relating to a complaint, the protective mandate may entail on-site visits or fact-finding missions to the place of the alleged violation.

In regard to its interpretive mandate, the African Commission is empowered to interpret authoritatively the provisions of the African Charter.[104] This mandate has been expounded as involving "giving sense, meaning and clarity to the provisions of the African Charter."[105] In the exercise of this mandate, the Commission has started to adopt General Comments in which it lays down authoritative interpretations of provisions of the African Charter.[106] This practice is progressive and constructive; it is a formal and non-contentious avenue for the Commission to clearly outline its perspective on the scope and content of a particular right so as to promote uniform interpretation and national implementation.[107] Of special relevance to the present analysis is the Commission's General Comment No. 3 which supplies interpretive guidance on the right to life under Article 4 of the African Charter, including during armed conflict.[108] A more detailed discussion of General Comment 3 and how it treats IHL is given further below.[109]

---

102 *See* 4.2 below.
103 African Charter, *supra* note 8, Articles 54 and 55.
104 *Ibid.*, Article 45(3); D. Long and R. Murray, 'The Role and Use of Soft Law Instruments in the African Human Rights System', in S. Lagoutte, T. Gamelltoft-Hansen and J. Cerone (eds.), *Tracing the Roles of Soft Law in Human Rights* (Oxford University Press, Oxford, 2016) p. 91.
105 Ntoubandi, *supra* note 44, p. 302.
106 African Commission on Human and Peoples' Rights, *General Comment No. 3 on the African Charter of Human and Peoples' Rights: The Right to Life (Article 4)*, 57th Ordinary Session, November 2015; African Commission on Human and Peoples' Rights, *General Comment No. 2 on Article 14.1(a), (b), (c), and (f) and Article 14.2(a) and (c) of the Protocol to the African Charter on Human and Peoples' Rights on the Rights of Women in Africa*; African Commission on Human and Peoples' Rights, *General Comment on Article 14(1)(d) and (e) of the Protocol to the African Charter on Human and Peoples' Rights on the Rights of Women in Africa*.
107 Murray and Long, *supra* note 96, p. 67.
108 General Comment No. 3, *supra* note 106.
109 *See* 4.3.2 below.

As a result of its broad mandate, the Commission has found it necessary to interpret the provisions of the African Charter with reference to general international law as well as other treaties not adopted within the framework of AU law.[110] Besides being necessary and useful, this outward-looking approach to treaty interpretation is explicitly supported by the African Charter. In comparison with other constitutive treaties of regional human rights treaty systems, the African Charter is far more receptive of external sources of law that originate outside the respective regional treaty frameworks.[111] The text of the American Convention on Human Rights only authorises the relevant treaty bodies to have regard to other treaties adopted under the Organization of American States ('OAS') system.[112] For its part, the European Convention on Human Rights does not specifically address the legal status and role of non-EU treaties.[113]

By contrast, Articles 60 and 61 of the African Charter provide the Commission with a clear legal basis to have recourse to sources of international law other than from the AU treaty system. Article 60 states that the "Commission shall draw inspiration from international law on human and peoples' rights", particularly those contained in the provisions of African human rights instruments, the UN Charter, the AU Charter, the Universal Declaration of Human Rights, and other relevant human rights instruments adopted by the UN and African States. Article 60 also requires the Commission to refer to "provisions of various instruments adopted by Specialised Agencies of the United Nations of which the parties to the present Charter are members." Apart from human rights instruments, Article 61 supplies a further basis for considering and relying on external sources of international law as subsidiary sources of legal guidance:

> The Commission shall also take into consideration, as subsidiary measures to determine the principles of law, other general or special international conventions, laying down rules expressly recognised by Member States of the [AU], African practices consistent with international norms on Human and Peoples' Rights, customs

---

110 Murray, *supra* note 97, p. 145.
111 Hailbronner, *supra* note 6, p. 346.
112 *"Other Treaties" Subject to the Consultative Jurisdiction of the Court (Art. 64 American Convention on Human Rights)*, 24 September 1982, IACtHR, Advisory Opinion, OC-1/82.
113 UN High Commissioner for Human Rights, *The European Union and International Human Rights Law* (2011) p. 11.

generally accepted as law, general principles of law recognised by African States as well as legal precedents and doctrine.

At a conceptual level, therefore, Articles 60 and 61 establish an obligation, where appropriate and in the interest of advancing human and peoples' rights, for the African Commission to take an outward-looking approach to interpretation by construing the Charter in light of general international law and other treaties.[114] This conclusion is supported by the approach taken by the Commission in its work. Indeed, in practice, Articles 60 and 61 of the African Charter have been interpreted by the African Commission as legal authorisation to draw guidance from broader international legal sources. In *Civil Liberties Organisation, Legal Defence Centre, Legal Defence and Assistance Project v. Nigeria* these articles were used to draw interpretive guidance from Article 14 of the ICCPR.[115] They were also relied on in *Africa Institute for Human Rights and Development (on behalf of Sierra Leonean refugees in Guinea) v. Republic of Guinea* to invoke the 1951 UN Convention on the Status of Refugees (hereafter '1951 Refugee Convention').[116] As will be shown in section 4.2, Articles 60 and 61 of the African Charter have been the primary basis on which the African Commission has used IHL in cases of alleged human rights violations committed in the context of armed conflict.

4.2   IHL in the African Commission's Adjudicative Jurisprudence

The adjudicative work of the African Commission mainly consists in hearing and determining individual and inter-State communications in which allegations are made concerning violations of human and peoples' rights.[117] Since its establishment, the Commission has only received one inter-State communication and has decided 96 communications on merit, with the majority being complaints brought by NGOs on behalf of individuals or communities. IHL has occasionally featured in the sub-

---

114   Ntoubandi, *supra* note 44, p. 309.
115   Communication No. 218/98, Fourteenth Annual Activity Report, 2000-2001, paras. 24 and 27.
116   Communication No. 249/2002, Twentieth Annual Activity Report, 2005-2006, paras. 37-38.
117   C.A. Odinkalu, 'The Individual Complaints Procedures of the African Commission on Human and Peoples' Rights: A Preliminary Assessment', 8 *Transnational Law and Contemporary Problems* (1998) p. 359.

missions of contesting parties or in the reasoning of the Commission.[118] In this section, a close analysis of the key instances where IHL has been used in the Commission's work is given in order to determine the status and effect of IHL in its jurisprudence.

4.2.1   Legal Basis for and Approach to Applying IHL
The African Charter does not clearly identify the 1949 Geneva Conventions and their Additional Protocols as applicable sources of law to which the African Commission may refer to in fulfilling its mandate. Nonetheless, the broad and inclusive wording of Articles 60 and 61 of the African Charter has been identified as providing a legal basis for the Commission to have regard to, and even apply, IHL.[119] As discussed above, the combined effect of Articles 60 and 61 authorises the Commission to refer to, draw inspiration from, or take into consideration external sources of international law, including IHL, in determining cases before it. In spite of this, the Commission has, in its practice, rarely specified on what authority it engages with IHL and to what effect. The only instance where it clarified the legal basis for using IHL is in *Democratic Republic of Congo v. Republics of Burundi, Rwanda and Uganda*.[120] Specifically, the Commission held that:

> By virtue of Articles 60 and 61 the Commission holds that the Four Geneva Conventions and the two Additional Protocols covering armed conflicts constitute part of the general principles of law recognized by African States, and take them into consideration in the determination of this case.[121]

It is noteworthy that reliance by the Commission on Articles 60 and 61 as its legal basis for applying IHL is consistent with its earlier jurisprudence. Previously, these two provisions have been used to draw inspiration from and take into consideration the International Covenant on Economic,

---

118   S. Sivakumaran, *The Law of Non-International Armed Conflict* (Oxford University Press, Oxford, 2012) p. 503.
119   Ntoubandi, *supra* note 44, p. 309.
120   Communication No. 227/99, 29 May 2003, ACHPR, Twentieth Activity Report of the African Commission, January-June 2006.
121   *Ibid.*, para. 70.

Social and Cultural Rights[122] as well as the 1951 Refugee Convention.[123] Although this shows that there is established precedence for using Articles 60 and 61 to refer to general international law in the African human rights system, it does not explain with sufficient precision how, nor does it specify the extent to which, IHL can be relied on.[124] Since no express mention is made in the African Charter of IHL as one of the external sources of law to which the Commission may refer to, consider, or rely on, it may have been beneficial for the Commission in *DRC* v. *Burundi, Rwanda and Uganda* to elaborate further on whether IHL constitutes: (a) international law on human and peoples' rights; (b) general or special international conventions laying down general rules expressly recognised by African States; (c) customs generally accepted as law; or (d) general principles of law.

Despite the fact that the Commission in *DRC* v. *Burundi, Rwanda and Uganda* held that the 1949 Geneva Conventions and their Additional Protocols are "special international conventions" stipulating rules expressly recognised by African States, it does not satisfactorily clarify the basis for invoking them. In particular, the Commission (a) neglected to specify whether the pertinent treaties are "expressly recognised" by member States, and (b) failed to substantiate how it concluded that the relevant treaties have come to be recognised as "general principles" by African States.[125] This oversight is all the more regrettable for the opportunity that it lost to clarify the status of IHL in the African human rights system. It is useful to recall that in most of its decisions relating to human rights violations in armed conflict, the Commission frequently acknowledges the factual existence of armed conflict,[126] occasionally uses language

---

122 *Social and Economic Rights Action Centre* v. *Nigeria*, 27 October 2001, ACHPR, Communication No. 155/96, Thirtieth Ordinary Session, 13th-27th October 2001, para. 63.

123 *African Institute for Human Rights and Development (on behalf of Sierra Leonean refugees in Guinea)* v. *Republic of Guinea*, Communication No. 249/2002, Twentieth Activity Report of the African Commission, 25th-29th June 2006, paras. 41, 45 and 52.

124 Viljoen, *supra* note 6, p. 314.

125 Viljoen, *supra* note 6, p. 315.

126 *Commission Nationale des Droits de l'Homme et des Libertés* v. *Chad*, 11 October 1995, ACHPR, Communication No. 74/92, paras. 21-22 (hereafter '*Chad Mass Violations*'); *Amnesty International, Comité Loosli Bachelard, Lawyers' Committee for Human Rights, and Association of Members of the Episcopal Conference of East Africa* v. *Sudan*, 15 November 1999, ACHPR, Communication No. 48/90-50/91-52/91-89/93, para. 50.

drawn from IHL treaty law,[127] but only rarely finds breaches of IHL that are analogous to violations of Charter rights.[128]

This conservative approach to IHL has been attributed to a number of reasons, including the failure by contending parties to plead IHL and modest acquaintance with IHL on the part of some Commissioners.[129] A more plausible explanation, however, may be that there remains much uncertainty about the legal basis for applying IHL. Support for this contention can be found in how the Commission has approached the application of IHL in its post-*DRC* v. *Burundi, Rwanda and Uganda* decisions. Its subsequent practice in *Sudan Human Rights Organisation* is a pertinent example.[130] While it found that the clashes in Darfur amounted to an armed conflict[131] and even repeatedly used the terms "civilians" and "civilian population",[132] it did not refer to IHL treaties. Nor did it couch its analysis of any alleged violations in the language of IHL treaty law.[133]

Equally viable as an explanation for the Commission's reticence to engage meaningfully with IHL in its adjudicative work may be the effect of its decisions in the communications procedure. Unlike the concluding observations in the State reporting process or findings of special mechanisms, which are not binding, decisions or individual communications of international courts are binding and are able to exert more political pressure on the parties at fault. Thus, the Commission may be less willing to apply IHL in determining a case in which its decision is analogous to a judicial finding and it would risk a potential backlash from affected States.[134] In this scenario, uncertainty as to the legal basis of applying IHL would be a key motivator for avoiding IHL. To demonstrate how the combined effect of uncertainty about the legal basis of applying IHL and the consequences of quasi-judicial decisions of the Commission, it is instructive to consider an instance where the Commission made dissimilar findings regarding the same facts when exercising distinct yet complementary functions.

---

127 *Sudan Human Rights Organisation and Centre on Human Rights and Evictions* v. *Sudan*, 27 May 2009, ACHPR, Communications No. 279/03-269/05, paras. 164-168.
128 *DRC* v. *Burundi, Rwanda and Uganda, supra* note 120, paras. 78 and 84.
129 Ntoubandi, *supra* note 44, p. 310.
130 *Sudan Human Rights Organisation, supra* note 127.
131 *Ibid.*, para. 201.
132 *Ibid.*, paras. 164, 168, 176, 178 and 223.
133 D. Steiger, 'Enforcing International Humanitarian Law through Human Rights Bodies', in Krieger, *supra* note 44, p. 296.
134 Murray and Long, *supra* note 96, p. 7.

A case in point is *Organisation Mondiale Contre La Torture, Association Internationale des Juristes (C.I.J), and Union Interafricaine des Droits de l'Homme* v. *Rwanda*.[135] In this case, the Commission's decision comprised the determination of four communications arising from alleged violations in the context of the armed conflict in Rwanda where the genocide occurred. One of the constituent communications detailed the alleged widespread massacres, extrajudicial executions, and arbitrary arrests of Tutsis by Rwandan security agents.[136] These allegations were partly confirmed by the Commission in the exercise of its promotional mandate; in its Resolution on the Situation in Rwanda at the material time, the Commission urged all parties to the armed conflict to respect the principles of IHL and condemned "the massacre of innocent civilians by the different armed factions."[137] However, it was rather circumspect in exercising its protective mandate in *Organisation Mondiale Contre La Torture*. Though finding that these massacres were a breach of the right to life in Article 4 of the African Charter, the Commission neither specified the legal nature of the conflict in Rwanda nor referred to IHL in any way.

4.2.2 Co-Application of IHL and Human Rights Law

Initially conceived as a means to protect individuals from the abusive excesses of States during peacetime, human rights law has since grown both in scope and pertinence.[138] It now applies both in times of peace as well as armed conflict, and regulates the conduct of State and non-State actors.[139] The continued application of human rights law in armed conflict has, however, been contested by a few States on the basis that, as the more specific law in armed conflict, IHL excludes the application and utility of human rights law.[140] Though the argument has often been advanced in other human rights systems,[141] it has only been advanced in one instance in the history of the African human rights system, and unsuccessfully. In *Article 19* v. *Eritrea* it was claimed by Eritrea that the

---

135 Communications Nos. 27/89, 46/91, 49/91 and 99/93, 31 October 1996, ACHPR.
136 Communication No. 49/91.
137 Resolution on the Situation in Rwanda, Seventh Annual Activity Report, 1993-94, ACHPR/APT/7th, Annex XII.
138 A. Clapham, 'Protection of Civilians under International Human Rights' in Willmot *et al.*, *supra* note 84, pp. 143-144.
139 L. Hill-Cawthorne, *Detention in Non-International Armed Conflict* (Oxford University Press, Oxford, 2016) pp. 217-218.
140 I. Park, *The Right to Life in Armed Conflict* (Oxford University Press, Oxford, 2018) p. 96.
141 Hill-Cawthorne, *supra* note 139, p. 114.

arbitrary arrest and prolonged detention of the victims was a necessary measure taken "against a backdrop of war when the very existence of the nation was threatened."[142] This argument suggests that Eritrea sought to exclude the application of human rights law in favour of IHL. This was, however, firmly rejected by the Commission.

The principal reason for the rarity in the African human rights system of challenges to the continued application of human rights law at all times is that, in contrast with other human rights treaties, the African Charter has no derogation clause.[143] Accordingly, it does not permit States Parties to suspend their human rights obligations during times of emergency or armed conflict.[144] It thus follows that the provisions of the African Charter continue to apply in armed conflict, a position confirmed by the consistent practice of African human rights treaty bodies. Indeed, the African Commission has repeatedly expressed the institutional view that since the Charter "does not allow for States Parties to derogate from their treaty obligations during emergency situations. Thus, even a situation of ... war ... cannot be cited as justification by the State violating or permitting violations of the African Charter."[145]

The inclusion of a legal right of all peoples' to peace and security in the African Charter might be another reason why the continued application of human rights law in armed conflict is not contested in the African human rights system.[146] This provision has inspired African human rights treaty bodies to stress a causal relationship between breaches of human rights and internal strife.[147]

In light of the foregoing, the question may be asked as to how the African Commission has elaborated the continued application of human rights in armed conflict, and the potential co-application of the African Charter alongside IHL. Apart from consistently holding that African Charter rights apply in situations of internal violence and armed conflict, the jurisprudence of the African Commission also recognises the parallel application of human rights law and IHL.[148] In *Chad Mass Violations*,

---

142 Communication 275/03, 30 May 2007, ACHPR, para. 87.
143 Hailbronner, *supra* note 6, p. 346.
144 R. Otto, *Targeted Killings and International Law* (Springer, Heidelberg, 2011) p. 143.
145 *Constitutional Rights Project, Civil Liberties Organisation and Media Rights Agenda v. Nigeria*, 5 November 1999, ACHPR, Communication Nos. 140/94, 141/94, 145/95, para. 41.
146 African Charter, *supra* note 8, Article 23.
147 Murray, *supra* note 97, p. 133.
148 Oberleitner, *supra* note 4, p. 312.

the African Commission not only found Chad responsible for the killings and disappearances, but it also applied the human rights law standard of a mandatory *ex post facto* investigation into the circumstances surrounding the loss of human life in the context of a civil war.[149] The African Commission reasoned that even where it could not be demonstrated that the killings were committed by State agents, "the government has a responsibility to ... conduct investigations into murders."[150] This illustrates a clear instance where the Commission applied a human rights norm in a situation of non-international armed conflict. No reference, however, was made to the potential applicability of IHL in determining the case.

A subsequent communication that arose from the non-international armed conflict in Sudan shows both how the African Commission insists on the continued application of human rights law in armed conflict and recognises a role for IHL in such situations. In *Amnesty International et al* the Commission not only upheld the application of the African Charter in armed conflict, but it also referred to IHL as one of the sources of legal obligations additional to the Charter.[151] In finding Sudan in violation of human rights in the African Charter, the African Commission also observed that "civilians in areas of strife are especially vulnerable and the state must take all possible measures to ensure that they are treated in accordance with [IHL]."[152] Having taken note of the widespread practice of arbitrary executions in Sudan, the Commission found it necessary to invoke IHL to remind African States of their obligation to respect and ensure respect for IHL in times of armed conflict.

Amnesty International Law et al thus establishes, albeit implicitly, that international legal responsibility may attach to States for not taking the reasonable steps to prevent breaches of IHL or human rights law, be they committed by its armed forces or by non-State armed groups. This judgment reflects the basic legal protections offered in armed conflict and the desire to secure accountability for it.[153] This view is supported by the African Commission's non-adjudicatory work, including its thematic resolutions and situation-specific statements, which reiterate the need for all parties to an armed conflict to respect the African Charter and IHL.[154]

---

149 *Chad Mass Violations, supra* note 126, para. 21.
150 *Ibid.*
151 *Amnesty International et al, supra* note 126, para. 50.
152 *Ibid.*, para. 50.
153 Sang-YK, *supra* note 6, p. 28.
154 *See* the discussion below section 4.3.

4.2.3 From Co-application to Concurrent Violations of IHL and Human Rights Law

A logical consequence of the continued application of human rights law in times of armed conflict and its co-application with IHL is the prospect of finding concurrent violations of IHL and human rights law.[155] Yet, as with other human rights treaty mechanisms,[156] the African Commission has been cautious about moving from acceptance of co-application to making explicit findings of African Charter-based and IHL-centred violations. Its jurisprudence shows that whereas it recognises, as a matter of principle, that concurrent violations of IHL and human rights law often occur simultaneously in armed conflict, it infrequently makes express findings of concurrent violations of the two sets of laws.[157]

Two communications concerning alleged breaches of both the African Charter and IHL norms in the context of incontestable armed conflict situations can be used to demonstrate the Commission's ambivalence towards the finding of concurrent violations. The first example is to be found in *DRC v. Burundi, Rwanda and Uganda* which arose from the unlawful occupation of the territory of the complainant State by the respective armed forces of the respondent States, thus giving rise to a situation of international armed conflict.[158] Apart from violations of the African Charter, the Commission specified the respective IHL provisions that were seriously breached by the armed forces of the respondent States. In particular, it found that "the killings, massacres, rapes, mutilations and other grave human rights abuses" committed by the armed forces of the foreign powers while occupying the eastern provinces of the DRC were "inconsistent with [the respondent States'] obligations under Part III of the Geneva Convention relative to the Protection of Civilian Persons in Time of War of 1949 and Protocol I of the Geneva Conventions."[159]

DRC v. Burundi, Rwanda and Uganda is also remarkable as the Commission went beyond simply identifying IHL treaties that impose legal obligations.[160] In an unprecedented manner, the Commission entered

---

155 Oberleitner, *supra* note 4, p. 312.
156 *Las Palmeras v. Colombia*, 6 December 2001, IACtHR, Series C No. 67, Preliminary Objections, 6 December 2001, paras. 32-34; *Ergi v. Turkey*, 28 July 1998, ECHR, Application No. 40/1993/435/514,.
157 Sang-YK, *supra* note 6, p. 34.
158 *Prosecutor v. Tadić*, 2 October 1995, ICTY, IT-94-1, Appeals Chamber, , para. 70.
159 *DRC v. Burundi, Rwanda and Uganda*, *supra* note 120, para. 79.
160 L. Doswald-Beck, *Human Rights in Times of Conflict and Terrorism* (Oxford University Press, Oxford, 2011) pp. 109-110.

into the specificities of the conduct that violated particular provisions of IHL treaties and, where appropriate, how such violations also breached human rights protections. The Commission found that: (a) the siege by the respondent States of the hydroelectric dam in the Lower Congo province violated the prohibitions contained in Article 56 of the First Protocol additional to the Geneva Conventions of 1949 and Article 23 of the Hague Convention (II) with respect to the Laws and Customs of War on Land;[161] (b) the raping of women and girls by the armed forces of the respondent States, which "is prohibited under Article 76 of the First Protocol Additional to the Geneva Conventions of 1949" and also offends both the African Charter and the Convention on the Elimination of All Forms of Discrimination Against Women;[162] and (c) the "indiscriminate dumping of and or mass burials of victims of the series of massacres and killings" are proscribed by Article 34 of the First Protocol Additional to the Geneva Conventions "which provides for the respect of the remains of such peoples and their gravesites", and also violates Article 22 of the African Charter.[163]

The extensive application of IHL in *DRC v. Burundi, Rwanda and Uganda* could not be more different than the Commission's approach in the subsequent communication of *Sudan Human Rights Organisation*.[164] This communication arose from the non-international armed conflict in Sudan between the Janjaweed militia supported by Sudanese government forces and the armed groups of the Nilotic tribes. The armed confrontation between the parties of the conflict resulted in extrajudicial killings, deliberate bombing of civilian populations, forced displacement, and destruction of civilian objects. The complainant's case made reference to a context of armed conflict where the "militia" assisted by "military fighter jets" bombarded the "civilian population".[165] The African Commission held that the government of Sudan was liable for targeting civilians as opposed to the "combatants" taking part in "the armed conflict."[166] Yet the Commission did not expressly refer to IHL as part of the applicable law in the matter. Nor did it indirectly apply it by interpreting African Charter provisions in light of IHL norms. This illustrates a puzzling departure from its reasoning in *DRC v. Burundi, Rwanda and Uganda*.

---

161   *DRC v. Burundi, Rwanda and Uganda, supra* note 120, paras. 83-84.
162   *Ibid.*
163   *Ibid.*
164   *Sudan Human Rights Organisation, supra* note 127.
165   *Ibid.*, para. 16.
166   *Ibid.*, para. 223.

One of the explanations given for the different approach taken in these two cases is that while the parties in *DRC v. Burundi, Rwanda and Uganda* explicitly pleaded IHL in their submissions, the applicants in *Sudan Human Rights Organisation* only used IHL-based terms in a descriptive sense.[167] Though this explanation is convincing, it is put into question by the Commission's decision in *Amnesty International et al* where, despite the fact that the parties did not rely on IHL in their submissions, the Commission referred to and took into consideration IHL in analysing alleged violations arising from the conflict in Sudan (the same conflict at the centre of *Sudan Human Rights Organisation*).[168] Even more detrimental to the 'deficient-party-submissions' argument is the fact that in its own fact-finding mission on the Darfur conflict, the African Commission characterised the situation as an "all out civil war",[169] observing the "continuing violations of human rights and [IHL] in Darfur and the continued depopulation of vast areas in the region of their indigenous owners".[170]

The African Commission's ambivalence towards finding concurrent violations of human rights law and IHL suggests a conflicted institution which, though recognising the potential role of IHL in determining a case, remains overly sensitive to and ultimately constrained by the political implications of applying IHL. In contrast, the Commission has been more willing to engage overtly with IHL in its non-adjudicative work. This has, in some respects, made up partially for the shortfalls of its IHL-related quasi-judicial jurisprudence and, more crucially, can contribute to the subsequent adoption of more principled approaches to IHL in the African human rights system.

4.3   *IHL in the African Commission's Non-Adjudicative Work*

In addition to its adjudicative function, the African Commission has an important role to play in standard-setting and adopting thematic or country-specific resolutions on human rights issues. This role has its legal basis in Article 45 of the African Charter which authorises the Commission to "give its views or make recommendations to Governments"[171] and to "formulate and lay down principles and rules"[172] in order to promote human rights and assist States to implement their treaty obligations. In

---

167   Viljoen, *supra* note 6, p. 331.
168   *Amnesty International et al*, *supra* note 126, para. 50.
169   *Ibid.*, para. 24.
170   *Ibid.*
171   African Charter, *supra* note 8, Article 45(1)(a).
172   *Ibid.*

the exercise of this non-adjudicative role, the African Commission has responded to armed conflicts where African Charter rights were violated by passing resolutions that urge all parties to the conflict to comply with IHL and human rights law, as well as by adopting general comments to clarify the interaction between IHL and the African Charter.[173] These developments are considered below.

4.3.1 Thematic Resolutions

Unlike when exercising its quasi-judicial function, the African Commission has been more ready to invoke IHL in its thematic and country-specific resolutions. It has, for instance, adopted some thematic resolutions calling for the dissemination and implementation of IHL in Africa on the basis of its common object with human rights law.[174] A notable example is the Resolution on the Promotion and the Respect of International Humanitarian Law and Human and Peoples' Rights which states, inter alia, that the African Commission:

> [c]onsidering that human rights and [IHL] have always, even in different situations, aimed at protecting human beings and their fundamental rights ... [r]ecognising the need for close cooperation in the field of dissemination of [IHL] and human and peoples' rights: 1. Invites all African States ... to adopt appropriate measures at the national level to ensure the promotion of the provisions of [IHL] and human and peoples' rights; 2. Stresses the need for specific instruction of military personnel and the training of the forces of law and order in [IHL] and human and peoples' rights respectively.[175]

Country-specific resolutions have also been used by the African Commission to invoke IHL directly. During the widespread and systematic attacks related to the 1994 genocide in Rwanda, the Commission passed a resolution that called on all parties to the armed conflict "to respect the African Charter ... the principles of [IHL] as well as the activities of the humani-

---

173 C. Heyns and T, Probert, 'Casting Fresh Light on the Supreme Right: The African Commission's *General Comment No. 3* on the Right to Life', in T. Maluwa, M. du Plessis and D. Tladi (eds.), *The Pursuit of a Brave New World in International Law: Essays in Honour of John Dugard* (Nijhoff, Leiden, 2017) pp. 63-66.

174 African Commission on Human and Peoples' Rights, *Resolution on the Promotion and Respect of International Humanitarian Law and Human and Peoples' Rights*, 14th Ordinary Session, 1-10 December 1993.

175 *Ibid.*

tarian organisations operating in the field."[176] In a statement issued concerning the armed conflict in Mali following the 2013 coup, the Commission called upon all parties to the conflict to respect human rights law at all times, and "to fully respect [IHL] and protect civilian populations and their property."[177] Likewise, in its 2011 resolution on the human rights situation in Libya, the Commission expressed concern over the violent suppression by Libyan government's armed forces of peaceful protests by civilians, which resulted in "loss of lives and the wanton destruction of buildings and property in violation of the African Charter and other relevant judicial, regional, international human rights instruments and [IHL]".[178]

4.3.2 General Comment No. 3 on the Right to Life

The African Commission has only recently started issuing general comments, which are soft law instruments designed to clarify the scope and content of particular rights as well as to elaborate on the corresponding State obligations. As with other thematic instruments, these general comments are authoritative interpretations of treaty law intended to "guide and modify state behaviour by enunciating principles and measures required to implement and comply with specific rights."[179] Of particular importance to the present discussion is General Comment No. 3 which outlines the perspective of the African Commission on the interpretation, application, and implementation of the right to life under Article 4 of the African Charter.[180]

In General Comment No. 3, the African Commission is explicit in affirming the continued application of the right to life in armed conflict situations: "The right to life continues to apply during armed conflict."[181] This confirms the consistent position adopted by the Commission in its practice. A more innovative aspect of General Comment No. 3 is the Commission's elaboration of the interaction between IHL and human rights law in armed conflict, which reflects four key advances in its IHL-related

---

176 African Commission on Human and Peoples' Rights, *Resolution on Rwanda*, Seventh Annual Activity Report, 1993-1994.
177 African Commission on Human and Peoples' Rights, *Statement by the African Commission on the Situation in Mali*, 18 January 2013.
178 African Commission on Human and Peoples' Rights, *Resolution on the Human Rights Situation in Libya*, ACHPR/Res.181 (EXT.OS/IX) 2011, 1 March 2011.
179 Long and Murray, *supra* note 104, p. 90.
180 General Comment No. 3, *supra* note 106.
181 *Ibid.*, para. 13.

jurisprudence. First, General Comment No. 3 recognises the need to construe the right to life in Article 4 of the African Charter in light of relevant IHL norms: "During the conduct of hostilities, the right to life *needs* to be interpreted with reference to the rules of international humanitarian law."[182] This signals a shift from the uncertain status of IHL in some of its decisions to a more principled affirmation of IHL as part of the applicable law in determining cases arising from armed conflict.

The second progressive aspect of General Comment No. 3 is how the African Commission, in a manner unprecedented in its IHL-related jurisprudence, stated that "arbitrary deprivation of life" must be defined with reference to IHL:

> In armed conflict, what constitutes an 'arbitrary' deprivation of life during the conduct of hostilities is to be determined by reference to [IHL]. This law does not prohibit the use of force in hostilities against lawful targets (for example combatants or civilians directly participating in hostilities) if necessary from a military perspective, provided that, in all circumstances, the rules of distinction, proportionality and precaution in attack are observed. Any violation of [IHL] resulting in death, including war crimes, will be an arbitrary deprivation of life.[183]

One implication of the above excerpt is that all decisions on whether loss of life resulting from combat operations is arbitrary, and thus contrary to Article 4 of the African Charter, must be made after having regard to the cardinal principles of IHL. It is also notable that the language used in General Comment No. 3 is drawn from the ICJ's *Nuclear Weapons* advisory opinion, which affirmed the applicability of the rules and principles of IHL as well as those of human rights law on the right to life to the use of lethal weapons.[184] The significance of IHL in deciding the justifiability of killings in armed conflict is also established in the practice of human rights treaty bodies.[185] Thus General Comment No. 3 consolidates the view that IHL provides the yardstick for evaluating when the use of lethal

---

182 *Ibid.*, para. 13.
183 *Ibid.*, para. 32.
184 *Nuclear Weapons, supra* note 25, para. 25.
185 Human Rights Committee, *General Comment No. 31: The Nature of General Legal Obligations Imposed on States Parties to the Covenant*, UN Doc. CCPR/C/21/Rev.1/Add. 13, para. 11; *Santo Domingo Massacre v. Colombia*, 30 November 2012, IACtHR, Ser. C No. 259, paras. 211-236.

force during hostilities constitutes "arbitrary deprivation of life in violation of relevant human rights norms."[186]

The third and, arguably, most important innovation of General Comment No. 3 is the fact that *lex specialis* is not presented as the principal interpretive tool for negotiating the relations between IHL norms and Article 4 of the African Charter. Even though *lex specialis* is a useful interpretive and norm-conflict-resolution device, its (mis)use is both notorious and deeply controversial. This has been cited as one of the reasons for its omission in the ICJ's *Armed Activities* judgment.[187] By avoiding the contested *lex specialis* principle, the African Commission seems to endorse the *pro homine* (priority to the most protective norm) principle which draws on the wider jurisprudence of the Inter-American human rights system.[188] This principle holds that where two or more norms simultaneously govern a disputed issue, priority should be given to the norm that offers the greatest protection to human beings.[189]

That the *pro homine* principle is advocated by General Comment No. 3 is clear in its position on the 'kill or capture' debate.[190] The Commission notes that in cases where military necessity does not demand the use of lethal force, "but allows the target for example to be captured rather than killed, the respect for the right to life can be best ensured by pursuing this option."[191] *Pro homine*-oriented reasoning is also evident in the requirement that the use of new technologies, and weapons systems, such as drones, during hostilities "should only be envisaged if they strengthen the protection of the right to life of those affected."[192] This indicates that the more restrictive human rights norms should prevail over IHL in cases where they offer better legal protection.

The final innovation of General Comment No. 3 is that it clarifies the legal implications of the co-application of IHL and the African Charter,

---

186 V. Todeschini, 'The Relationship between International Humanitarian Law and Human Rights Law in the African Commission's General Comment on the Right to Life', EJIL: Talk! 7 June 2016.
187 *Armed Activities*, supra note 28, para. 216.
188 T. Antkowiak and A. Gonza, *American Convention on Human Rights: Essential Rights* (Oxford, Oxford University Press, 2017) p. 3.
189 L. Lixinski, 'Treaty Interpretation by the Inter-American Court of Human Rights: Expansionism at the Service of the Unity of International Law', 21 *European Journal of International Law* (2010) p. 588.
190 R. Goodman, 'The Power to Kill or Capture Enemy Combatants', 24 *European Journal of International Law* (2013) p. 819.
191 General Comment No. 3, *supra* note 106, para. 34.
192 *Ibid.*, para. 35.

particularly where loss of life results from a breach of IHL norms. General Comment No. 3 provides that "[a]ny violation of [IHL] resulting in death, including war crimes, will be an arbitrary deprivation of life."[193] This is novel development in the practice of human rights treaty mechanisms. The African Commission advances a view that, though established in international criminal jurisprudence,[194] has never been adopted explicitly by a universal or regional human rights treaty body.[195] The African Commission thus enunciates the position that, even where more pertinent IHL norms override human rights norms, breaches of IHL norms will entail violations of the corresponding human rights norms, thereby triggering accountability measures under the pertinent human rights treaty law.[196]

5 IHL in the Jurisprudence of the African Court on Human and Peoples' Rights

Despite the important work done by the African Commission, as early as in the mid-1990s serious concerns were raised about the critical shortfalls of its enforcement capacity.[197] This was triggered by widespread non-compliance of African States with the African Commission's decisions and the Commission's lack of means to enforce compliance.[198] Thus in 1998 the Protocol to the African Charter on Human and Peoples' Rights[199] (hereafter '1998 Protocol') was adopted to establish a court with legally binding force to complement the African Commission's work.[200]

---

193 *Ibid.*, para. 32.
194 *Prosecutor* v. *Kupreskić et al.*, 14 January 2000, ICTY, Case No. IT-95-16-T, Trial Chamber, , para. 518.
195 *Hassan* v. *United Kingdom*, 16 September 2016, ECHR, Application No. 29750/09, para. 105, para. 105; *Santo Domingo Massacre, supra* note 185, paras. 230 and 237.
196 Heyns and Probert, *supra* note 173, p. 64.
197 F. Viljoen and L. Louw, 'State Compliance with the Recommendations of the African Commission on Human and Peoples' Rights, 1994-2004', 101 *American Journal of International Law* (2007) pp. 1-2.
198 Murray and Long, *supra* note 96, pp. 4-5.
199 African Commission on Human and Peoples' Rights, *Protocol to the African Charter on Human and Peoples' Rights on the Establishment of an African Court on Human and Peoples' Rights*, June 9, 1998, OAU Doc. AU/LEG/EXP/AFCHPR/PROT (III).
200 G.J. Naldi, 'The Role of the Human and Peoples' Rights Section of the African Court of Justice and Human Rights', in A. Abass (ed.), *Protecting Human Security in Africa* (Oxford University Press, Oxford, 2010) p. 284.

This section examines how the African Court has contributed towards securing better compliance with the African Charter's provisions in cases where IHL is simultaneously applicable. In order to do so, the jurisdiction and functions of the African Court are outlined, and its approach to IHL is reviewed.

5.1 Functions and jurisdiction of the African Court

Established by a Protocol to the African Charter, the African Court is a judicial organ of the AU that is mandated to complement and reinforce the functions of the African Commission. It was intended as a means to address weaknesses in the enforcement capacity of the Commission and to complement its protective mandate. Thus the role envisaged for the Court includes the settlement of legal disputes arising from obligations in African human rights treaty law, interpreting and applying other legal instruments pertaining to human rights, and making pronouncements on relevant aspects of multilateral treaties.[201]

In regard to its jurisdiction, the African Court is competent to exercise dual and complementary jurisdiction; it can settle contentious disputes and issue advisory opinions. Article 3(1) of the 1998 Protocol specifies that the Court's jurisdiction covers all cases and disputes that are submitted to the Court and which entail the interpretation and application of the African Charter, as well as the Protocol and any other human rights instruments ratified by States Parties to the 1998 Protocol. Article 3(2) also affirms the Court's competence to decide its own jurisdiction over a particular matter. Article 34(6) of the 1998 Protocol further qualifies the scope of the Court's contentious jurisdiction. It states that the Court may only adjudicate complaints which have been instituted against States that have explicitly accepted the Court's jurisdiction.

As for the Court's advisory jurisdiction, Article 4 of the 1998 Protocol empowers the Court to prepare opinions on any legal matter relating to the African Charter or any other relevant human rights instrument when requested by the AU, a member State of the AU, one of the AU bodies, or any other organisation recognised by the AU.[202] Where the Court agrees to such a request (to prepare an opinion), it must substantiate its position and individual judges of the Court may express their dissenting views.[203] The scope of issuing advisory opinions is broader than that in conten-

---

201 1998 Protocol, *supra* note 199, Article 3.
202 Naldi, *supra* note 200, p. 303.
203 1998 Protocol, *supra* note 199, Article 4(2).

tious cases because while the subject-matter of the latter is restricted to human rights instruments ratified by the concerned States, the former is not. Hence, when the opportunity arises, the Court should utilise advisory opinions to clarify the status of IHL in the African human rights system.

Like the African Charter, the 1998 Protocol does not explicitly state that IHL is one of the applicable sources of law to which the relevant African human rights treaty bodies may have recourse. But both treaties refer to other relevant human rights instruments adopted by African States. The Commission has, in its practice, read these references as a legal basis for taking IHL into consideration in determining cases involving armed conflict.[204] However, some commentators argue that the phrase "other human rights instruments" should be accorded a narrow interpretation and limited to only such human rights instruments ratified by all the States that have accepted the competence of the African Court.[205] This latter approach is overly restrictive and unsupported by both the drafting history of the 1998 Protocol and the practice of the Court. Indeed, the emerging jurisprudence of the Court indicates that it is willing to refer to other sources of general international law, such as treaties not adopted under the auspices of the AU legal framework as well as non-human rights instruments.[206]

5.2   *Conservative application of IHL by the African Court*

The African Court rendered its first judgment in 2009, almost 10 years after adoption of the 1998 Protocol and five years after its coming into force.[207] Despite this slow start, the African Court has seen an exponential increase in the number of decided cases in recent years. A combination of the Court's robust approach to its mandate and greater awareness of its work in the AU led to a rapidly expanding docket. The Court's ju-

---

204   *DRC v. Burundi, Rwanda and Uganda, supra* note 120, para. 70; *Amnesty International et al, supra* note 126, para. 50.

205   I. Östardahl, 'The Jurisdiction Materiae of the African Court of Human and Peoples' Rights' (1998) 7 *RACHPR* 132-50, p. 136.

206   T.G. Daly and M. Wiebusch, 'The African Court on Human and Peoples' Rights: Mapping Resistance against a Young Court', 14 *International Journal of Law in Context* (2018) pp. 294-313.

207   *Michelot Yogogombaye v. the Republic of Senegal* Application 001/2008, 2010, ACHPR, 49 I.L.M. 850; B. Sang-YK, 'Improving the Protection of Human and Peoples' Rights in Africa: Reflections from the *Yogogombaye* Case', 20 *African Journal of International and Comparative Law* (2012) pp. 348-352.

risprudence has grown in areas such as fair trial guarantees,[208] political rights,[209] and freedom of expression rights.[210] But for all the advances in its jurisprudence, the Court has not yet contributed meaningfully to the debate and discourse on the interplay between IHL and human rights law. One of the reasons for this is that compared to other issues such as fair trial rights that have been raised in numerous cases, few applications have dealt with issues of human rights violations in armed conflict where IHL becomes relevant. Even so, the Court's approach in instances where IHL may be applicable has been conservative at most.[211]

A key case where the Court showed its reluctance to engage with IHL is *African Commission on Human and Peoples' Rights* v. *Great Socialist People's Libyan Arab Jamahiriya*.[212] This case arose out of the 2011 armed conflict in Libya between forces loyal to the incumbent leader, Muamar Gaddafi, and armed opposition groups. The applicant (African Commission) sought an order of the Court to restrain the Libyan government's security forces from continuing its violent suppression of anti-government protests, including the aerial bombardment of civilian populations, and systematic detention of opponents. Such actions, urged the African Commission, constituted serious violations of the right to life and physical integrity of persons.

It is significant that the African Court in *Libya Provisional Measures* explicitly observed the existence of a situation of "ongoing conflict" in Libya during the course of which the AU Peace and Security Council had noted that violations of the African Charter rights and IHL had been perpetrated by agents of the Libyan government.[213] In spite of this acknowledgement, the Court elected not to contextualise its analysis within the backdrop of an armed conflict, nor did it have regard to IHL even in respect to the aerial bombardment of civilians. Rather, it avoided "any IHL-

---

208 *Jonas* v. *Tanzania*, Application No. 011/2015, 28 September 2017, ACHPR; *Onyango* v. *Tanzania*, Application 006/2013, 18 March 2016, ACHPR; *Abubakari* v. *Tanzania*, Application No. 007/2013, 3 June 2016, ACHPR.
209 *Actions Pour La Protection des Droits de l'Homme (APDH)* v. *The Republic of Côte d'Ivoire*, Application No. 001/2014, 18 November 2016, ACHPR, para. 65; *Mtikila* v. *Tanzania*, Application No. 009/2011 and 011/2011, 14 June 2013, ACHPR.
210 *Ingabire* v. *Rwanda*, Application No. 003/2014, 24 November 2017; *Zongo* v. *Burkina Faso*, Application No. 013/2011, 28 March 2014.
211 Viljoen, *supra* note 6, p. 325.
212 *African Commission on Human and Peoples' Rights* v. *Great Socialist People's Libyan Arab Jamahiriya*, Case No. 4/11, 25 March 2011, ACtHR, Provisional Measures, [2011] AHRLR 175.
213 *Ibid.*, para. 13.

related language and focused on and framed the violations within the language of human rights" law.²¹⁴ Ultimately, the Court ordered Libya to "refrain from any action that would result in loss of life or violation of physical integrity of persons, which could be a breach of the [African] Charter or any other human rights instrument to which it is a party".²¹⁵ *Libya Provisional Measures* is a significant decision in terms of the status of IHL in the African human rights system because of what the Court said as well as what it omitted to say. On the one hand, by ordering Libya to refrain from violating specific provisions of the African Charter and other human rights treaties, the Court confirmed the continued application of human rights law in cases of collective violence, including armed conflict. For this finding, the Court is to be commended for fulfilling its mandate and complementing and reinforcing the Commission's jurisprudence.²¹⁶ On the other hand, by steering clear of IHL in its analysis and failing to restate the obligation of all belligerents to respect IHL, the Court created uncertainty regarding the normative role of IHL in its jurisprudence.²¹⁷ This is a regrettable aspect of *Libya Provisional Measures* as it represents a missed opportunity where the Court could have clarified the legal basis for referring to IHL, as has been partially done by the African Commission.

While the African Commission has made IHL a relevant part of its work in analysing human rights obligations in armed conflict situations, the conservative approach taken in the Court's jurisprudence seems to detract somewhat from the use of IHL in the African human rights system. The Court may have made its decision in order to be prudent; Libya and other actors may have contested the characterisation of the relevant situation as an armed conflict, thereby placing compliance with its future decisions at risk. However, such concerns should surely have been allayed by the AU Peace and Security Council's description of the situation as an armed conflict in which serious violations of IHL and human rights had been committed by Libyan agents.²¹⁸ As a result of its overly cautious approach, it remains unclear how and, if so, the extent to which IHL should be used in the Court's future work. This has not been helped by the fact

---

214   Viljoen, *supra* note 6, p. 325.
215   *Libya Provisional Measures, supra* note 140, para. 25.
216   *Chad Mass Violations, supra* note 26, paras. 21-22; *Amnesty International et al, supra* note 26, para. 50.
217   Sang-YK, *supra* note 6, p. 34.
218   *Libya Provisional Measures, supra* note 140, para 13.

that there have been no further cases decided by the Court arising from alleged violations of the African Charter in situations of armed conflict.

6 The Potential Role of IHL in the Future Work of the African Court of Justice and Human Rights

Concerned about the proliferation of AU institutions and the onerous financial cost that such a development would create, in 2004 the AU decided to merge the African Court of Human and Peoples' Rights with the "not-yet-existent" Court of Justice of the African Union.[219] Another key consideration that informed the integration of these two courts was the need to remedy one of the African human rights system's most significant challenges: the lack of "an authoritative, robust, and effective supervisory and enforcement mechanism."[220] The merger of the two courts was given legal effect through the Protocol on the Statute of the African Court of Justice and Human Rights (hereafter '2008 Protocol').[221] This Protocol is, however, yet to come into force as it has not been ratified by 15 Member States.[222]

Nonetheless, the African Court of Justice and Human Rights will in the near future become the principal judicial organ of the AU, a fact supported by the recent extension of its subject-matter jurisdiction to encompass genocide, war crimes, and crimes against humanity.[223] This development is of key relevance to the present inquiry because this newfound subject-matter jurisdiction will necessarily require the Court to engage with IHL. But since the African Court of Justice and Human Rights is not yet operational, the most constructive approach to determining what potential role IHL may have in the Court's future work is to: (a) examine its structure, jurisdiction and functions, and (b) analyse the legal basis for engaging with IHL in its future work.

---

219 Kioko and Wambugu, *supra* note 84, p. 283.
220 Naldi, *supra* note 200, p. 311.
221 African Union, *Protocol on the Statute of the African Court of Justice and Human Rights*, 1 July 2008.
222 The 2008 Protocol has been ratified by only six Member States of the African Union, nine short of the number needed to trigger its entry into force. Ratifications have been made by the following States: Benin; Burkina Faso; Congo; Libya; Liberia; and Mali.
223 C.C. Jalloh, 'The Nature of the Crimes in the African Criminal Court', 15 *Journal of International Criminal Justice* (2017) p. 799.

6.1 *Structure, Jurisdiction, and Function*

Established by Article 2 of the 2008 Protocol, the African Court of Justice and Human Rights will ultimately be the principal judicial organ of the AU. It is thus necessary to consider carefully the implications of its institutional organisation, jurisdiction, and functions for the protection of human rights in Africa. This section will examine whether the Court's mandate and operational structure is sufficiently robust to ensure respect for human rights and IHL in times of armed conflict, particularly in light of the recent creation of a chamber with international criminal jurisdiction.

The institutional merger of the African Court of Human and Peoples' Rights with the Court of Justice of the African Union resulted in a new court that retained the jurisdictional competencies of its two precursors. In particular, this new court was originally composed of two chambers: a General Affairs Section and a Human Rights Section. The International Criminal Law Section was only incorporated later in response to the perceived targeting of African leaders by the International Criminal Court (hereafter 'ICC').[224] The initial plan was to have the General Affairs section exercise the jurisdiction analogous to that of the Court of Justice of the African Union, while the Human Rights Section, like the African Court of Human and Peoples' Rights, would exercise jurisdiction over alleged human rights violations. With the introduction of an expanded criminal jurisdiction, the African Court of Justice and Human Rights will have greater scope to consider IHL in its adjudicative work.

The General Affairs Section will be competent to exercise jurisdiction over all cases and legal disputes that are specified in Article 28 of the 2008 Protocol, "save those concerning human and/or peoples' rights issues".[225] Thus the General Affairs Section shall have competence over matters relating to: the interpretation and application of the Constitutive Act of the AU; the interpretation, application, and validity of other AU treaties as well as subsidiary legal instruments; any question of international law except those relating to human rights law; the content of agreements concluded between States Parties, between themselves or with the AU, and which confer jurisdiction on the Court; and the nature or extent of reparations to be made for breaches of international obligations. This indicates that the General Affairs Section will play a role comparable to that

---

224 *Ibid.*
225 2008 Protocol, *supra* note 221, Article 17(1).

of the European Court of Justice which decides questions of EU law,[226] as the General Affairs Section will make decisions on questions of AU law and is expected to develop jurisprudence on general principles of AU law.

In contrast to the broad subject-matter jurisdiction of the General Affairs Section, the Human Rights Section can only determine cases concerning human or peoples' rights. Article 17(2) of the 2008 Protocol specifies that the "Human Rights Section shall be competent to hear all cases relating to human and/or peoples' rights." The jurisdiction of the Human Rights Section is defined by Article 17, which specifies the competence of the General Affairs and Human Rights Sections, and Article 28 of the 2008 Protocol, which indicates that the Human Rights Section shall have jurisdiction over all legal disputes relating to: (a) the interpretation and application of the African Charter, the African Children's Charter, the African Protocol on Women's Rights, the Kampala Convention, or any other legal instrument relating to human rights ratified by the States Parties concerned,[227] and (b) any question of international law that raises human rights issues.[228]

It is thus conceivable that the Human Rights Section of the African Court of Justice and Human Rights will be competent to engage with IHL insofar as it applies alongside human rights law. Indeed, as has been discussed above,[229] the African treaty regime for women, children and IDPs integrate human rights law and IHL, thereby providing a normative basis for relevant human rights mechanisms to have regard to IHL in their respective supervisory and monitoring work. In the case of the African Court of Justice and Human Rights which is designed expressly to have legally binding authority, IHL will potentially acquire a much-needed enforcement mechanism to ensure compliance with fundamental rights in armed conflict.

A more recent development that will like have even more far-reaching implications for IHL in the African human rights system is the establishment of a third chamber in the African Court of Justice and Human Rights which has the competence to try core international crimes such as genocide, war crimes, and crimes against humanity: the International Criminal Law Section. In June 2014, at its summit in Malabo, Equatorial

---

226   M. Parish, 'International Courts and the European Legal Order', 23 *European Journal of International Law* (2012) p. 142.
227   2008 Protocol, *supra* note 221, Article 28(c).
228   *Ibid.*, Article 28(d).
229   *See* Sections 3.1, 3.2 and 3.3 above.

Guinea the AU adopted the Protocol on Amendments to the Protocol on the Statute of the African Court of Justice and Human Rights ('Malabo Protocol').[230] The principal judicial effect of the Malabo Protocol was to extend the jurisdiction of the Court to encompass core international crimes falling within the jurisdiction of the ICC, as well as other transnational crimes including corruption, money laundering, human trafficking, and the illicit exploitation of natural resources.[231]

Most relevant to our present discussion is the fact that, once it becomes operational, the International Criminal Law Section will be the African regional equivalent of the ICC; it will operate "in a manner akin to the [ICC] but within a narrowly defined geographical scope, and over a massively expanded list of crimes."[232] Genocide, crimes against humanity and, chiefly, war crimes are often committed in those conflict situations in which IHL may apply. Thus to the extent that IHL applies to a relevant situation, the International Criminal Law Section of the African Court of Justice and Human Rights will be competent to decide on any question of international law relating to grave breaches of IHL, including serious violations of human rights, during armed conflict.

Alongside its contentious jurisdiction, the African Court of Justice and Human Rights is competent to exercise an advisory jurisdiction. Article 53 of the 2008 Protocol authorises the Court to "give an advisory opinion on any legal question at the request of the Assembly, the Parliament, the Executive Council, the Peace and Security Council, the Economic, Social and Cultural Council (ECOSOCC), the Financial Institutions, or any other organ of the Union as may be authorised by the Assembly." The Peace and Security Council is the organ of the AU most likely to find IHL pertinent to its work because among its objectives are the protection and promotion of human rights and humanitarian law.[233] Equally, the African Commission, at the request of individuals or NGOs, may have the occasion to seek advisory opinions on legal questions relating to human rights in armed conflict.

Having shown that the institutional structure and jurisdictional competence of the African Court of Justice and Human Rights admits engagement with IHL, particularly by the Human Rights Section and Interna-

---

230 *Protocol on Amendments to the Protocol on the Statute of the African Court of Justice and Human Rights*, AU Doc. No. Assembly/AU/Dec.529 (XXIII).
231 Jalloh, *supra* note 218, pp. 799-826.
232 Amnesty International, *Malabo Protocol: Legal and Institutional Implications of the Merged and Expanded African Court* (Amnesty International, London, 2016) p. 5.
233 Kioko and Wambugu, *supra* note 84, p. 279.

tional Criminal Law Section, the next logical step would be to specify on what basis the Court may apply or interpret IHL in its work.

6.2   Legal Basis for Applying IHL

The sources of applicable law that the African Court of Justice and Human Rights must have regard to in determining cases submitted to it are specified in descending order of priority in the 2008 Protocol.[234] Article 31(1) provides that in carrying out its functions, the Court must take into account:

(a) The Constitutive Act [of the AU];
(d) International treaties, whether general or particular, ratified by the contesting States;
(c) International custom, as evidence of a general practice accepted as law;
(e) The general principles of law recognised universally or by African States;
(f) Subject to the provisions of paragraph 1 of Article 46 of the present Statute, judicial decisions and writings of the most highly qualified publicists of various nations as well as regulations, doctrines and decisions of the Union, as subsidiary means for the determination of the rules of law;
(g) Any other law relevant to the determination of the case."

Article 31(2) further provides that, where the parties agree, it has the power to "decide a case *ex aequo et bono*". This means that in addition to the sources of law expressly enumerated in Article 31(1), the Court can also refer to the principles of equity and good conscience.[235]

A striking feature of Article 31 of the 2008 Protocol is its remarkable similarity to Article 38 of the Statute of the International Court of Justice,[236] which likewise recognises as sources of law international treaties, custom, general principles of law, judicial decisions, and writings of the most highly qualified publicists of international law. However, the main difference between the two instruments is the regional vis-à-vis

---

234   Naldi, *supra* note 200, p. 300.
235   F. Ouguergouz, 'The African Court of Justice and Human Rights', in A. Yusuf and F. Ouguergouz (ed.), *The African Union Legal and Institutional Framework: A Manual on the Pan-African Organisation* (Brill, Leiden, 2012) p. 133.
236   *Statute of the International Court of Justice* (33 U.N.T.S. 993), Article 38; 2008 Protocol, *supra* note 221, Ouguergouz, *supra* note 235, p. 133.

international contexts in which the two courts apply. Still, an objective and holistic reading of Article 31 of the 2008 Protocol suggests that the jurisdiction of the ICJ mirrors the jurisdiction envisaged for the African Court of Justice and Human Rights. Four reasons support the contention that, though there are some differences in the text and language, the applicable law that Article 31 of the 2008 Protocol requires the African Court of Justice and Human Rights to apply is functionally equivalent to that which Article 38 of the ICJ Statute requires the ICJ to apply. These reasons in turn provide the entry point for arguing that IHL is part of the applicable law to which the African Court of Justice and Human Rights may have recourse in its future work.

First, the reference in Article 31(1)(b) of the 2008 Protocol to international treaties ratified by the contesting States may include the Kampala Convention, the African Women's Protocol, and the African Children's Charter, as well as the 1949 Geneva Conventions and their Additional Protocols. Second, a number of IHL norms have attained the status of customary international law, a fact that has been confirmed in binding decisions of international tribunals and courts.[237] This means that such IHL norms may be applied in the reasoning and findings of the Court. Third, the common core of IHL and human rights norms, including the prohibition of torture and restriction on arbitrary killings, are codified in the national laws of an overwhelming majority of States. This qualifies them as general principles of law, and to the extent that they reflect IHL norms they are applicable to the work of the African Court of Justice and Human Rights. Fourth, judicial decisions may bind the parties of a particular dispute in subsequent proceedings between them. Therefore, the African Commission's IHL-related findings in *DRC v. Burundi, Rwanda and Uganda* may bind the States involved in the case in future. In sum, it is therefore conceivable that IHL will have an important role in the future work of the not-yet-operational African Court of Justice and Human Rights.

---

237 *Prosecutor* v. *Martić*, Case No. IT-95-11-T, paras. 67-69 (prohibition on attacking civilians); *Prosecutor* v. *Galić*, Case No. IT-98-29-A, paras. 190-192 (prohibition on attacking civilians) and para. 58 (verification of targets).

7 A Critique of the Status, Use, and Effect of IHL in the Jurisprudence of African Human Rights Treaty Bodies

An argument may be made that the case law and other non-adjudicative work of African human rights treaty bodies on how IHL interacts with the AU and universal and regional human rights treaty frameworks is limited. Thus, it is difficult to determine decisively the status, use, and effect of IHL in the African human rights system. It is true that the IHL-related jurisprudence of African human rights treaty bodies is not as voluminous or varied as that of the equivalent bodies in the Inter-American or European human rights systems. Yet the limited case law argument can be challenged because there is no bright-line test for determining the number, type, and character of cases required to meet the relevant volume threshold.

It is submitted here that the better argument is that, though modest in number or variety, the IHL-related decisions and other work of the African Commission, African Court of Human and Peoples' Rights, and the African Children's Rights Committee is a sufficient basis from which to draw useful conclusions on the role and contribution of IHL in the African human rights system. In particular, a critical analysis of the existing jurisprudence enables certain general observations to be made and specific trends to be mapped, which in turn provides the opportunity to analyse what should be reformed. An analysis of this sort is given below.

7.1 Increasing Relevance, Inconsistent Use, and Indeterminate Utility of IHL

The increasing relevance of IHL in the work of African human rights treaty bodies is one of the key trends that characterise the IHL-human rights relations in the African human rights system. That the role and effect of IHL has grown both in scope and import is supported by a chronological review of the jurisprudence of the African Commission. In the period of the early to mid-1990s, IHL was not at all referred to in decisions on human rights violations in armed conflict, like *Chad Mass Violations*[238] and *Organisation Mondiale Contre La Torture*.[239] By the late 1990s until the early 2000s, the Commission had begun referring to IHL as applicable law in considering alleged breaches of the African Charter in armed con-

---

238 *Chad Mass Violations*, supra note 126.
239 *Organisation Mondiale Contre La Torture*, supra note 135.

flict. A decision that illustrates this point is *Amnesty International et al*.[240] This trend reached its height in the mid-2000s in *DRC* v. *Burundi, Rwanda and Uganda* where the Commission made extensive reference to IHL and found concurrent violations of IHL as well as of the African Charter.

However, this general tendency towards the increasing relevance of and engagement with IHL in the work of African human rights treaty bodies has neither been uniform nor coherent. Instead, the IHL-related practice discloses a divergence of approaches within and across the jurisprudence of the African Commission and Court. The African Commission has frequently referred to concepts or the language of IHL, whether descriptively or substantively, in its assessment of human rights violations. By contrast, the African Court has avoided it entirely. Even within the jurisprudence of the Commission, one can find instances of marked inconsistency in engaging with IHL. Two decisions relating to the civil war in Sudan can suitably illustrate this. In *Amnesty International et al*, the Commission found that in order to protect vulnerable civilians in conflict zones, the State must take "all possible measures to ensure that they are treated in accordance with IHL."[241] Yet in *Sudan Human Rights Organisation* the Commission only used words like "civilians" or "civilian population" in a descriptive manner without invoking substantive IHL.[242] The African Commission even applied IHL in contradictory ways in assessing violations of the African Charter in the context of a single armed conflict occurring in the same country (Sudan).

The inconsistent use of IHL by African human rights treaty bodies may lead to uncertainty as to its status and role in determining cases. This is a worrisome outcome as it casts the utility of IHL into doubt at a time when its contribution to the protection of human rights in the African regional system can be most beneficial. It is necessary, therefore, to give IHL a more principled basis in the African human rights treaty system. The African Commission's General Comment No. 3, which clarifies that during armed conflict the African Charter rights need to be interpreted with reference to the rules of IHL, is a move in the right direction.[243]

---

240   *Amnesty International et al, supra* note 126.
241   *Ibid.*, para. 50.
242   *Sudan Human Rights Organisation, supra* note 127.
243   General Comment No. 3, *supra* note 106, para. 13.

7.2 Acute and pervasive absence of a systematic analysis

The question may be posed as to why, despite its growing relevance and increasing use, the full potential of IHL in the African human rights system remains unrealised. This can be explained by the pervasive absence of a methodical analysis by African human rights treaty bodies of the interaction of IHL and the African human rights treaties, and its implications for implementing fundamental rights in armed conflict.[244] In particular, the jurisprudence surveyed in this article, which oscillates between engagement and avoidance, demonstrates that African human rights treaty bodies have neglected to systematically analyse and articulate clearly the following key aspects of the co-extensive application of IHL and human rights law: (a) the legal basis of their competence to apply IHL; (b) the extent to which IHL can or should influence the interpretation of African human rights treaties; (c) the body of law (IHL or African human rights law) or, alternatively, the specific legal rule that should prevail in case of a conflict of norms; and (d) the appropriate methodology for resolving conflicts if norms of IHL and human rights law diverge.

Comparative practice regarding the application of IHL by regional human rights treaty bodies also demonstrates the need to clarify these issues. Reviews of the IHL-related jurisprudence of the Inter-American Commission on Human Rights, the Inter-American Court of Human Rights, and the European Court of Human Rights have revealed the absence of a systematic and in-depth analysis of the nature and implications of the interplay of IHL and human rights law.[245] In common with these treaty bodies, the African Commission and African Court have not offered substantive or satisfactory elaboration of the legal reasoning process that determines why either IHL or human rights norms should be given priority in armed conflict-related contexts.[246] Yet, unlike their African equivalents, the treaty bodies of the European and Inter-American and human rights systems have acknowledged this shortcoming, and have since taken the initiative to adopt technical and interpretive approaches that promote the application of both IHL and human rights law.[247]

The jurisprudence of the Inter-American human rights system has developed the *pro homine* rule as an innovative and pragmatic way of

---

244   Sang-YK, *supra* note 6, p. 34.
245   Van den Herik and Duffy, *supra* note, pp. 401-402; Sang-YK, *supra* note 4, p. 26.
246   Sang-YK, *supra* note 6, pp. 34-35.
247   Sang-YK, *supra* note 4, pp. 20 and 25.

negotiating the IHL-human rights law relationship.[248] According to this rule, where two norms of both sets of law apply, compete or conflict, priority is to be accorded the norm that offers the best protective standard in the circumstances.[249] The ECHR has, for its part, invoked the principle of systemic integration as an interpretive tool for resolving conflicts between IHL and human rights norms.[250] Derived from Article 31(3)(c) of the Vienna Convention on the Law of Treaties,[251] this principle holds that competing or conflicting norms should be "interpreted so as to give rise to a single set of compatible obligations".[252] Thus in *Hassan* v. *United Kingdom*, which concerned the detention of an individual by British forces during the armed conflict in Iraq, the ECHR used human rights law standards to inform the application and implementation of IHL norms on deprivation of liberty in armed conflict.[253] A similar norm conflict resolution method has been espoused by the UN Human Rights Committee, which advocates that when laws from the two bodies of law conflict, the norm from either body of law that provides better protection for victims should be applied.[254]

These progressive examples offer instructive templates on which African human rights treaty bodies can model their future analytical approaches. Already the African Commission is making headway in this crucial process. It has clarified in General Comment No. 3 on the right to life that if a lawful target can be captured rather than killed, "the respect for the right to life can be best ensured by pursuing this option."[255] This is consistent with progressive international practice reflective of customary international law and also indicates an encouraging first step towards the institutionalisation of an interpretive approach that has aims to secure the greatest protection for human beings.

---

248 Lixinski, *supra* note 189, p. 593.
249 *Ibid.*, p. 588.
250 McCosker, *supra* note 9, pp. 165-166.
251 *Vienna Convention on the Law of Treaties* (1155 U.N.T.S. 331): Article 31(3)(c) provides, in relevant part, that in the interpretation of a treaty "there shall be taken into account [...] any relevant rules of international law applicable in the relations between the parties."
252 C. McLachlan, 'The Principle of Systemic Integration and Article 31(3)(c) of the Vienna Convention', 54 *International and Comparative Law Quarterly* (2005) p. 280.
253 *Hassan* v. *United Kingdom*, Application 29750/09, 16 September 2014, ECHR, para. 106.
254 General Comment No. 31, *supra* note 185, para. 11.
255 General Comment No. 3, *supra* note 106, para. 34.

8 Conclusion

In answering the question as to the legal status, role, and effect of international humanitarian law in the jurisprudence of African human rights treaty bodies, this article has analysed treaty law as well as the practice of the African Commission and Court. Its discussion has demonstrated a disparity between the openness with which the treaty law in the African human rights system incorporates IHL as part of its applicable law and the ambivalent approach of its treaty bodies to IHL. Although there are remarkable instances where the beneficial role of IHL is recognised and utilised, for the most part African human rights treaty bodies have not systematically elaborated the conceptual and normative interactions between IHL and human rights law. Nor have the practical implications of IHL-human rights law relations been clearly articulated.

The inevitable result of this lack of methodical analysis of what IHL means for the African human rights system is that African human rights treaty bodies have not been consistent in the way they engage with IHL. This observation is supported by the conflicting decisions of these treaty bodies. As demonstrated in this article, there are instances in which recourse is made, directly or indirectly, to IHL as an aid in interpreting provisions of the African Charter, other instances where IHL is applied alongside the African Charter's provisions to determine a case, and yet other decisions where IHL is presumably applicable but is only superficially referred to, or is ignored altogether. Given its comparatively modest IHL-related case law, the recent prodigious output of the African Court and the promising developments in the jurisdiction of the African Court of Justice of Human Rights, it is not possible to conclusively pronounce on the approach of African human rights treaty bodies to IHL. Still, the emerging jurisprudence of the African Commission and Court provides some indication of how IHL and human rights law will interact in the African human rights system now as well as in the future. While IHL is progressively gaining importance in the practice of African human rights treaty bodies, its utility is not uniformly recognised.

2   Against the Law: Turkey's Annexation Efforts in Occupied Cyprus

Ilias Kouskouvelis* and Kalliopi Chainoglou**

Abstract

The article considers the legal aspects of Turkey's activities in the occupied territory of Cyprus and claims that Turkey has violated its obligations under public international law. The article critically assesses the (il)legality of economic and other activities such as the construction of the electricity and water-pipeline projects that Turkey has been carrying out in the occupied territory while providing the "Turkish Republic of Northern Cyprus" ("TRNC") with political, financial, and military support over the past 40 years. For this purpose, the article establishes first that the "TRNC" is a non-existent entity under international law. Secondly, it affirms Turkey's status in the occupied territory of the Republic of Cyprus as one of a belligerent occupying power, violating specific obligations of international law. Thirdly, it examines the validity of the delimitation agreement between the "TRNC" and Turkey, and the agreements for the construction of the underwater pipeline and the electricity supply lines. Finally, the article asserts the rights of the occupied sovereign State, the Republic of Cyprus, under general public international law, international humanitarian law, occupation law, and the law of the sea.

---

*   Professor of International Relations, Department of International and European Studies, University of Macedonia; Dean of the School of Social Sciences, Humanities and Arts; Director of the "International Relations and European Integration Research Laboratory"; Chair-Holder of "Thucydides – The Hellenic National Defense General Staff Chair in Strategic Studies"; Former Rector of the University of Macedonia.
** Assistant Professor of International Law and International Institutions, Department of International and European Studies, University of Macedonia; Visiting Research Fellow, Centre on Human Rights in Conflict, University of East London.

1 Historical and Factual Background

In 1974, Turkey invaded the territory of the Republic of Cyprus ('RoC'), thus violating Article 2(4) of the United Nations ('UN') Charter[1] and making it illegal under international law. The invasion resulted in the forcible expulsion by Turkey of 180,000 Greek-Cypriots from the north of Cyprus and the partitioning of the island. The presence of a large force of Turkish occupation troops in the north led to a unilateral declaration of independence, in 1983, in an attempt to set up illegally the "Turkish Republic of Northern Cyprus" ('"TRNC"'). Since then and with the aim of strengthening its control of the RoC's occupied territory, Turkey has systematically provided the "TRNC" with political, financial and military support.

The relationship that Turkey has enforced on the "TRNC" has been described as one of "infant-land", as part or as an extension of the "motherland" Turkey or an "overseas province" of Turkey.[2] The economy of the "TRNC" is aid-dependent, relying heavily on annual cash handouts from Turkey, with the direct financial aid reaching $US 1.2 billion in the period 2016-2018.[3] Turkey's policy to dominate and control the occupied

---

[1] United Nations, *Charter of the United Nations*, 24 October 1945, 1 UNTS XVI.

[2] See U. Bozkurt, 'Turkey: From the 'Motherland' to the 'IMF of Northern Cyprus'?', 26:1 *The Cyprus Review* (2014) p.84 where it is explained how the economic dependence of the TRNC on Turkey is such that the latter has even imposed austerity programmes on the occupied territory. Bozkurt states: "[i]n its quest to tame the 'cumbersome' state in the "TRNC", Turkey imposed economic programmes that included austerity measures, slashing salaries and the privatisation of state enterprises". Political dependence was again demonstrated when, following the failed military coup, the AKP Turkish government issued arrest warrants against dissidents of the Erdogan government or anyone allegedly connected to the Fettulah Gulen movement in the occupied territory. See T. Gumrukcu, 'Turkey Issues Arrest Warrants for 25 Soldiers in Post-Coup Probe – Sources', *Reuters*, 12 October 2017, <www.reuters.com/article/us-turkey-security/turkey-issues-arrest-warrants-for-25-soldiers-in-post-coup-probe-sources-idUSKBN1CH0XC/>, visited on 12 July 2018.

[3] The "TRNC's" sole reliance on Turkey is admitted even by Turkish-Cypriot and Turkish politicians. In his written evidence to the UK Parliament Select Committee on Foreign Affairs, An states that: "Bulent Akarcali, Deputy President of the mainland Turkish party ANAP, was quoted by *Yeni Demokrat* (2 September 2001) as saying that: "Today the "TRNC" is a republic only on paper. The money, everything goes there from Turkey. Even the Turkish ambassador cannot do anything without the permission of the military commander there. All the large investments in Northern Cyprus are given to tenders, directly in Ankara. This means that Northern Cyprus is governed like a province of Turkey. It is foolish and wrong to think that the Greek Cypriots, the Greeks and other members of the EU do not know this.

territory is evidenced through the economic and development activities pursued by national Turkish political institutions and private companies affiliated with the government. Within this context, a number of economic protocols and other agreements have been signed by Turkey and the "TRNC" authorities. In a further effort to extinguish the physical and politico-economic links of the occupied territory with the RoC,[4] Turkey has embarked on designing, funding and carrying out projects in the occupied territory. This article argues that such projects, when analysed in light of international law, can be arguably viewed as aimed at undermining the sovereignty of the RoC, bolstering the continuing *de facto* division, upgrading the secessionist entity's status, and further strengthening the "TRNC's" dependence on Turkey. After all, these projects are taking place while Turkey continues even to this day to contest the existence of the RoC and the legitimacy of the RoC's actions in its maritime zones, including the exploration of the natural resources in its Exclusive Economic Zone ('EEZ').[5] As a consequence, the matter has also drawn the attention of the European Union ('EU') as it falls within the ambit of the EU-Turkey accession negotiations.[6]

   They know it very well".'' See A. An, 'How Many Turkish Cypriots Remain in Cyprus', *UK Parliament Select Committee on Foreign Affairs Written Evidence*, (2004-2005), <publications.parliament.uk/pa/cm200405/cmselect/cmfaff/113/113we33.htm>, visited on 12 July 2018; 'Turkey, Northern Cyprus $1,2B Deal Enters Into Force', *Anadolu Agency*, 29 June 2016, <aa.com.tr/en/economy/turkey-northern-cyprus-12b-deal-enters-into-force/599750>, visited on 4 October 2017.

4 Turkey's nationalistic aspirations for the annexation of territories belonging to Cyprus and Iraq have resurfaced during the last few years. See N. Danforth, 'Turkey's New Maps are Reclaiming the Ottoman Empire', *Foreign Policy*, 23 October 2016, <foreignpolicy.com/2016/10/23/turkeys-religious-nationalists-want-ottoman-borders-iraq-erdogan/>, visited on 4 October 2017; A. Anastasiou, 'Annexation Up For Discussion, Says Turkey', *Cyprus Mail Online*, 9 October 2017, <cyprus-mail.com/2017/10/09/annexation-discussion-says-turkey/>, visited on 26 October 2017; S. Cameron-Moore 'Turkey Says It Could Annex North if Cyprus Stays Split', *Reuters*, 4 March 2012, <www.reuters.com/article/us-turkey-cyprus/turkey-says-could-annex-north-if-cyprus-stays-split-idUSTRE8230IR20120304>, visited on 26 October 2017.

5 It is reported that Turkey is referring to the Republic of Cyprus as the 'Greek Cypriot Administration of Southern Cyprus'. See Y. Inan and P. Gözen Ercan, 'Maritime Relations of Peninsular Turkey: Surrounded by Hostile or Peaceful Waters', in P. Gözen Ercan (ed.), *Turkish Foreign Policy: International Relations, Legality and Global Reach* (Palgrave Macmillan, Basingstoke, 2017) p. 297.

6 *E.g.,* European Parliament, *Resolution on Turkish Actions Creating Tensions in the Exclusive Economic Zone of Cyprus*, 2014/2921(RSP), <www.europarl.europa.eu/

The "TRNC" currently benefits from a massive Turkish infrastructure investment: the construction of the water supply pipeline, the electricity plant and the upgraded airport, along with the ongoing housing projects, are aimed at accommodating the needs of the few Turkish Cypriots left in occupied territory and the numerous new arrivals of the settlers from mainland Turkey.[7] All these projects have been allocated in a monopolistic manner only to private Turkish companies with close ties to the AKP government.[8]

The first project concerns the supply of water through an underwater pipeline from mainland Turkey (Alaköprü Dam) to the "TRNC" (Geçitköy Dam). The preparation for the project started in 1998, but it was officially launched in 2011, and its construction finished in 2015. The project has three main parts or structures: the part on Turkey, the underwater sea-crossing, and the part on the "TRNC". The pipeline is to supply 75 million cubic meters per year for domestic and industrial use, and 37.24 million cubic meters per year will be distributed for irrigation for the next 50 years.[9]

The second project aims to supply electricity via underwater cables. The project connects the Teknecik power plant in the north of Cyprus with the transformer station at Turkey's Akkuyu power plant.[10] The project was planned to start transferring power by the end of 2017, and it is part of the Energy Protocol that was signed in October 2016 between the "TRNC" and Turkey; the said agreement also provides for "the renewal of electricity infrastructure, development of electricity supply security, the construction of an interconnected system, mutual cooperation on re-

---

sides/getDoc.do?type=MOTION&reference=P8-RC-2014-0211&language=EN>, visited on 4 October 2017.

7   Kohelet Policy Forum, *Who else profits? The Scope of European and Multinational Business in the Occupied Territories*, June 2017, <www.ngo-monitor.org/nm/wp-content/uploads/2017/06/WhoElseProfits_final.pdf>, visited on 24 August 2017.

8   *Ibid.*, p. 43 *et seq*. For example, the construction of the water supply pipeline was allocated to Kalyon group (a privately held Turkish conglomerate that operates in the construction, energy, and infrastructure sectors). Trelleborg's Engineers manufactured buoys for the Mediterranean Subsea Water Pipeline project. Reiner-ritz GMBH was responsible for building durable pipelines for the water supply project.

9   'Turkish Pipelines to Provide Cyprus With Water After Agreement Signed', *Daily Sabah*, 2 March 2016, <www.dailysabah.com/business/2016/03/03/turkish-pipelines-to-provide-cyprus-with-water-after-agreement-signed>, visited on 3 March 2016.

10   E. Binici, 'Turkey's Cooperation with Northern Cyprus to Expand Horizon in Regional Energy Politics', *Daily Sabah*, 16 October 2017, <www.dailysabah.com/energy/2017/10/17/turkeys-cooperation-with-northern-cyprus-to-expand-horizon-in-regional-energy-politics>, visited on 20 October 2017.

newable energy, the application of energy regulations, as well as exploration of new oil and natural gas resources."¹¹

These two underwater projects were paralleled by the conclusion of another agreement between the "TRNC" and Turkey providing for the delimitation of maritime boundaries.¹² The latter is a follow-up to the 2015 illegal thirty-years concession to Turkey of exploration rights into the sea, north of the RoC, where, in fact, Turkey's seismic vessel Barbaros Hayreddin has been conducting surveys ever since.

This article discusses the legal aspects of the aforementioned projects in the "TRNC"; the article argues that the water and electricity supply projects as well as other Turkish activities in the "TRNC" constitute violations of international law which do not only give rise to claims of international responsibility of Turkey but also set a bad precedent for the non-compliance with and non-enforcement of international law. Moreover, such projects in the occupied territory could be viewed as annexation efforts by Turkey that are aimed at consolidating Turkey's political and economic control over the occupied part of Cyprus, which is legally an EU area,¹³ thus deepening the existing division on the island and creating

---

11   'Northern Cyprus Ratifies Energy Agreement with Turkey', *Balkan Green Energy News*, 20 January 2017, <balkangreenenergynews.com/northern-cyprus-ratifies-energy-agreement-turkey/>, visited on 25 March 2017.

12   *Ibid.* For the text of the agreement see 'Türkiye Cumhuriyeti ile Kuzey Kıbrıs Türk Cumhuriyeti Arasında Akdeniz'de Kıta Sahanlığı Sınırlandırılması Hakkında Anlaşma', 21 September 2011, <http://www.resmigazete.gov.tr/eskiler/2012/10/20121010-3-1.pdf>, visited on 22 August 2018.

13   EU law has been suspended in the territory of Cyprus that is outside the effective control of its sole legitimate Government of RoC until a comprehensive settlement to the Cyprus Question is reached. See Case C-432/92, *Anastasiou I, The Queen* v. *Minister of Agriculture, Fisheries and Food, Cypfruvex (UK) Limited (intervening) and Cyprus Fruit and Vegetable Enterprises Limited (Cypfruvex) (intervening), ex parte SP Anastasiou (Pissouri) Limited*, 5 July 1994, ECJ, Judgment, (1994), ECR-I, vol. 7, p. 3087; Case C-219/98, *Anastasiou II, Regina* v. *Minister of Agriculture, Fisheries and Food), ex parte SP Anastasiou (Pissouri) Limited*, 4 July 2000, ECJ, Judgment, (2000), ECR-I, p.5241; *Meletis Apostolides* v. *David Charles Orams and Linda Elizabeth Orams*, 28 April 2009, ECJ, Judgment (Grand Chamber), para. 1, <curia.europa.eu/juris/document/document.jsf?text=&docid=78109&pageIndex=0&doclang=en&mode=lst&dir=&occ=first&part=1&cid=455152>, visited on 3 March 2016: "The suspension of the application of the *acquis communautaire* in those areas of the Republic of Cyprus in which the Government of that Member State does not exercise effective control, provided for by Article 1(1) of Protocol No 10 on Cyprus to the Act concerning the conditions of accession [to the European Union] of ... the Republic of Cyprus, ... and the adjustments to the Treaties on which the European Union is founded, does not preclude the application of Council Regula-

new *faits accomplis* on the ground. Despite the political repercussions of the Turkish activities on the resolution of the Cyprus issue, the analysis herein asserts that the rights of the occupied sovereign state, that is the RoC, under general public international law, international humanitarian law, occupation law, and the law of the sea, remain intact.

2 The Status of the "TRNC" under International Law

The most authoritative criteria for statehood under international law to date are codified by the 1933 Montevideo Convention on the Rights and Duties of States.[14] It is stated therein that a State must possess a defined territory, a permanent population, a government, and a capacity to enter into relations with other states. Entities that are created through the unlawful use of force are effectively barred from gaining Statehood under international law. On 15 July 1974, Turkey invaded the territory of Cyprus, thus violating Article 2(4) of the UN Charter, a rule of international law that is considered to be *jus cogens*. The creation of the "TRNC" was the *de facto* result of the unlawful use of force which disrupted the territorial unity of the RoC and in effect violated the RoC's founding agreements. Furthermore, the "TRNC" has never been recognised by any other member State of the international community, except for Turkey, bringing up thus the question as to what is the legal status of "TRNC's" actions. For example, the legal status of bilateral agreements between "TRNC" and Turkey and Turkey's economic and other activities in the "TRNC" are uncertain under international law. As will be analysed below, a number of UN Security Council Resolutions as well as international jurisprudence demonstrate that the "TRNC" has never gained 'statehood' status under international law and general international practice.

2.1 *UN Security Council Resolutions*

The UN Security Council Resolutions apply *ratione personae* to all member States of the UN, including "those members of the Security Council which voted against it and those Members of the United Nations who

---

tion (EC) No 44/2001 of 22 December 2000 on jurisdiction and the recognition and enforcement of judgments in civil and commercial matters to a judgment which is given by a Cypriot court sitting in the area of the island effectively controlled by the Cypriot Government, but concerns land situated in areas not so controlled".

14 International Conference of American States, *Montevideo Convention on the Rights and Duties of States*, 165 *LNTS* 19.

are not members of the Council",¹⁵ and, when applicable, to the specific addressee of the resolution. As to their application *ratione materiae*, international legal scholarship tends to agree that Security Council Resolutions that have not been adopted under Chapter VII of the UN Charter, but whose wording purports to create international obligations for member States, are considered to be legally binding. To put it simply, such Resolutions that are in the form of *decisions* of the Security Council are legally binding upon all UN member States, independent of whether the text of the resolution refers explicitly or not to Chapter VII. The famous passage of the *Namibia Advisory Opinion* illustrates this:

> It has been contended that Article 25 of the Charter applies only to enforcement measures adopted under Chapter VII of the Charter. It is not possible to find in the Charter any support for this view ... It has also been contended that the relevant Security Council resolutions are couched in exhortatory rather than mandatory language and that, therefore, they do not purport to impose any legal duty on any State nor to affect any right of any State. The language of a resolution of the Security Council should be carefully analysed before a conclusion can be made as to its binding effect. In view of the nature of the powers under Article 25, the question whether they have been in fact exercised is to be determined in each case, having regard to the terms of the resolution to be interpreted, the discussions leading to it, the Charter provisions invoked and, in general, all circumstances that might assist in determining the legal consequences of the resolution of the Security Council.¹⁶

International legal scholarship further agrees that Security Council Resolutions lacking reference to Chapter VII of the UN Charter will be considered binding when the Security Council has used such wording as to command the member States to abide by their obligations under interna-

---

15 *Legal Consequences for States of the Continued Presence of South Africa in Namibia (South West Africa) Notwithstanding Security Council Resolution*, 21 June 1971, ICJ, Advisory Opinion, para. 116, <www.icj-cij.org/en/case/53>, visited on 31 March 2017; *Reparation for Injuries Suffered in the Service of the United Nations*, 11 April 1949, ICJ, Advisory Opinion, (1949) *I.C.J. Reports* 174, at 178. *See* M. Divac Oberg, 'The Legal Effects of Resolutions of the UN Security Council and General Assembly in the Jurisprudence of the ICJ', 16:5 *European Journal of International Law* (2005) pp. 879–906.

16 *Namibia Advisory Opinion*, *supra* note 15, paras. 113-114.

tional law or to abide by newly created obligations that do not exist elsewhere in international law. Within this context, the International Court of Justice ('ICJ') and various scholars have identified that using language such as 'demand' or 'call upon' within the text of Security Council Resolutions will make it legally-binding.[17]

The Security Council Resolutions on Cyprus have not been adopted under Chapter VII. However, this does not mean that they are not legally binding.[18] As the *Namibia Advisory Opinion* provides, the wording of these Resolutions as well as the surrounding circumstances (the illegality of the occupation of Northern Cyprus and the international community's refusal to recognise the "TRNC" as a State for more than 40 years) indicate that these Security Council Resolutions are legally binding upon all UN member States, including Turkey. Since the invasion of northern Cyprus, the UN Security Council has maintained a consistent objection to the emergence of the "TRNC" and has called for States to respect of the sovereignty of RoC. In Resolution 541, the Security Council unequivocally called upon all States "to respect the sovereignty, independence, territorial integrity and non-alignment of the Republic of Cyprus; ... [and] not to recognize any Cypriot State other than the Republic of Cyprus".[19] In

---

17 In the *Namibia Advisory Opinion*, the Court found the operative paragraph 5 of the Security Council Resolution which began with the words "Calls upon all States" to be legally binding. *Ibid.*

18 *See* R. MacDonald, 'International Law and the Conflict in Cyprus', 29 *Canadian Yearbook of International Law*, (1981), pp. 3-49. *See also* F. Hoffmeister, *Legal Aspects of the Cyprus Problem: Annan Plan and EU Accession*, (Martinus Nijhoff Publishers, Leiden, 2006) at p. 72 who reaches the wrong conclusion when he claims that that "Greek Cypriot claims that any Security Council resolution would be mandatory to the parties are unfounded in international law". A similarly unfounded argument is made by Raic where he misguidedly claims that "[b]oth Security Council Resolution 541 and 550 cannot be considered to be binding instruments, however, because they were not adopted under Chapter VII and did not contain a reference to Article 25 of the Charter. Nor did their terms imply that the resolutions were intended to be binding". *See* D. Raic, *Statehood and the Law of Self-Determination* (Kluwer Law International, The Hague, 2002) p.24.

19 UN Security Council, Security Council Resolution 541 (1983), 18 November 1983, S/RES/541 (1983), paras. 6-7; UN Security Council, Security Council Resolution 550 (1984), 11 May 1984, S/RES/550 (1984), paras. 3-4. At the time, a number of international organisations and governments expressed their support to the Government of the RoC as the sole legitimate government of Cyprus. *See e.g.*, Resolution (83) 13 on Cyprus (adopted by the Committee of Ministers of the Council of Europe on 24 November 1983 at its 73rd Session); Parliamentary Assembly, Recommendation 974, 23 November 1983; Parliamentary Resolution, 21 March 1984; EC Bulletin 11-1983 (16 November 1983), points 2.2.34, 2.4.1-2.4.2, OJ 1983 C342/52; EC Bulletin

1984, the Security Council in Resolution 550 reaffirmed Resolution 541 and, again, in identical terms, called upon "all States to respect the sovereignty, independence, territorial integrity and non-alignment of the Republic of Cyprus" and "not to recognize any Cypriot State other than the Republic of Cyprus".[20] The Security Council has characterised "the declaration of the Turkish Cypriot authorities of the purported secession of part of the Republic of Cyprus" as "legally invalid" and has called for Turkey's withdrawal from the territory.[21]

With regard to the said Security Council Resolutions, member States of the UN have interpreted these resolutions as imposing on them an obligation of non-recognition of the "TRNC". National courts have also consistently upheld the decisions of their governments not to recognise the "TRNC". In *Autocephalous Church of Cyprus* v. *Golberg and Feldman Fine Arts* (1990),[22] the US Court of Appeals held that it would not give effect to confiscatory decrees issued by the unrecognised "Turkish Federated State of Cyprus" (later called "TRNC") due to the US' non-recognition of the "TRNC". In *Caglar* v. *Billingham* it was affirmed that: "the only state on the island of Cyprus is the Republic of Cyprus ... [i]t would be contrary to domestic statute law to hold that the Turkish Republic of Northern Cyprus is a foreign state. The absence of recognition by any state other than Turkey was evidence of the fact that the Turkish Republic of Northern Cyprus had failed to meet the criteria of statehood."[23] In *R* v. *Secretary of*

3-1984, point 2.4.3, OJ 1994 C 289/13. *See also* European Parliament, *Report of the Committee of Foreign Affairs, Human Rights, Common Security and Defence Policy*, 22 June 1995, PE-DOC-A4-1995/156-1EN, p. 9. Relevant jurisprudence from the then European Court of Justice affirms that that cooperation between the authorities of an entity such as the "TRNC" "which was recognized neither by the Community nor by the member states" could not serve the purposes of the relevant EU directives and other legal instruments; in effect, the ruling resulted in the prohibition of the illegal import of products originating from the occupied part of Cyprus. *See* Case C-432/92, *Anastasiou II*, supra note 13.

20   UN Security Council Resolution 550, *supra* note 19, paras. 2, 6-7.
21   *Ibid.*, paras. 1-2.
22   *Autocephalous Greek-Orthodox Church of Cyprus* v. *Goldber and Feldman Fine Arts Inc.*, 3 August 1989, S.D. Ind., (1989) 717 F. Supp. 1374, <http://www.uniset.ca/microstates/717FSupp1374.htm>, visited on 24 June 2018; *Autocephalous Greek-Orthodox Church of Cyprus and The Republic of Cyprus, Plaintiffs-Appellees* v. *Goldberg and Feldman Fine Arts Inc and Peg Golberg, Defendants-Appellants* 24 October 1990, USA Court of Appeals Seventh Circuit, 917 F. 2d 278, <www.uniset.ca/microstates/917F2d278.htm>, visited on 24 June 2018.
23   *Caglar and ors* v. *Billingham (Inspector of Taxes)*, 7 March 1996, Special Commissioners of Income Tax, Appeal decision, ILDC 2128 (UK 1996), (1996) STC (SCD)

State for Transport the Court held: "A legal duty exists whereby the Government of the United Kingdom is obliged not to recognise the "TRNC" or its Government. Further the Government of the United Kingdom has consistently refused to recognise the "TRNC". This court is obliged to refuse to give effect to the validity of acts carried out in a territory which is unrecognised".[24] Thirdly, not only have States refrained from recognising the claim of the "TRNC" to statehood, but international organisations have done so too (see discussion above and below). To add, violating binding UN Security Council Resolutions, as is the case with Turkey and its activities in the "TRNC", opens up the possibility that the UN Security Council will take measures under Chapter VII of the UN Charter. Whether this will be done in the near future is a political matter, not a question of law.

Even if one takes the view that UN Security Council Resolutions 541 and 550 are not legally binding, but rather stand as persuasive authoritative expressions of the view that the "TRNC" is not a State, they are nonetheless evidence that the "TRNC" could never meet the criteria of statehood. The status of the "TRNC" under international law is that of an illegal regime which does not have functional and legal independence as it cannot enter into relations with other States; it operates on the side

---

150, (1996) 1 LRC 526, (1998) 108 ILR 510, paras. 44, 134-150, 163. It was held that "the absence of recognition by any state other than Turkey was evidence of the fact that the Turkish Republic of Northern Cyprus had failed to meet the criteria of statehood", para. 163.

24   See e.g., *R (On the Application of Kibris Turk Hava Yollari and CTA Holidays Limited)* v. *Secretary of State for Transport (Republic of Cyprus, Interested Party)*, 28 July 2009, High Court, Queen's Bench Division (2009), EWHC 1918; 12 October 2010, Court of Appeal, (2010) EWCA Civ 1093. The case was concerned with whether the grant of the permits sought to take on board and discharge passengers, baggage and cargo at a point or points in the United Kingdom carried or to be carried on services from the United Kingdom to Northern Cyprus and *vice versa* would render the United Kingdom Government in breach of its duty not to recognise the "TRNC". The High Court originally held (para. 90): "This Court is obliged to refuse to give effect to the validity of acts carried out in a territory which is unrecognised unless the acts in question can properly be regarded as regulating the day to day affairs of the people within the territory in question and can properly be regarded as essentially private in character. I have reached the conclusion that the grant of the permits in this case would be a breach of the United Kingdom Government's duty not to recognise the "TRNC". I cannot categorise the acts of the "TRNC" which are relevant to international aviation as acts which regulate the day to day affairs of the people who live within the area controlled by the Government of the "TRNC"; the acts in question are essentially public in nature." It should be noted that the Court of Appeal upheld the High Court judgment and dismissed the claim.

lines of the international community.[25] This is bolstered by the fact that the "TRNC" has never been recognised by any State except Turkey since its inception and hence no other State or international organisation has officially entered into international relations with the "TRNC". However, Turkey has tried to deny its obligations under international law by alleging that "none of the Security Council resolutions on Cyprus refer to the presence of the Turkish troops on the island as an 'occupation'"[26] even though the UN General Assembly has condemned in Resolution 33/15[27] the presence of foreign military troops in the RoC. Furthermore, the General Assembly has employed the term 'occupation' in both Resolutions 34/30[28] and 37/253[29] and has specifically demanded "the immediate withdrawal of all occupation forces from the Republic of Cyprus".

Conversely, the RoC continues to enjoy international recognition as the sole legitimate government of the island by the international community. All projects that Turkey has agreed to carry out in the "TRNC" are in effect violating the 'the letter and the spirit' of the UN Security Council Resolutions. To start, the UN Security Council Resolutions have affirmed that the sole legitimate authority on the territory of Cyprus is the government of the Republic of Cyprus. The RoC has always enjoyed recognition as a State having a single international legal personality and sovereignty. This means that the only competent authorities to conclude interstate agreements for projects to be carried out in the north of Cyprus are the authorities of the RoC. Further, if such projects are carried out without the consent of the sole legitimate authority, which is the RoC, then they can only be deemed to support the "secessionist acts in the occupied part of the Republic of Cyprus".[30]

---

25 See M. Kohen, *Secession: International Law Perspectives* (Cambridge University Press, Cambridge 2006) p. 119, note 78, p. 133.

26 Letter dated 14 December 2016 from the Permanent Representative of Turkey to the United Nations addressed to the Secretary-General, A/71/693–S/2016/1067, 16 December 2016, <undocs.org/A/71/693%E2%80%93S/2016/1067>, visited on 24 June 2018.

27 UN General Assembly, Resolution 33/15 (1978), 9 November 1978, para. 3.

28 UN General Assembly, Resolution 34/30 (1979), 20 November 1979, A/RES/34/30, para. 5.

29 UN General Assembly, Resolution 37/253 (1983), 16 May 1983, A/RES/37/253, paras. 7-8.

30 *See* UN Security Council Resolution 541, *supra* note 19, paras. 1-2; UN Security Council Resolution 550, *supra* note 19, para. 2.

2.2 The Republic of Cyprus' Founding Agreements

The duty of non-recognition of the "TRNC" also arises by virtue of the Treaties of Establishment and the Treaty of Guarantee (applicable to the signatory parties of the said Treaties). Under Article 1 of both Treaties, the RoC undertook to ensure, *inter alia*, the maintenance of its independence, territorial integrity and security, and, under Article 2 of the Treaty of Guarantee, Greece, Turkey and the United Kingdom undertook to prohibit, so far as concerned them, *"any activity aimed at promoting, directly or indirectly, either union of Cyprus with any other State or partition of the island."*[31] Turkey has alleged that "Turkey's intervention and its subsequent presence on the island is legitimate under international law since it was conducted in accordance with Turkey's rights and obligations emanating from the 1960 Treaty of Guarantee."[32] Despite this statement, it is quite clear that Turkey has violated Article 2 of the 1960 Treaty of Guarantee through its unlawful use of force under Article 2(4) of the UN Charter which has inevitably resulted in the partitioning of the island.[33]

Furthermore, Turkey has repeatedly questioned the competence of the government of the RoC to represent both Greek-Cypriots and Turkish-Cypriots, and has claimed that "there is no single authority which in law or in fact is competent to represent ... Cyprus as a whole".[34] For example,

---

31 *Treaty of Guarantee (Cyprus, Greece, Turkey, United Kingdom)*, 16 August 1960, 382 UNTS 5475; *Treaty Concerning the Establishment of the Republic of Cyprus*, 16 August 1960, 382 UNTS 5476.

32 *See* Letter dated 14 December 2016 from the Permanent Representative of Turkey to the United Nations addressed to the Secretary-General, A/71/693–S/2016/1067, 16 December 2016, <undocs.org/A/71/693%E2%80%93S/2016/1067>, visited on 31 March 2017.

33 Article 4 of the Treaty of Guarantee, *supra* note 31, provides that when concerted action is not possible, each of the signatory parties has the right to take action "with the sole aim of re-establishing the state of affairs created by the Treaty". It should be noted that the 2017 Gutierrez Report has described "the unilateral right of intervention, as "unsustainable": "[A] new system of security was needed for Cyprus, as was a credible framework for monitoring the implementation of the agreement in which the current guarantors would play a role. On the question of the presence of Greek and Turkish troops in Cyprus, it was agreed that any outstanding issues regarding troops would best be addressed at the highest political level involving the Prime Ministers of the three guarantor Powers". *See* UN Secretary General, *Report of the Secretary-General on His Mission of Good Offices in Cyprus*, S/2017/814, 28 September 2017, para. 24, <www.refworld.org/docid/59dddıcf4.html>, visited on 4 October 2017.

34 *See* Letter dated 17 March 2016 from the Permanent Representative of Turkey to the United Nations addressed to the Secretary-General, A/70/788–S/2016/257, 17 March 2016, <undocs.org/a/70/788>, visited on 31 March 2017.

in a letter dated 14 December 2016 from the Permanent Representative of Turkey to the UN, Turkey argued that the RoC has acted "on the false premise that the Greek Cypriot administration has the right to speak on behalf of the whole island."[35] It seems that Turkey might be arguing that the Turkish Cypriots are exercising their right to self-determination under Turkey's control. However, international law has consistently prevented an entity from gaining statehood if it has emerged out of the violation of a peremptory norm or if "its creation violates the local population's right of self-determination".[36] As noted by Henriksen:

> it remains a fact that the exact relationship between the use of force and self-determination is unclear. While a territorial entity created through the illegal force in violation of the right to self-determination of the population on the territory is unlikely to be accepted as a state, the result may be different if the unlawful use of force is used in order to further the realization of the self-determination of a population.[37]

Self-determination, though, does not support secessionist acts; in other words, the right to self-determination does not validate claims of a segment of the local population to form a new, independent State. Only in exceptional cases can the right to self-determination be exercised and only under the condition that "it is exercised within the existing state".[38] In this case, the local population consists of both Turkish-Cypriots and Greek-Cypriots and the right to self-determination has to be exercised by both communities forming the local population. Furthermore, for the right to self-determination to be exercised through the creation of a new State there has to be evidence of gross human rights violations against the local population, i.e. the Turkish-Cypriots and Greek-Cypriots, and this has never been corroborated by any evidence in the case of Cyprus. But even in exceptional cases where there are gross human rights viola-

---

35   "Needless to say, the democratically elected Government of the Turkish Republic of Northern Cyprus has the sole authority and discretion to sign and conclude such agreements in order to address the needs of the Turkish Cypriot people. Hence, the Greek Cypriot administration of Southern Cyprus has no moral or legal right of say over these issues." *See* Letter dated 14 December 2016 from the Permanent Representative of Turkey to the United Nations, *supra* note 32.
36   A. Henriksen, *International Law* (Oxford University Press, Oxford, 2017) p. 68.
37   *Ibid.*, p. 69.
38   *Ibid.*, p. 71.

tions, the creation of a new state remains controversial under international law. The illegal use of force by Turkey in this case disrupted and negated any claims to the right to self-determination of the local population and created a settlement whereby it is expected that there will be a *de jure* and *de facto* restoration of the territorial unity of the State, that is the RoC.

2.3 Jurisprudence and International Practice

The duty of non-recognition of the "TRNC" arises for all UN member States, including Turkey, by virtue of the established rule of customary international law not to recognise any illegal entity brought about by the illegal use of force.[39] The ICJ has also clearly stated that unilateral declarations of independence are *a priori* illegal when they are connected to an illegal use of force, as in the case of the "TRNC".[40]

The illegality of the acts of the Turkish regime in the "TRNC" is quite clear.[41] From an international law perspective the non-recognised "TRNC"

---

39 H. Lauterpacht, *Recognition in International Law* (Cambridge University Press, Cambridge, 1947) p. 420; J. Dugard, *Recognition and the United Nations* (Cambridge University Press, Cambridge, 1987) p. 135; T. Franck, *Fairness in International Law and Institutions* (Oxford University Press, Oxford, 1995) p. 158; V. Gowlland-Debbas, *Collective Responses to Illegal Acts in International Law* (Martinus Nijhoff Publishers, Dordrecht, 1991) p. 294; ILC Special Rapporteur on State Responsibility, *First Report on State Responsibility*, UN Doc. A/CN.4/490/Add.1, para. 51; ILC Special Rapporteur on State Responsibility, *Third Report on State Responsibility*, UN Doc. A/CN.4/507/Add.4, para. 410.

40 *See Accordance with International Law of the Unilateral Declaration of Independence in Respect of Kosovo*, 22 July 2010, ICJ, Advisory Opinion, para. 81, <www.icj-cij.org/en/case/141>, visited on 31 March 2017, where it is stated that: "Several participants have invoked resolutions of the Security Council condemning particular declarations of independence: see, *inter alia*, Security Council resolutions 216 (1965) and 217 (1965), concerning Southern Rhodesia; Security Council resolution 541 (1983), concerning northern Cyprus; and Security Council resolution 787 (1992), concerning the Republika Srpska. The Court notes, however, that in all of those instances the Security Council was making a determination as regards the concrete situation existing at the time that those declarations of independence were made; the illegality attached to the declarations of independence thus stemmed not from the unilateral character of these declarations as such, but from the fact that they were, or would have been, connected with the unlawful use of force or other egregious violations of norms of general international law, in particular those of a peremptory character (*jus cogens*)."

41 International legal scholarship affirms that the duty of non-recognition applies to all States. The recognition of acts of the illegal regime, such as the judicial organs of the "TRNC", has been accepted by the European Court of Human Rights only in order "to avoid in the territory of northern Cyprus the existence of a vacuum in the

does not exist as a sovereign State. In *Cyprus* v. *Turkey* the European Court of Human Rights acknowledged that the regime in the north of Cyprus "is unlawful under international law" and held that it operates under the effective control of Turkey.[42] Accordingly, the acts of the "TRNC" are null and void of legal force.[43] This is in line with the long-standing legal principle of *ex injuria jus non oritur* – an illegality cannot, as a rule, become a source of legal right to the wrongdoer. In other words, any international agreements entered into by the "TRNC" lack legal effect and they are invalid *ab initio*. Moreover, because Turkey is the only power with effective control over the "TRNC", this means that all of the "TRNC's" actions are imputed to Turkey and such control is sufficient to establish Turkey's international responsibility for the policies and actions of the "TRNC" (for example, the agreements on the construction of the underwater pipeline, the electricity supply pipeline, the exploitation of the natural resources of the occupied territories, and the maritime delimitation between the "TRNC" and Turkey). As a consequence, any agreements between Turkey and the "TRNC" are non-effective and stand in violation of fundamental principles of international law.

---

protection of the human rights guaranteed" by the European Convention on Human Rights and Fundamental Freedoms. The recognition is necessary only in order to not endanger the survival of the people living under the control of the illegal authority or in order to not deny the right to property of the Greek Cypriots in the occupied territory of Cyprus. The Court stated that "this in no way amounts to an indirect legitimization of a regime which is unlawful under international law". This is based on the so-called "doctrine of necessity" and it concerns the recognition of the acts of the unlawful regime for humanitarian reasons or matters of routine administration, *i.e.* registration of births, marriages, etc. See *Cyprus* v. *Turkey*, 10 May 2001, ECHR, Judgment, no. 25781/94, paras. 91-101, <hudoc.echr.coe.int/eng#{%22itemid%22:[%22001-59454%22]}>, visited on 4 October 2017; *Loizidou* v *Turkey*, 18 December 1996, ECHR, Judgment Merits, no. 15318/89, para. 45, <hudoc.echr.coe.int/app/conversion/pdf/?library=ECHR&id=001-58007&filename=001-58007.pdf&TID=nnqbcpodfy>, visited on 4 October 2017.

42 *Cyprus* v. *Turkey*, *supra* note 41, para. 101. These kind of entities have been termed "puppet States" in the legal literature. In *Ilascu and Others* v. *Moldova and Russia*, 8 July 2004, ECHR, Grand Chamber Judgment, no. 48787/99, paras. 392-393, <hudoc.echr.coe.int/eng#{%22itemid%22:[%22001-61886%22]}>, visited on 4 October 2017, the Court found that puppet States can be under the effective control of another State not only through military occupation but even through the subordination of the puppet State's administration, *i.e.* by virtue of economic, financial, and political support given to it by the sponsor State.

43 See Lauterpacht, *supra* note 39, pp. 145, 420; F.A. Mann, 'The Judicial Recognition of an Unrecognised State', 36 *ICLQ* (1987) p. 348 *et seq.*

An example of the non-existent status of the "TRNC" as a sovereign State under international law is perhaps best illustrated with the case of the delimitation agreement between Turkey and the "TRNC". The particular agreement was ratified by Turkey on 29 June 2012. Turkey, despite not having signed the United Nations Convention on the Law of the Sea ('UNCLOS'), decided to act in accordance with Article 84(2) of UNCLOS and transmit the (illegally) agreed coordinates to the UN Secretary-General and to have them published in the Law of the Sea Bulletin.[44] As the UN and all its organs (including the Department of Oceans and the Law of the Sea – 'DOALOS') do not recognise the "TRNC", the delimitation agreement was never published on the deposit of the DOALOS website.[45]

Finally, it should be borne in mind that the agreements that Turkey has forced on the "TRNC" in exchange of economic support entail terms that are not in the best interests of the Turkish-Cypriots and Greek-Cypriots, the 'people' of the State concerned according to international law. The terms in these agreements, in particular those concerned with the exploitation of natural resources in Cyprus by Turkey for the next 30 years, infringe the principle of self-determination, a peremptory norm which is non-derogable even in times of military occupation, and the rule on the prohibition of the use of force, a long-established peremptory norm.[46] These agreements set up projects that will sustain the "TRNC" under military occupation. Accordingly, these agreements are violating *jus cogens*

---

44 UN General Assembly, *Convention on the Law of the Sea*, 10 December 1982, 1833 UNTS 3. *See also* Letter dated 19 May 2014 from the Permanent Representative of Cyprus to the United Nations addressed to the Secretary-General, A/68/883, 20 May 2014, <undocs.org/A/68/883>, visited on 3 March 2016. *See* E. Franckx and M. Benatar, 'Turkish Objections to Exclusive Economic Zone Agreements Concluded by Cyprus', in P. Pazartzis and M. Gavouneli, *Reconceptualising the Rule of Law in Global Governance, Resources, Investment and Trade* (Hart Publishing, Oxford, 2016), pp. 217-242.

45 *See* N. Ioannidis, The Continental Shelf Delimitation Agreement between Turkey and "TRNC", *EJIL TALK*, 26 May 2014, <ejiltalk.org/the-continental-shelf-delimitation-agreement-between-turkey-and-trnc/>, visited on 4 October 2017.

46 As to the peremptory status of self-determination *see e.g.*, UN General Assembly, *Declaration on Principles of International Law concerning Friendly Relations and Cooperation among States in accordance with the Charter of the United Nations*, 24 October 1970, A/RES/2625(XXV). As to the peremptory status of the rule on the prohibition of the use of force see *Legal Consequences of the Construction of a Wall in the Occupied Palestinian Territory*, 9 July 2004, ICJ, Advisory Opinion, 43 *ILM* 1009, (Separate Opinion of Judge Elaraby).

norms and are not valid under Article 53 of the Vienna Convention on the Law of the Treaties.[47]

3 Turkey's Obligations under Belligerent Occupation Law

As has been affirmed by international and national courts,[48] the northern territory of Cyprus is, since the unlawful Turkish invasion in 1974 and to this day, under belligerent occupation. This means that the territory is under the effective control of the foreign occupying force without the consent of the sovereign of the territory, the RoC. Thus, any agreement between the invading force and any authority of the occupied area, as those under discussion, are illegal if they violate the specific rules of the belligerent occupation law, as it will be shown below.

Article 42 of the Hague Regulations provides that a "territory is considered occupied when it is actually placed under the authority of the hostile army. The occupation extends only to the territory where such authority has been established and can be exercised".[49] Any claims by

---

47   United Nations, *Vienna Convention on the Law of Treaties*, 23 May 1969, UNTS 1155, p. 331.

48   See *Cyprus v. Turkey*, *supra* note 41, para. 77: "Having effective overall control over northern Cyprus, [Turkey's] responsibility cannot be confined to the acts of its own soldiers or officials in northern Cyprus but must also be engaged by virtue of the acts of the local administration which survives by virtue of Turkish military and other support." It is interesting to note that even the "TRNC's" judicial authorities have applied the law of occupation when addressing the legal claims of Greek-Cypriots for their private property in northern Cyprus. *See e.g.*, *National Unity Party (Ulusal Birlik Partisi) v. TRNC Assembly of the Republic (KKTC Cumhuriyet Meclisi)*, "TRNC" Constitutional Court, ILDC 499 (TCC 2006), cited in S. Power, 'Occupying the Continental Shelf? A Note Considering the Status of the Continental Shelf Delimitation Agreement Concluded between Turkey and the "TRNC" during the Belligerent Occupation of Northern Cyprus', 9 *Irish Yearbook of International Law* (2014) p. 95, note 30.

49   The law of belligerent occupation is codified in the 1907 Hague Regulations, the 1949 Fourth Geneva Convention (IV GC) (Arts. 27-34, 47-78), and the 1977 First Protocol Additional to the 1949 Geneva Conventions (AP I). The Hague Regulations are considered to reflect customary international law. *See* Second International Peace Conference, *Convention (IV) Respecting the Laws and Customs of War on Land and its Annex: Regulations concerning the Laws and Customs of War on Land*, The Hague, 18 October 1907, <www.ihl-databases.icrc.org/applic/ihl/ihl.nsf/Treaty.xsp?action=openDocument&documentId=4D47F92DF3966A7EC12563CD002D6788>, visited on 25 March 2018; International Committee of the Red Cross, *Geneva Convention Relative to the Protection of Civilian Persons in Time of War* (IV GC), 12 August 1949,

Turkey that its presence in northern Cyprus is legitimate under international law are highly doubtful; furthermore, irrespective of whether Turkey has declared the territory in question to be occupied or disputes this fact, the applicable law is the law of belligerent occupation.[50] The international consensus is that Turkey is an occupying force and is bound by all relevant provisions of international humanitarian law applicable on belligerent occupation.[51]

Several provisions of international humanitarian law affirm that the occupying power cannot acquire sovereignty over the occupied territory. During an occupation the government of the original State retains sovereignty over the territory that is occupied even if it does not control that area anymore. A corresponding obligation for the occupying power is to maintain the *status quo ante bellum* and not to interfere with the fundamental institutions of government in the occupied territory or force changes on the occupied territory that may have enduring consequences even after the end of military occupation.[52] The construction of the wa-

---

75 UNTS 287; International Committee of the Red Cross, *Protocol Additional to the Geneva Conventions of 12 August 1949, and relating to the Protection of Victims of International Armed Conflicts (Protocol I)*, 8 June 1977, 1125 UNTS 3.

50 See Y. Arai-Takahashi, *The Law of Occupation: Continuity and Change of International Humanitarian Law and Its Interaction with International Human Rights Law* (Martinus Nijhoff Publishers, Leiden, 2009); E. Benvenisti, *The International Law of Occupation*. 2d ed. (Oxford University Press, Oxford, 2012); R. Kolb and S. Vité, *Le droit de l'occupation militaire: Perspectives historiques et enjeux juridiques actuels* (Bruylant, Brussels, 2009); T. Ferraro, (ed.) *Occupation and Other Forms of Administration of Foreign Territory* (International Committee of the Red Cross, Geneva, 2012). Furthermore, in a note prepared by the International Committee of the Red Cross legal team it has been clarified that "[o]nce a situation exists which factually amounts to an occupation the law of occupation applies – whether or not the occupation is considered lawful. Therefore, for the applicability of the law of occupation, it makes no difference whether an occupation has received Security Council approval, what its aim is, or indeed whether it is called an "invasion", "liberation", "administration" or "occupation" ... The rules of international humanitarian law relevant to occupied territories become applicable whenever territory comes under the effective control of hostile foreign armed forces, even if the occupation meets no armed resistance and there is no fighting." See International Committee of the Red Cross, *Occupation and International Humanitarian Law: Questions and Answers*, 4 August 2004, <www.icrc.org/eng/resources/documents/misc/634kfc.htm>, visited on 24 July 2018.

51 See B. Ivanen, 'Puppet States: A Growing Trend of Covert Occupation', in T. D. Gill et al (eds.) 18 *Yearbook of International Humanitarian Law* (2015) pp. 43-65.

52 See e.g., *Dweikat et al v. Government of Israel*, Supreme Court of Israel, HCJ 390/79, 34(1) PD 1, 22 October 1979, cited in J. Crawford, *Opinion: Third Party Obligations with respect to Israeli Settlements in the Occupied Palestinian Territories*, p. 5, <www.

ter pipeline project in the "TRNC" is one of the measures that is prohibited under occupation law. The impact it had on the occupied territory is irreversible and will have transformative effect for the years to come. It has been reported that "the countryside and many of the roads in north Cyprus have been torn apart to lay the total of 478 kilometres of pipes that deliver the water throughout the island".[53]

Even though the occupied territory in the north of the island is not under the control of the RoC, the latter has not relinquished its sovereignty over the territory that is under the *de facto* control of Turkey. To the contrary, the RoC continues to maintain *de jure* sovereignty over the whole of the island, including the occupied territory and the population. Furthermore, the RoC has exclusive sovereignty over the airspace[54] above the whole of the island and the territorial waters adjacent thereto, irrespective of whether some parts of the island are under the control of another entity.[55] Consequently, any international agreements that are signed and

---

tuc.org.uk/sites/default/files/tucfiles/LegalOpinionIsraeliSettlements.pdf>, visited on 24 July 2018.

53   Z. Doğan, 'Water War Could Leave Turkish Cyprus High and Dry', *Al-Monitor*, 11 January 2016, <www.al-monitor.com/pulse/originals/2016/01/turkey-cyprus-water-row-threatens-peace-process.html#ixzz53rD5urU6>, visited on 24 June 2018; R. Bryant, 'Cyprus 'peace water" project: how it could affect Greek-Turkish relations on the island', 28 October 2015, <www.eprints.lse.ac.uk/70893/1/blogs.lse.ac.uk-Cyprus%20peace%20water%20project%20how%20it%20could%20affect%20Greek-Turkish%20relations%20on%20the%20island.pdf>, visited on 24 June 2018.

54   Turkey has repeatedly violated the national airspace of the RoC, infringed international air traffic regulations and harassed civilian and military aircraft within the Nicosia flight information region (FIR) via radio calls. *See* Letter dated 31 October 2017 from the Permanent Representative of Cyprus to the United Nations addressed to the Secretary-General, A/72/550–S/2017/912, 31 October 2017, <undocs.org/en/A/72/550>, visited on 8 November 2017; Letter dated 7 August 2018 from the Permanent Representative of Cyprus to the United Nations addressed to the Secretary-General, A/72/947-S/2018/760, 10 August 2018, <undocs.org/en/S/2018/760>, visited on 11 August 2018.

55   *See* Institut de Droit International, *Bruges Declaration on the Use of Force*, 2 September 2003, <www.idi-iil.org/app/uploads/2017/06/2003_bru_en.pdf>, visited on 24 July 2018: "Belligerent occupation of a territory entails the application of the rules of international humanitarian law codified in the Hague Regulations of 1907, the Fourth Geneva Convention of 1949 and the First Additional Protocol:
– belligerent occupation does not transfer sovereignty over territory to the occupying power,
– the occupying power can only dispose of the resources of the occupied territory to the extent necessary for the current administration of the territory and to meet the essential needs of the population; -the occupying power has the obligation to respect the rights of the inhabitants of the occupied territory which

ratified by the territorial sovereign, the RoC, such as the Exclusive Economic Zone ('EEZ') delimitation agreements with Egypt (2003), Lebanon (2007), and Israel (2010), are enforceable over the whole territory, including the occupied territory.

Under occupation law, the character of the occupation is meant to be temporary. Any measures that contribute towards the unlawful occupation becoming a *fait accompli* are prohibited; on the contrary, it is expected that even the occupying power will act in such a manner as to prevent the occupation from becoming permanent. Turkey has tried to rewrite or rather override this principle of occupation law. The water pipeline project, the delimitation agreement between the "TRNC" and Turkey, the exploitation of the natural resources agreement, and the electricity pipeline project violate the sovereignty of the RoC over the occupied territory in the north, and purport to create a situation where (even if unity is achieved between Turkish-Cypriots and Greek-Cypriots), Turkey will still be able to assert a dependency-nexus with Cyprus. For example, Article 2 of the Framework Treaty for the Water Supply of the "TRNC" states that: "the construction of the sea passage through the pipeline as well as land structures within the Party of the "TRNC" shall be built by the Republic of Turkey. From the very start of the project, the given land structures and all of the structures as well as the pipeline with a sea-pass shall be property of the Republic of Turkey".[56] The wording herein could be construed as a violation of belligerent occupation law, as it could be viewed as an attempt by Turkey to acquire sovereign title in the occupied territory and thus violate the sovereignty of the RoC over the occupied territory. This barely falls short of annexation. The term in the Framework Agreement for the Water Supply of the "TRNC" provides for the illegal land appropriation (that is, an illegal title of possession and ownership) over (1) the land structures in the occupied territory, (2) the pipeline itself, which is built at a depth of 250 meters (820 feet) in the Mediterranean Sea, and (3) the sea-pass that goes through the maritime zones of the Republic of Cyprus, that is the EEZ and the territorial waters. Furthermore, since the RoC maintains sovereignty over its northern territory, such agreements

---

are guaranteed by international humanitarian law and international human rights law, the minimum content of which is codified in Article 75 of the First Additional Protocol".

56 Framework Treaty Between the Government of Republic of Turkey and the Government of the "Turkish Republic Northern Cyprus" to Provide for the Water Supply of the "Turkish Republic Northern Cyprus", signed 19 July 2010, translated by the Press and Information Office of the Republic of Cyprus, on file with the authors.

should have been negotiated only between Turkey and the RoC. For the reasons we have analysed above, the "TRNC" cannot enter into any kind of international agreements. Moreover, Article 47 of the Geneva Convention IV provides that:

> protected persons who are in occupied territory shall not be deprived, in any case or in any manner whatsoever, of the benefits of the present Convention by any change introduced, as the result of the occupation of a territory, into the institutions or government of the said territory, nor by any agreement concluded between the authorities of the occupied territories and the Occupying Power, nor by any annexation by the latter of the whole or part of the occupied territory.[57]

This provision should be read in conjunction with Article 7 of the Geneva Convention IV when assessing the illegality of the agreements concluded on behalf of the occupied territory and Turkey. Accordingly, the maritime delimitation agreement between the "TRNC" and Turkey, the agreement on the exploitation of natural resources, the agreement on the construction of the water pipeline, and other similar agreements bear no legal effect.

Furthermore, Article 47 of the Geneva Convention IV prohibits any measures taken by the occupying power that will have a negative impact on the life of the population in the occupied territory and imposes an obligation on both the occupying power and the authorities of the occupied territories from reaching agreements that will have a detrimental effect on the lives and legal status of the population. The reactions of the local municipalities in the "TRNC" with regard to the distribution and sale rights of the water from Turkey, the privatisation of the water system in the occupied territory cutting an important source of revenue for the local municipalities and high price of water also suggest that the Framework Agreement for the Water Supply of the "TRNC" will solely benefit the Turkish economy, rather than the Turkish-Cypriots and Greek-Cypriots.[58] Disagreements over the price of water and the terms of ownership

---

57 Geneva Convention Relative to the Protection of Civilian Persons in Time of War (IV GC), *supra* note 49.
58 *See* A. Calik, 'The Power Struggle Over the North's Electricity', *Cyprus Mail Online*, 27 November 2016, <www.cyprus-mail.com/2016/11/27/power-struggle-norths-electricity/>, visited on 24 July 2018.

of the water and the relevant installation, as well as the terms of its management and the monopoly regime of its exploitation, were voiced by the "TRNC's" local municipalities throughout the negotiations and the construction of the project.[59] In fact, the distribution of the water brought by the pipeline is intended to change the legal and political regime of the water distribution in the occupied territory and practically unify it with the regime of the water distribution in Turkey. This will only result in depriving the local authorities of the occupied territory control over water distribution[60] and it seems to be an act of indirect annexation of the occupied territory by Turkey.[61]

It is noteworthy that the terms of the Framework Agreement for the Water Supply of the "TRNC" encompass several terms as to how the water will be distributed, sold and billed that might be deemed unfair towards the local municipalities under the international[62] and European[63] water law regulation framework: (a) the distribution and sale of water is to be under a monopoly scheme, ran by a private Turkish company for the next 50 years; (b) other companies are denied the right to sell and distribute water;[64] and (c) the "TRNC" has an obligation to buy on an annual basis 75 billion cubic meters of water without a prearranged price. The reactions of the local municipalities in the "TRNC" with regard to the high price of water also indicate that they believe the Framework Agreement for the Water Supply of the "TRNC" will solely benefit Turkey.[65] Furthermore, Article 2(4) of the Framework Agreement for the Water Supply of the "TRNC" states that: "the Republic of Turkey … reserves the right to sell water to third countries. Consultation meeting shall be made with the

---

59 Y. Kanli, 'Water Issues with Northern Cyprus', *Hurriyet Daily News*, 7 December 2015, <www.hurriyetdailynews.com/water-issues-with-northern-cyprus.aspx?PageID=238&NID=92136&NewsCatID=425>, visited on 24 July 2018.
60 *Ibid.*
61 *Ibid.*
62 See R. Bates, 'The Trade in Water Services: How does GATS apply to the Water and Sanitation Services?', 31 *Sydney Law Review* (2009) 121.
63 EU, *Directive 2000/60/EC of the European Parliament and of the Council, of 23 October 2000 Establishing A Framework For Community Action In The Field Of Water Policy*, OJ L 327, 22 December 2000, pp. 1-73.
64 "According to rumors circulating in Nicosia, the AKP has already decided which company will get the water. There will be a tender, of course, but everyone knows how tenders work in the Turkish lands." *See* Doğan, *supra* note 53.
65 *Ibid.*

"TRNC" Party at the case of a water sale to a third country, a possible usage of territories of the "TRNC" or usage of the water pipeline".[66]

From an international law perspective, the occupying power cannot exploit the inhabitants, the natural resources, including the land, or the infrastructure of the land that it has occupied for its domestic benefit, *i.e.* to benefit its own economy.[67] Under the Framework Agreement for the Water Supply of the "TRNC", the "TRNC" authorities have made concessions under the pressure of Turkey to the detriment of Turkish-Cypriots and Greek-Cypriots, as they have accepted terms that allow Turkey to exercise sovereign rights over their land and resources. Similarly, the "TRNC" authorities have signed an energy agreement that gives Turkey exploration rights for 30 years. Turkey's permanently taking over of resources, such as land, or reshaping the territory's economy to the occupied population's detriment is contrary to international law. International responsibility over the conclusion of such illegal and unfair agreements arises solely for Turkey as the occupying power.

During an occupation, the sovereignty of the territorial State over its occupied territory is neither ended nor suspended. After all, the occupation is purported to be only temporary. The nature of belligerent occupation is a situation in which governmental functions are exercised on the basis of *de facto* control over a territory. Within this context, Article 43 of the Hague Regulations provides that "the authority of the legitimate power having in fact passed into the hands of the occupant, the latter shall take all the measures in his power to restore, and ensure, as far as possible, public order and safety, while respecting, unless absolutely prevented, the laws in force in the country".[68]

In addition, under Article 55 of the Hague Regulations, the occupying power is obliged to act "only as administrator and usufructuary of

---

66   Framework Treaty Between the Government of Republic of Turkey and the Government of the "Turkish Republic Northern Cyprus" to Provide for the Water Supply of the "Turkish Republic Northern Cyprus", *supra* note 56.

67   A. Cassese, 'Powers and Duties of an Occupant in Relation to Land and Natural Resources', in E. Playfair (ed.) *International Law and the Administration of Occupied Territories: Two Decades of Israeli Occupation of the West Bank and Gaza Strip* (Oxford University Press, Oxford, 1992) p. 422 *et seq*. On the contrary, the exploitation of natural resources should solely benefit both communities in Cyprus. *See* UN Secretary General, *Report of the Secretary-General Progress a Settlement in Cyprus*, S/2018/61, 14 June 2018, para. 30, <undocs.org/S/2018/610>, visited on 22 August 2018.

68   Convention (IV) Respecting the Laws and Customs of War on Land and its Annex: Regulations concerning the Laws and Customs of War on Land, *supra* note 49.

public buildings, real estate, forests, and agricultural estates belonging to the hostile State, and situated in the occupied country. It must safeguard the capital of these properties, and administer them in accordance with the rules of usufruct."[69] This provision encompasses the obligation of the occupying force to protect the natural resources *inter alia* from exploitation. Natural resources can be categorised as either public or private property depending on the domestic law of the occupied territory in force before the beginning of the occupation. Natural resources that are considered public property fall within the protection of Article 55 of the Hague Regulations. An exception stands for movable natural resources that may be used only for military operations under Article 53 of the Hague Regulations.[70] The principle of permanent sovereignty (of the territorial State) over its natural resources, including land, water and energy resources, is applicable even in times of belligerent occupation.[71] The UN Security Council and the General Assembly have affirmed this principle on several occasions and have demanded that the occupying power cease the exploitation, damage, cause of loss, depletion, and endangerment of the natural resources.[72] The ICJ has found that such acts

---

69 *Ibid.*

70 "[A]n army of occupation can only take possession of [...] all movable property belonging to the State which may be used for military operations", *ibid*. Note though Article 46 of the Hague Regulations which provides that "private property cannot be confiscated", *ibid*. See M. Longobardo, 'State Responsibility for International Humanitarian Law Violations by Private Actors in Occupied Territories and the Exploitation of Natural Resources', 63 *Netherlands International Law Review* (2016) pp. 251-274, p. 255, note 24, where he cites national case law according to which crude oil in the ground could not be termed as movable property pursuant to Art. 53 of the Hague Regulations. See *N.V. De Bataafsche Petroleum Maatschappij & Ors v. The War Damage Commission*, 13 April 1956, Singapore Court of Appeal, 23 *ILR* 810, p. 822.

71 See G. Schwarzenberger, *International Law as Applied by International Courts and Tribunals: Volume II The Law of Armed Conflict* (Stevens & Sons, London, 1968) p. 248.

72 See UN General Assembly, Resolution 1803 (XVII) *Permanent Sovereignty Over Natural Resources*, 14 December 1962; UN General Assembly, Resolution 3171, A/RES/3171, 17 December 1973; UN General Assembly, Resolution 64/185, UN Doc. A/RES/64/185, 29 January 2010; UN General Assembly, Resolution 66/225, UN Doc. A/RES/66/225, 29 March 2012; UN General Assembly, Resolution 67/229, UN Doc. A/RES/67/229, 9 April 2013; UN General Assembly, Resolution 69/241, UN Doc. A/RES/69/241, 2 February 2015; UN Security Council, Resolution 1483, UN Doc. S/RES/1483, 22 May 2003; UN Security Council, Resolution 1511, UN Doc. S/RES/1511, 16 October 2003; UN Security Council, Resolution 1546, UN Doc. S/RES/1546, 8 June 2004.

may constitute a form of pillaging too.[73] According to Article 47 of the Geneva Convention IV and Article 47 of the Hague Regulations, "pillage is formally forbidden."[74] Also, pillaging amounts to a war crime under Article 8(2)(b)(xvi) of the Rome Statute of the International Criminal Court ('ICC') and there is scholarly support that it may encompass acts of illegal exploitation of natural resources.[75]

In addition, an occupying power is prohibited from confiscating, exploiting or using the natural resources, including the land, of the territory it occupies for its own benefit. This means that any Turkish companies that are operating in or extracting resources from the occupied territory, and thus receiving taxes, royalties or other fees companies paid to Turkey for their business, should be reserved for the benefit of the protected population.

Belligerent occupation laws also necessitate that any funds that are accrued from resource-based business must be independently monitored and administered solely to benefit the protected population.[76] Finally,

---

73   *See Case Concerning Armed Activities on the Territory of the Congo (Democratic Republic of the Congo v Uganda)*, 19 December 2005, ICJ, Judgment, paras. 222-250, <www.icj-cij.org/files/case-related/116/116-20051219-JUD-01-00-EN.pdf>, visited on 24 July 2018; R. Dufresne, 'Reflection and Extrapolation on the ICJ's Approach to Illegal Resource Exploitation in the Armed Activities Case', 3 *IILJ Emerging Scholars Paper* (2007), <www.iilj.org/publications/reflections-and-extrapolation-on-the-icjs-approach-to-illegal-resource-exploitation-in-the-armed-activities-case/>, visited on 24 July 2018.

74   See Convention (IV) Respecting the Laws and Customs of War on Land and its Annex: Regulations concerning the Laws and Customs of War on Land and Geneva Convention Relative to the Protection of Civilian Persons in Time of War (IV GC), *supra* note 49. *See* also E. Benvenisti and E Zamir, 'Private Claims to Property Rights in the Future Israeli-Palestinian Settlement', 89 *American Journal of International Law* (1995) p. 295: "international law recognizes the power of the occupant to take possession of, and to administer, the private property of absent individuals...the administration of the property does not sever the legal tie between absentees and their property"; E. Benvenisti, *The International Law of Occupation* (Oxford: OUP, 2012) p. 81; H. Dichter, 'The Legal Status of Israel's Water Policies in the Occupied Territories', 35 *Harvard International Law Journal* (1994), pp. 565, 592-3.

75   UN General Assembly, *Rome Statute of the International Criminal Court* (last amended 2010), 17 July 1998, <www.refworld.org/docid/3ae6b3a84.html> visited on 21 May 2017. *See* Longobardo, *supra* note 70, pp. 257-258, 269-271.

76   *See* S. Saadoun, 'Responsible Business in Occupied Territories', *Harvard International Law Review*, 21 June 2016, <http://hir.harvard.edu/article/?a=13429>, visited on 21 May 2017, who explains that: "[b]usinesses need to ensure that any revenues paid to the occupying state for use or exploitation of resources are reserved for the protected population. One possible way to do this is for the occupying state to divert all financial benefits into an independently managed and audited fund,

the obligations of Turkey, as an occupying power, are extended over the acts of illegal exploitation of natural resources committed by its *de jure* or *de facto* organs. This triggers Turkey's State responsibility for the violations of international humanitarian rules regarding the exploitation of natural resources in the occupied territory by the Turkish companies if they qualify as State organs (as their acts can be attributed to the State). Individually, these State organs can be prosecuted for the war crime of pillaging. Further, these Turkish private companies could face international criminal prosecution for their acts of illegal exploitation. In this case, Turkey has an indisputable 'duty of vigilance' regarding private actors' acts in breach of international humanitarian law.[77] According to Article 43 of the Hague Regulations,[78] Turkey has to prevent individuals in the occupied territory from illegally exploiting the natural resources of the territory.

Article 43 of the Hague Regulations has been interpreted to also encompass services concerning health, education, welfare, *etc* that meet

---

and make revenue and expenditures public. Companies should also publish all payments to governments under contractual or other agreements. If an occupying state does not set up such a fund, and companies pay taxes or other fees that flow into the state's coffers and are then disbursed as part of its general budget, companies need to ensure that such funds are independently monitored and administered solely to benefit the protected population."

[77] *Eritrea-Ethiopia Claims Commission, Partial Award: Central Front – Eritrea's Claims 2, 4, 6, 7, 8 & 22*, 28 April 2004, Eritrea-Ethiopia Claims Commission, Decision, para. 67, <legal.un.org/riaa/cases/vol_XXVI/115-153.pdf>, visited on 25 March 2017: "Whether or not Ethiopian military personnel were directly involved in the looting and stripping of buildings in the town, Ethiopia, as the Occupying Power, was responsible for the maintenance of public order, for respecting private property, and for preventing pillage. Consequently, Ethiopia is liable for permitting the unlawful looting and stripping of buildings in the town during the period of its occupation". *See Congo* v. *Uganda, supra* note 73, p. 168, paras. 158, 248 where the Court held that "Uganda was under an obligation, according to Art. 43 HR, to take all the measures in its power to restore, and ensure, as far as possible, public order and safety in the occupied area ... This obligation comprised the duty to secure respect for the applicable rules of international human rights law and international humanitarian law, to protect the inhabitants of the occupied territory against acts of violence, and not to tolerate such violence by any third party ... [t]he fact that Uganda was the occupying Power in Ituri district extends Uganda's obligation to take appropriate measures to prevent the looting, plundering and exploitation of natural resources in the occupied territory to cover private persons in this district and not only members of Ugandan military forces".

[78] Convention (IV) Respecting the Laws and Customs of War on Land and its Annex: Regulations concerning the Laws and Customs of War on Land, *supra* note 49.

the needs of people who live in a modern and civilized society.[79] Articles 43 and 55 of the Hague Regulations not only create positive obligations for the occupying power but also negative obligations to refrain from measures that will severely affect the survival of the civilian population or will cause them to move away.[80] There is no obligation arising under occupation law for the occupying power to carry out construction projects in the occupied territory, especially when these projects may outlast the military occupation. On the contrary, international legal scholars have expressed their serious reservations concerning the construction of water and electricity plants or roads and rail systems[81] in occupied territories, as such measures can change the temporary character of the occupation and can directly or indirectly facilitate the immigration of foreign settlers into the occupied territory, hence constituting a violation of Article 49(6) of Geneva Convention IV.[82]

It is also prohibited under occupation law to change the demographic structure of the occupied territory, as this can not only prolong the mili-

---

79 Convention (IV) Respecting the Laws and Customs of War on Land and its Annex: Regulations concerning the Laws and Customs of War on Land, *supra* note 49. *See also* Article 55 of the Geneva Convention Relative to the Protection of Civilian Persons in Time of War (IV GC) under which the occupying power "has the duty of ensuring the food and medical supplies of the population", *supra* note 49. *See Jami'at Ascan et al* v *IDF Commander in Judea and Samaria et al.*, Supreme Court of Israel, HCJ 393/82,37(4) PD, p. 785, 786 (1983); *Tabib* v *Minister of Defense*, Supreme Court of Israel, HCJ 202/81 (1981); *Abu Itta et al* v *Commander of Judea and Samaria et al*, Supreme Court of Israel, HCL 493/81, PD 37(2), 197, 313 (1983) cited in The Association for Civil Rights in Israel, *The Right to Water in Occupied Territories: Legal Background*, (2016), <www.acri.org.il/en/wp-content/uploads/2016/02/Right-to-water-in-the-OPT-Legal-Background.pdf>, visited on 21 May 2017.

80 Convention (IV) Respecting the Laws and Customs of War on Land and its Annex: Regulations concerning the Laws and Customs of War on Land, *supra* note 49. *See* for example, Article 54 (2) of Protocol I and Article 53 Geneva Convention Relative to the Protection of Civilian Persons in Time of War (IV GC) whereby it is stated that "[a]ny destruction by the Occupying Power of real or personal property belonging individually or collectively to private persons, or to the State, or to other public authorities, or to social or cooperative organizations, is prohibited, except where such destruction is rendered absolutely necessary by military operations", *supra* note 49.

81 *See* C. Greenwood, 'The Administration of Occupied Territory in International Law', in E. Playfair, (ed.) *International Law and the Administration of Occupied Territories – Two Decades of Israeli Occupation of the West Bank and Gaza Strip* (Clarendon Press, Oxford, 1992) pp. 244-245.

82 Geneva Convention Relative to the Protection of Civilian Persons in Time of War (IV GC), *supra* note 49.

tary occupation but eventually lead to the annexation of the occupied territory. An occupying power is prohibited from transferring its own civilians into the occupied territory and facilitating the move of settlers by providing services, such as water and electricity, or financing infrastructure, such as housing. In particular, under Article 7(2)(d) of the Rome Statute of the ICC deportation or forcible transfer of population (*i.e.* the forced displacement of the persons concerned by expulsion or other coercive acts from the area in which they are lawfully present) without grounds permitted under international law constitutes a crime against humanity and, when in violation of the Geneva Conventions, under Article 8(2)(b)(viii) of the Rome Statute of the ICC, deportation or forcible transfer of population, amounts to a war crime.[83]

Thus, the RoC is facing a systematic policy of demographic manipulation of the population in the occupied territory by Turkey.[84] The construction of the underwater pipeline project will, first, contribute to the prolongation of the military occupation and, second, will assist in the continuation of the movement of people from Turkey to the "TRNC". These acts by Turkey seem to not only systematise the illegal settlement-related activities in the region, but also disregards the decisions of international organisation[85] and courts, which have condemned the transfer of people by Turkey and the expulsion of Greek-Cypriots from their

---

83   Rome Statute of the International Criminal Court, *supra* note 75.
84   Amb. R. Schlicher, *Turkish Cypriot Census Debate Focuses on Natives versus "Settlers"*, May 2007, <www.wikileaks.ikiru.ch/cable/07NICOSIA434/Census%20Debate>, visited on 24 July 2018. Cyprus has expressed its concern over the enforced colonization and "Turkification" of the population in the occupied territory: "In this connection, we have witnessed, lately, an intensification of Turkish attempts to change the demographics of the occupied areas of Cyprus through colonization and a "citizenship" granting process for Turkish citizens. Illegal Turkish settlers, brought to Cyprus from Anatolia, consciously or unconsciously assume the role of a catalyst for the advancement and implementation of AKP policies intended to further integrate the Turkish Cypriot" community into Turkey and to "Turkify" the occupied areas of Cyprus, with far-reaching repercussions in the Government-controlled areas of the Republic". See Letter dated 3 October 2017 from the Permanent Representative of Cyprus to the United Nations addressed to the Secretary-General, A/72/507–S/2017/831, 5 October 2017, <undocs.org/A/72/507>, visited on 24 July 2018; Letter dated 18 October 2017 from the Permanent Representative of Turkey to the United Nations addressed to the Secretary-General, A/72/542–S/2017/878, 19 October 2017, <undocs.org/A/72/542>, visited on 24 July 2018.
85   *See* A. de Zayas, *The Status of Turkish Settlers in Northern Cyprus-The Implantation of Turkish Settlers in Northern Cyprus*, (2005), <www.alfreddezayas.com/Lectures/Cypruslimassol.shtml>, visited on 24 July 2018.

homes.⁸⁶ Perhaps this is best illustrated by the Framework Agreement for the Water Supply of the "TRNC", which does not mention restitution or compensation for any damages caused by the construction of the pipeline on the land of Greek-Cypriots. This kind of infrastructure project in the occupied territory of Cyprus can be viewed as aggravating the human rights situation of the Greek-Cypriots as it may perpetuate their forced displacement.

The ICJ's, as well as other international judicial bodies', case law affirm the extraterritorial obligations of occupying powers to enforce human rights obligations in the occupied territories.⁸⁷ For example, the right to water has been recognised in a number of human rights instruments⁸⁸ and it has been confirmed as being one of the obligations of the occupying powers in occupied territories. RoC has repeatedly expressed concern over the fact that it is not in a position to apply and ensure the implementation of human rights in the whole of its territory due to the military occupation of Turkey.⁸⁹ Turkey has tried to justify the underwater pipeline and the electricity supply project in the occupied territory, as projects that will alleviate the suffering of the Turkish Cypriots,⁹⁰ However, it is doubtful whether the underwater pipeline or the electricity un-

---

86 See Council of Europe, *Parliamentary Assembly, Committee on Legal Affairs and Human Rights, Forced Population Transfer as Human Rights Violation*, (Mr. Egidijus Vareikis, AS/Jur (2011) 49), 5 December 2011, note 19: "It was only in December 2003 that Titina Loizidou received from Turkey 1.3 million Euros in compensation for the lost use of her property located in the occupied northern part of Cyprus. However, she has still [in 2011] not been allowed to return to her home. The remedy of compensation ordered by the ECtHR to Titina Loizidou had remained unimplemented for over five years. It required three resolutions by the Committee of Ministers to convince Turkey to make reparation payments pursuant to the judgment of 1998."

87 *Legal Consequences of the Construction of a Wall in the Occupied Palestinian Territory*, 9 July 2004, ICJ, Advisory Opinion, *supra* note 46, paras.108-111, 120.

88 See e.g., UN General Assembly, *International Covenant on Economic, Social and Cultural Rights*, 16 December 1966, UNTS 993, p. 3, Article 11; Committee on Economic, Social and Cultural Rights, *General Comment No. 15 Substantive Issues Arising in the Implementation of the International Covenant on Economic, Social and Cultural Rights-The right to water (arts. 11 and 12 of the International Covenant on Economic, Social and Cultural Rights*, 20 January 2003, E/C.12/2002/11.

89 UN Human Rights Committee, *List of issues in relation to the fourth periodic report of Cyprus – Addendum – Replies of Cyprus to the list of issues*, 19 January 2015, CCPR/C/CYP/Q/4/Add.1, para. 6, <documents-dds-ny.un.org/doc/UNDOC/GEN/G15/006/11/PDF/G1500611.pdf?OpenElement>, visited on 4 October 2017.

90 See Letter dated 14 December 2016 from the Permanent Representative of Turkey to the United Nations addressed to the Secretary-General, A/71/693–S/2016/1067,

derwater cable have been constructed to protect the human rights of the population in the occupied territory of Cyprus.[91] On the one hand, it is clear that these projects are effectively making the Turkish Cypriots dependent on Turkey which is the occupying power. On the other hand, it seems strange that Turkey has chosen to protect the rights to water and electricity of the the occupied population while it has sidelined or even ignored other human rights of the Turkish-Cypriots and Greek-Cypriots. In support of this, one should note that Turkey has been under constant pressure by the UN and the Council of Europe for the past 10 years "to implement without further delay all the relevant judgments of the European Court of Human Rights, where grave human rights violations by Turkey had been established in the occupied areas of Cyprus under the effective control of Turkey".[92] Perhaps human rights courts and bodies, despite their mandate to protect and guarantee human rights, are not effective enough to put an end to Turkey's human rights violations in the north of Cyprus.[93]

---

16 December 2016, <undocs.org/A/71/693%E2%80%93S/2016/1067>, visited on 4 October 2017.

[91] The right to water in occupied territories refers to basic aspects of water services that guarantee the right to live in dignity of the civilian population in the occupied territory (for example, connection to water systems, water supply and storage and water consumption levels). *See* Y. Lein, *Disputed Waters: Israel's Responsibility for the Water Shortage in the Occupied Territories* (The Israeli Information Center for Human Rights in the Occupied Territories, Jerusalem, September 1998), <www.btselem.org/publications/summaries/199809_disputed_waters>, visited on 4 October 2017.

[92] UN Human Rights Committee, *List of issues in relation to the fourth periodic report of Cyprus- Addendum -Replies of Cyprus to the list of issues*, 19 January 2015, CCPR/C/CYP/Q/4/Add.1, para. 6, <documents-dds-ny.un.org/doc/UNDOC/GEN/G15/006/11/PDF/G1500611.pdf?OpenElement>, visited on 4 October 2017; Human Rights Council, *Report of the Office of the United Nations High Commissioner for Human Rights, Question of Human Rights in Cyprus*, A/HRC/31/21, 11 February 2016, para. 10, <documents-dds-ny.un.org/doc/UNDOC/GEN/G16/015/26/PDF/G1601526.pdf?OpenElement>, visited on 18 January 2018; Human Rights Council, *Report of the Office of the United Nations High Commissioner for Human Rights, Question of Human Rights in Cyprus*, A/HRC/25/21, 22 January 2014, <documents-dds-ny.un.org/doc/UNDOC/GEN/G14/104/78/PDF/G1410478.pdf?OpenElement>, visited on 18 January 2018; Human Rights Council, *Report of the Working Group on the Universal Periodic Review- Turkey*, A/HRC/29/15, 13 April 2015, <documents-dds-ny.un.org/doc/UNDOC/GEN/G15/076/33/PDF/G1507633.pdf?OpenElement>, visited on 18 January 2018.

[93] *See* K. Chainoglou, B. Collins, M. Phillips, and J. Strawson, *Injustice, Memory and Faith in Human Rights* (Routledge, Abingdon, 2017). There are other human rights issues that have not been addressed in the present text and they are of equal importance to the issues raised herein, such as the destruction of cultural heritage in

4 Turkey's Objections to Cyprus' Maritime Zones and the Law of the Sea

The UNCLOS sets out a comprehensive legal framework and establishes rules governing all uses of the oceans and their resources. The EU has ratified the UNCLOS and it is now an integral part of its *acquis communautaire*. Turkey has been repeatedly called by EU to ratify UNCLOS as it is now both part of EU and international law.[94] Until Turkey ratifies UNCLOS, Turkey is bound only by the customary rules on the law of the sea.

For more than 15 years, Turkey has embarked on a number of questionable actions in the east of the Mediterranean. The European Council and other EU bodies have called Turkey to cease all illegal activities in the east of the Mediterranean that violate the sovereign rights of EU member States and their sovereignty over their territorial sea and airspace.[95] Specifically, the EU has called Turkey to respect the sovereign rights of Cyprus to enter into bilateral agreements and "to explore and exploit its natural resources in accordance with EU and International Law".[96] For instance, in early 2018 Turkey was accused of preventing foreign energy companies licensed to drill for gas and oil from accessing Cypriot waters, which has been condemned by the EU (see discussion below).[97]

---

the occupied territory and the cultural rights of the affected population. On the subject of cultural dimensions of human rights *see* K. Chainoglou, A. Wiesand, A. Sledzinska-Simon, and Y. Donders, *Culture and Human Rights: The Wroclaw Commentaries*, (De Gruyter, Berlin, 2016).

94   *See e.g.* Council, *Conclusions on Enlargement and Stabilisation and Association Process*, 15356/15, 15 December 2015, <data.consilium.europa.eu/doc/document/ST-15356-2015-INIT/en/pdf>, visited on 12 July 2018.

95   *Ibid.*

96   European Council, *Conclusions on the Western Balkans and actions by Turkey in the Eastern Mediterranean and the Aegean Sea*, 22 March 2018, <www.consilium.europa.eu/en/press/press-releases/2018/03/22/european-council-conclusions-on-the-western-balkans-and-actions-by-turkey-in-the-eastern-mediterranean-and-the-aegean-sea-22-march-2018/>, visited on 12 July 2018. With regard to the European Council Conclusions of 22 March 2018 on the illegal actions by Turkey, Federica Morgherini has affirmed that the European Council will remain seized of this matter and the Commission will continue to monitor the situation closely. *See* EU, *Parliamentary Questions, Answer given by Vice-President Mogherini on behalf of the Commission*, 31 May 2018, <www.europarl.europa.eu/sides/getAllAnswers.do?reference=E-2018-001721&language=EN>, visited on 12 July 2018.

97   *See* 'Turkish Warships Block Drilling Rig Near Cyprus', *Deutsche Welle*, 13 February 2018 <www.dw.com/en/turkish-warships-block-drilling-rig-near-cyprus/a-42559676>, visited on 3 March 2018.

It has been part of the Turkish rhetoric since the 1970s that islands do not enjoy the right to generate maritime zones of their own. Turkey has disputed Cyprus' right to the continental shelf and an EEZ around the whole of the island. In a number of letters to the UN, Turkey has claimed sovereignty over the maritime zone in the sea that lies between the eastern Aegean region and Cyprus, and in particular has attempted to delimit "the outer limits of Turkey's continental shelf in the eastern Mediterranean that are west of longitude 32°16'18"E".[98]

The Turkish claim is premised on a dubious interpretation of international law as Turkey argues against the opinion that islands can generate full maritime zones and that Cyprus has a right to generate maritime zones off its western coast. Turkey's position on this matter is that the maritime zone situated in Blocks 1, 4, 5, 6, and 7 of Cyprus' continental shelf/EEZ overlap with Turkey's alleged continental shelf outer limits. This position by Turkey seems to suggest that it is rather pursuing an annexation policy as it is treating the western coast of Cyprus and the occupied territory as part of Turkey.

Article 121(2) of the UNCLOS clearly provides that islands, irrespective of their size,[99] generate the same maritime rights as any other land territory. The wording of this provision states that "the territorial sea, the contiguous zone, the exclusive economic zone and the continental shelf of an island are determined in accordance with the provisions of this Convention applicable to other land territory".[100] Customary international law is aligned with the UNCLOS on this matter; the ICJ has confirmed that Article 121 of the UNCLOS reflects customary international law.[101]

---

98   See Turkish notes verbales No. 2004/Turku no DT/4739, dated 2 March 2004, and No. 2013/14136816/22273, dated 12 March 2013, cited in Power, *supra* note 48, p.92; *See also* Letter dated 29 September 2016 from the Permanent Representative of Turkey to the United Nations addressed to the Secretary-General, A/71/421, 30 September 2016, <undocs.org/A/71/421>, visited on 2 April 2018.

99   Convention on the Law of the Sea, *supra* note 44. Article 121(3) of the Convention on the Law of the Sea, mentions though that "[r]ocks which cannot sustain human habitation or economic life of their own shall have no exclusive economic zone or continental shelf", *ibid*.

100 *Ibid*.

101 *Ibid. See also Maritime Delimitation and Territorial Questions between Qatar and Bahrain (Qatar v. Bahrain),* 13 March 2001, ICJ, Judgment, para. 185, <www.icj-cij.org/files/case-related/87/087-20010316-JUD-01-00-EN.pdf>, visited on 24 June 2018; *Territorial and Maritime Dispute (Nicaragua v. Colombia),* 19 November 2012, ICJ, Judgment, *I.C.J. Reports* 624, para. 139.

This means that as a rule it binds also non-State parties to the UNCLOS, like Turkey.

4.1 Cyprus' Exclusive Economic Zone

The RoC has established an EEZ with the enactment of the Exclusive Economic Zone and Continental Shelf Law (Law No. 64(I)/2004), which was been deposited with the UN Secretary-General of the UN in accordance with the UNCLOS. Pursuant to the Exclusive Economic Zone and Continental Shelf Law (which has been amended by Law 97(I)/2014), the outer limit of the EEZ of the RoC is to be found 200 nautical miles from the baselines from which the breadth of the territorial sea is measured. However, in the event that any part of the EEZ of the RoC covers part of the EEZ of any other State whose coast lies opposite Cyprus (as is the case in the eastern Mediterranean), the limit of the EEZ of the RoC and the EEZ of the other State is determined in accordance with an agreement between them. In the absence of such an agreement, the limit of the EEZ is the median line. The RoC has signed EEZ delimitation agreements with Egypt (2003),[102] Lebanon (2007),[103] and Israel (2010).[104] The delimitation effected with these agreements is based on the median line method which is widely accepted under international law and through State practice.[105]

---

102 Agreement between the Republic of Cyprus and the Arab Republic of Egypt on the Delimitation of the Exclusive Economic Zone, 17 February 2003, <www.un.org/depts/los/LEGISLATIONANDTREATIES/STATEFILES/CYP.htm>, visited on 12 June 2018.

103 Lebanon has never disputed the maritime delimitation between Lebanon and Cyprus but has expressed its disagreement of Israel's geographical coordinates which partially overlap with Lebanon's geographical points and EEZ. *See* Letter dated 20 June 2011 from the Minister for Foreign Affairs and Emigrants of Lebanon addressed to the Secretary-General of the United Nations concerning the Agreement between the Government of the State of Israel and the Government of the Republic of Cyprus on the Delimitation of the Exclusive Economic Zone, 17 December 2010, <treaties.un.org/doc/Publication/UNTS/Volume%202740/v2740.pdf>, visited on 12 June 2018.

104 Agreement between the Government of the State of Israel and the Government of the Republic of Cyprus on the Delimitation of the Exclusive Economic Zone, 17 December 2010, <treaties.un.org/doc/Publication/UNTS/Volume%202740/v2740.pdf>, visited on 12 June 2018.

105 The Ministry of Foreign Affairs of the Republic of Cyprus states that "[t]aking into account that in the Mediterranean Sea the distances between the coastal states are smaller than 400 nautical miles and that it is not practically possible to claim EEZ/continental shelf up to 200 nautical miles, the limit of the EEZ of the Republic of Cyprus, as well as its continental shelf, is the median line between its coasts and

Turkey, however, has expressed a different opinion on the current state of law of the sea. Specifically, Turkey has claimed that

> [i]t has never been sanctioned by international law on maritime delimitation to cut a coastal State off from its access to the high seas. Similarly, it is well established in international court rulings that islands do not necessarily generate full maritime jurisdiction zones (continental shelf and/or exclusive economic zone) when they are competing against continental land areas.[106]

It is true that, in a small number of cases, international courts, and tribunals have chosen to restrict the right of islands to generate full maritime zones, but they have done so in view of the special circumstances of each case, *i.e.* if their zones would reduce the size of zones created by adjacent or opposite continental land masses.[107] For example, the ICJ has found that uninhabited tiny islands or otherwise "insignificant maritime features" could not have a disproportionate effect on the choice of a maritime delimitation line.[108] However, neither international courts nor

---

the coasts of the opposite states (unless there is an agreement to the contrary). Pursuant to the legislation, the two zones overlap, as the limits thereof coincide, whilst the relevant sovereign rights and jurisdictions of the Republic of Cyprus as a coastal state, also, coincide according to the 1982 United Nations Convention on the Law of the Sea; nevertheless they remain two distinctive maritime zones". See Ministry of Foreign Affairs, *Exclusive Economic Zone and Continental Shelf*, (2016), <www.mfa.gov.cy/mfa/mfa2016.nsf/mfa86_en/mfa86_en?OpenDocument&print>, visited on 24 June 2018.

106 Letter dated 15 June 2016 from the Chargé d'affaires a.i. of the Permanent Mission of Turkey to the United Nations addressed to the Secretary-General, A/70/945–S/2016/541, 17 June 2016, <undocs.org/A/70/945>, visited on 4 October 2017.

107 *Delimitation of the Maritime Boundary in the Bay of Bengal (Bangladesh/Myanmar)*, International Tribunal for the Law of the Sea, Judgment, *ITLOS Reports* 2012, p. 4, para. 137, <www.itlos.org/cases/list-of-cases/case-no-16/>, visited on 24 June 2018.

108 See *Continental Shelf, Libya v. Malta*, 3 June 1985, ICJ, Judgment Merits, *I.C.J. Reports* 13, p.48, para. 64 <www.icj-cij.org/files/case-related/68/068-19850603-JUD-01-00-EN.pdf>, visited on 24 June 2018, where the Court "refused to give full effect to Malta's main island, which is the size of Washington, D.C., and contains hundreds of thousands of individuals, and adjusted the median line northward because of the longer length of the Libyan coast and its resulting greater power to generate a maritime zone". In *Maritime Delimitation and Territorial Questions between Qatar and Bahrain (Qatar v. Bahrain)*, 13 March 2001, ICJ, Judgment, para. 219, the Court admitted that "[it] has sometimes been led to eliminate the disproportionate effect of small islands (see *North Sea Continental Shelf*, Judgment, *I.C.J. Reports* 1969, p. 36, para. 57; *Continental Shelf (Libyan Arab Jamahiriya/Malta)*, Judgment, *I.C.J. Reports*

international legal scholars have suggested that such restrictions on islands' rights could be imposed on island States with the geographical and security considerations of Cyprus.

Turkey has also repeatedly used the argument that the Mediterranean sea is particular in that it is . a semi-closed sea. Turkey has argued that:

> the delimitation in the eastern Mediterranean should therefore be effected by agreement of all the related parties on the basis of the principle of equity so as not to prejudice the sovereign rights and jurisdiction of other interested States/entities. Furthermore, concepts like "land dominates the sea" and "cut-off effect" still continue to be among the essential principles of international law and jurisprudence in the context of the delineation of maritime jurisdiction areas.[109]

Although States may have the right to avoid being totally suffocated by the ocean zone of a coastal State that cuts them off from access to the seas altogether, this is not the case with Cyprus' continental shelf and EEZ. With the RoC, the maritime delimitation decisions need to protect the vital security interests of all interested parties, not only Turkey's.[110] To add, in *Libya* v. *Malta*, the ICJ stated that "the delimitation in question was not so near the coast of either party as to make questions of security

---

1985, p. 48, para. 64)", <www.icj-cij.org/files/case-related/87/087-20010316-JUD-01-00-EN.pdf>, visited on 24 June 2018. It should be noted though that a number of States have expressed their belief that islands are *mutatis mutandis* in the same position as continental territories as regards to rights and obligations under international law and that islands should enjoy at least the same rights, if not some form of special privileges, as continental territories. The rationale for this belief lies in the fact that islands tend to rely more on the resources in their maritime zones than non-island territories. See generally A/Conf. 62/C.2/L/50, 2 Official Records (1974) p. 84 *et seq* cited in C. R. Symmons, *The Maritime Zones of Islands in International Law*, (Martinus Nijhoff Publishers, The Hague, 1979), p. 213, note 25; UN Special Committee on Geographical Disadvantage, *A Comprehensive Proposal for Accommodation of Geographically Disadvantaged States*, 1974.

109   Letter dated 15 June 2016 from the Chargé d'affaires of the Permanent Mission of Turkey to the United Nations addressed to the Secretary-General, A/70/945–S/2016/541, 17 June 2016, <undocs.org/A/70/945>, visited on 24 June 2018.

110   *Case Concerning Maritime Delimitation in the Area Between Greenland and Jan Mayen (Denmark* v. *Norway)*, 14 June 1993, ICJ, Judgment, *I.C.J. Reports* 38; *Land, Island and Maritime Frontier Dispute (El Salvador/Honduras; Nicaragua intervening)*, 11 September 1992, ICJ, Judgment, *I.C.J. Reports 351*, paras. 415-20.

a particular consideration in the present case".[111] As it has been pointed out, "this could be redrawn where considerations of security require the boundary to be established further away from one state".[112] In the case of Cyprus' EEZ, three more States (Egypt, Lebanon, and Israel) whose security interests should be also be equally taken into consideration, have agreed on the maritime boundary delimitation with the RoC.[113] Any efforts to annul these agreements on the part of Turkey are not possible under international law and the Vienna Convention on the Law of the Treaties.

Turkey, further, has proceeded with a unilateral delimitation which is prohibited under international law. The ICJ has held that there can be no unilateral delimitations:

> No maritime delimitation between states with opposite or adjacent coasts may be effected unilaterally by one those states. Such delimitation must be sought and effected by means of an agreement, following negotiations conducted in good faith and with the genuine intention of achieving a positive result. Where, however, such agreement cannot be achieved, delimitation should be effected by recourse to a third party possessing the necessary competence. In either case, delimitation is to be effected by the application of equitable criteria and by the use of practical methods capable of en-

---

[111] *Libya* v. *Malta, supra* note 108, para. 51, cited in Power, *supra* note 48, p.105.

[112] Power, *supra* note 48, p. 105.

[113] On 21 November 2017, Greece, Cyprus, and Egypt signed a Joint Declaration which was communicated to the UN. The Joint Declaration stated *inter alia* that the three parties "emphasized the universal character of the UNCLOS and stressed their commitment to proceed expeditiously with the negotiations on the delimitation of their common maritime boundaries as appropriate". *See* Letter dated 13 February 2018 from the Permanent Representatives of Cyprus, Egypt and Greece to the United Nations addressed to the Secretary-General, A/72/760, 23 February 2018, <undocs.org/A/72/760>, visited on 24 June 2018. Some days later, Turkey objected to the Joint Declaration and claimed that "the reference to so-called "common maritime boundaries" is void and unfounded under the terms of international law, including both customary and case law ... Turkey is committed to protecting its *ipso facto* and *ab initio* sovereign rights over its continental shelf emanating from international law". *See also* Letter dated 27 March 2018 from the Permanent Representative of Turkey to the United Nations addressed to the Secretary-General, A/72/820, 6 April 2018, <undocs.org/en/a/72/820>, visited on 24 June 2018.

suring, with regard to the geographic configuration of the area and other relevant circumstances, an equitable result.[114]

Turkey claims sovereignty over the maritime area are between 32°16'18"E longitude and 33°40'N latitude. This has not been negotiated between Turkey and the other States in the region (as the RoC has done). The delimitation agreement concluded between the "TRNC" and Turkey is not a valid international agreement; at best, it can be described as a unilateral declaration. Furthermore, the longitude 32°16'18"E that Turkey claims is just outside the RoC's twelve nautical mile territorial sea; as it has been correctly pointed out, this "disregard[s] the Republic of Cyprus' inherent right to a continental shelf and its capacity to declare an EEZ".[115] A State's right to continental shelf exists by virtue of its sovereignty; as the Court has said, "the continental shelf can be declared, but does not need to be constituted".[116] Hence, according to Power, Turkey's unilateral delimitation declaration and "extension of jurisdiction over the maritime space of the occupied northern Cyprus" can be viewed as a violation of Article 2(4) of the UN Charter.[117]

4.2 *Cyprus' Sovereignty over Territorial Waters*

The RoC is a State party to the UNCLOS. Under Article 2 of the UNCLOS, a coastal State has the right to establish the breadth of its territorial sea up to 12 nautical miles, measured from the territory's baseline.[118] Accordingly, the RoC has sovereignty over a 12 nautical miles belt of sea (covering also the occupied territory in the north) which includes the airspace above and the seabed and subsoil below.

Under the UNCLOS, the only limit to a coastal State's sovereignty over its territorial waters is the right of innocent passage of ships. However, the carrying out of research or survey activities and "any other activity not having a direct bearing on passage" shall not be considered an "innocent

---

114 *Case Concerning Delimitation of the Maritime Boundary in the Gulf of Maine Area (Canada v. United States)*, 12 October 1984, ICJ, Judgment, para. 112, <www.icj-cij.org/files/case-related/67/067-19841012-JUD-01-00-EN.pdf>, visited on 24 June 2018.
115 N. Ioannidis, 'The Law of the Sea Dimension of the Cyprus Problem', 12:4 *In Depth* (2015) p. 30, <cceia.unic.ac.cy/wp-content/uploads/IN_DEPTH-_2015_12_4.pdf>, visited on 3 February 2018.
116 *North Sea Continental Shelf Cases (Federal Republic of Germany v. Denmark; Federal Republic of Germany v. Netherlands*, 20 February 1969, ICJ, Judgment, *I.C.J. Reports* 1969, p. 3, para. 19.
117 Power, *supra* note 48, p. 105.
118 Convention on the Law of the Sea, *supra* note 44.

passage" (Article 19(2)(j) and (l) of the UNCLOS[119]). Survey activities of cable routes by third States' ships, the laying of cables and pipelines and maintenance activities of cables and pipelines in the territorial waters of a coastal State are considered to fall within the definition of "survey activities" that do not enjoy a right of "innocent passage".[120] Coastal States are entitled to impose conditions for pipelines and cables that enter their territory and territorial waters. They regulate any cable operations as it is in their security and economic interests. State practice indicates that coastal States will grant permits or licenses before such operations can be carried out.[121] To add, negotiations between the coastal State and the third State as to the purported route of the cable or pipeline is a *sine qua non* condition for the granting of the permit of the pipeline or cable laying operation.

The construction of the underwater water-supply pipeline and the underwater electricity cable therefore violates the RoC's sovereignty over its territorial waters "TRNC's". Since it is sovereign over its territorial waters, only the RoC has the authority to regulate the activities of third States in cable and pipeline operations. The RoC has the right to control survey activities of cable routes by third States' ships, the laying of cables and pipelines, and maintenance activities of cables and pipelines. As discussed above, the cable laying operation in the territorial waters of Cyprus cannot enjoy the status of "innocent passage"; to the contrary, the RoC must consent to the laying and the route of the cable or pipeline in its territorial waters and territory. In this case, the RoC has repeatedly objected to the laying of the underwater cable and pipeline and has raised the issue before the UN.[122]

---

119 *ibid.*

120 *Ibid.* Under Article 21 of the Convention on the Law of the Sea a coastal State can impose regulations on the innocent passage through its territorial waters, *ibid. See* T. Davenport, 'Submarine Communications Cables and Law of the Sea: Problems in Law and Practice', 43: 3 *Ocean Development and International Law* (2013), pp. 201-242. Under Article 21 of the Convention on the Law of the Sea a coastal State can impose regulations on the innocent passage through its territorial waters, *supra* note 44.

121 Davenport notes that "a more uncommon type of condition imposed as part of the permitting processes in territorial waters is the requirement that either the crew or vessel carrying out cable operations have the same nationality as the coastal state". *See* T. Davenport, *supra* note 120, pp. 201-242.

122 *See* Letter dated 10 November 2016 from the Chargé d'affaires a.i. of the Permanent Mission of Cyprus to the United Nations addressed to the Secretary-General, A/71/611–S/2016/955, 11 November 2016, <undocs.org/A/71/611-S/2016/955>, visited

4.3 Cyprus' Sovereign Rights over its Continental Shelf

A number of the UNCLOS provisions affirm that coastal States enjoy exclusive sovereign rights over their continental shelf. Article 56(1)(a) and (3) of the UNCLOS provides that

> in the exclusive economic zone, the coastal State has:
> (a) sovereign rights for the purpose of exploring and exploiting, conserving and managing the natural resources, whether living or non-living, of the waters superjacent to the seabed and of the seabed and its subsoil, and with regard to other activities for the economic exploitation and exploration of the zone, such as the production of energy from the water, currents and winds;
>
> ....
>
> 3. The rights set out in this article with respect to the seabed and subsoil shall be exercised in accordance with Part VI [Articles 76-85].[123]

Article 77(1) of the UNCLOS provides that "the coastal State exercises over the continental shelf sovereign rights for the purpose of exploring it and exploiting its natural resources" and Article 77(2) of the UNCLOS states that "the rights referred to in paragraph 1 are exclusive in the sense that if the coastal State does not explore the continental shelf or exploit its natural resources, no one may undertake these activities without the express consent of the coastal State".[124] Article 81 of the UNCLOS stipulates that "the coastal State shall have the exclusive right to authorize and regulate drilling on the continental shelf for all purposes."[125] Thus, under the UNCLOS, the RoC enjoys exclusive sovereign rights over its EEZ and continental shelf; this means that it is the only legitimate authority that can explore and exploit (or give its consent for another entity to explore and exploit) the natural resources in its seabed and subsoil.

Turkey makes two claims that have little support in international law, whether customary or conventional law. First, Turkey argues that the "TRNC" can independently have a right to the underwater natural re-

---

on 24 July 2018; Letter dated 8 October 1996 from the Permanent Representative of Cyprus to the United Nations addressed to the Secretary-General, A/51/487 S/1996/846, 11 October 1996, <undocs.org/A/51/487>, visited on 24 July 2018.

123 Convention on the Law of the Sea, *supra* note 44.
124 *Ibid.*
125 *Ibid.*

sources; and second, that Turkey argues that it has the right to explore and exploit the natural resources that are found in the RoC's continental shelf.

As to the first claim, it has been explained above that the "TRNC" territory is under Turkey's occupation. Hence, sovereignty over the water (and any) natural resources belongs to the people of the territorial State concerned, that is the RoC only. This means that ownership of hydrocarbons and any other natural resources in the continental shelf and the Cyprus' EEZ (including the occupied territory) rests solely in the RoC. Furthermore, the protection guaranteed under Article 55 of the Hague Regulations[126] could be perhaps extended over the continental shelf only on the precondition that natural resources will be treated as public property over which the occupying power, Turkey, cannot acquire sovereign rights.

As to the second claim, Turkey has been carrying out illegal seismic surveys in the territorial waters, as well as in the EEZ and the continental shelf of the RoC, and has unlawfully granted hydrocarbon exploration licenses to TPAO.[127] Thus, Turkey has attempted to interfere with the RoC's sovereignty.[128] For example, in a letter from Turkey to the UN it was al-

---

126   Convention (IV) Respecting the Laws and Customs of War on Land and its Annex: Regulations concerning the Laws and Customs of War on Land, *supra* note 49.

127   *See* Letter dated 13 February 2014 from the Permanent Representative of Cyprus to the United Nations addressed to the Secretary-General, A/68/759, 18 February 2014, <undocs.org/a/68/759>, visited on 3 June 2017; Letter dated 5 December 2013 from the Permanent Representative of Cyprus to the United Nations addressed to the Secretary-General, A/68/644–S/2013/720, 5 December 2013, <undocs.org/S/2013/720>, visited on 3 June 2017; Letter dated 29 October 2013 from the Permanent Representative of Cyprus to the United Nations addressed to the Secretary-General, A/68/555–S/2013/634, 29 October 2013, <undocs.org/S/2013/634>, visited on 3 June 2017; Letter dated 17 October 2013 from the Permanent Representative of Cyprus to the United Nations addressed to the Secretary-General, A/68/537–S/2013/622, 18 October 2013, <undocs.org/S/2013/622>, visited on 3 June 2017.

128   *See* Letter dated 15 June 2012 from the Permanent Representative of Cyprus to the United Nations addressed to the Secretary-General, A/66/851, 19 June 2012, <www.cyprusun.org/?p=4728>, visited on 3 June 2017. *See also* RoC's protest to the Barbaros' activities in the RoC's EEZ: "More precisely, the Turkish scientific ship Barbaros Hayreddin Pasa, accompanied by two other support vessels, will carry out a seismic survey from 20 October to 30 December 2014 in the southern sea of Cyprus and more specifically in blocks 1, 2, 3, 8 and 9 of the exclusive economic zone of the Republic of Cyprus. For that purpose, Turkey already issued a navigational telex directive, through which it designated certain areas of the exclusive economic zone of the Republic of Cyprus as reserved. It is worth noting that blocks 2, 3 and 9 have been assigned by the Government of the Republic of Cyprus to the Eni and Kogas companies for exploration and exploitation of possible hydrocarbon reserves in

leged that "the so-called offshore licence granted by the Greek Cypriot Administration for "Block 6" on 6 April 2017 bears no legal effect on Turkey's *ipso facto* and *ab initio* sovereign rights over its continental shelf for the purposes of exploration and exploitation of its natural resources".[129] In addition to these activities, Turkey has interfered with vessels that were lawfully carrying out operations in the RoC's EEZ. Since 2003, threatening acts by Turkish ships have taken place outside the context of police enforcement measures and within the maritime zones of the RoC.[130] These acts have been accompanied by the use of threatening language in official letters issued by Turkey. For example, in a letter from 2017 Turkey states that it "is committed to protecting its sovereign rights emanating from international law and will not allow foreign companies to conduct unauthorized hydrocarbon exploration and exploitation activities on its continental shelf, as it was strongly underlined in several statements on the issue by the Turkish Ministry of Foreign Affairs, most recently on 6 April 2017."[131] In early 2018, when Turkish warships obstructed a ship

---

the seabed subsoil. Suffice it to add that Eni and Kogas have already commenced a drilling operation in block 9 in order to explore the possibility of the existence of hydrocarbon reserves, in accordance with an agreement they signed with the Government of the Republic of Cyprus. This is the culmination of a continued provocative policy of disputing and interfering with the sovereign rights of the Republic of Cyprus in its exclusive economic zone through the exploration and exploitation of this zone's natural resources in accordance with international law, including the United Nations Convention on the Law of the Sea. It is recalled that this provocative policy included, apart from continued verbal threats and rhetoric, the harassment of vessels performing lawful activities authorized by the Government of the Republic of Cyprus, by Turkish warships and military aircraft, and unlawful seismic surveys within the western exclusive economic zone of Cyprus by Turkish vessels." *See* Letter dated 6 October 2014 from the Chargé d'affaires of the Permanent Mission of Cyprus to the United Nations addressed to the Secretary-General, A/69/425–S/2014/723, 8 October 2014, <undocs.org/a/69/425>, visited on 3 June 2018.

129   Letter dated 12 April 2017 from the Permanent Representative of Turkey to the United Nations addressed to the Secretary-General, A/71/875–S/2017/321, 13 April 2017, <undocs.org/A/71/875>, visited on 3 June 2018.

130   *See* Y. Inan and P. Gözen Ercan, *supra* note 5, pp. 297-298; 'Cypriot research vessel being shadowed by Turkish frigate off Paphos', *Cyprus Mail*, 18 December 2015, <cyprus-mail.com/2015/12/18/cypriot-research-vessels-being-shadowed-by-turkish-frigate-off-paphos/>, visited on 24 July 2018; 'Italian vessels was harassed by Turkish navy off Pafos', *Cyprus Mail*, 31 July 2013, <cyprus-mail.com/2013/07/31/italian-vessel-was-harassed-by-turkish-navy-off-paphos/>, visited on 24 July 2018.

131   Letter dated 12 April 2017 from the Permanent Representative of Turkey to the United Nations addressed to the Secretary-General, *supra* note 129.

(contracted by Italian oil company Eni to explore for natural gas) from approaching an area in Cypriot waters,[132] Turkish President Erdogan was reported to have stated in the Turkish Parliament that: "right now, our warships, air force and other security units are following developments in the region closely with the authority to make any kind of intervention if necessary ... We advise the foreign companies who are conducting activities off Cyprus, relying on the Greek side, not to be an instrument to businesses that exceed their limit and power."[133]

It should be noted that in an arbitral award case from 2007, the use of threatening language from Suriname was found to be tantamount to a threat of use of force which is prohibited under Article 2(4) of the UN Charter; an analogy might be made with Turkey's behaviour towards Cyprus regarding the maritime zone. It could arguably amount to an international wrongful act and engage the international responsibility of Turkey.[134] In response to the 2018 incident mentioned above,[135] President Juncker on behalf of the EU Commission stated that:

> The Commission recalls the position of the EU, expressed at various occasions including in the Negotiating Framework and Council conclusions that Turkey needs to commit itself unequivocally to good neighbourly relations and to the peaceful settlement of disputes in accordance with the United Nations (UN) Charter, having

---

132 M. Kampas, 'Standoff in High Seas as Cyprus Says Turkey Blocks Gas Drill Ship', *Reuters*, 11 February 2018, <www.reuters.com/article/us-cyprus-natgas-turkey-ship/standoff-in-high-seas-as-cyprus-says-turkey-blocks-gas-drill-ship-idUSKBN1FV0X5>, visited on 3 March 2018.

133 See 'Turkish Warships Block Drilling Rig Near Cyprus', *Deutsche Welle*, 13 February 2018 <www.dw.com/en/turkish-warships-block-drilling-rig-near-cyprus/a-42 559676>, visited on 3 March 2018. Along these lines, the "TRNC" Deputy Prime Minister and Minister of Foreign Affairs, Kudret Özersay, has stated that "if the Greek Cypriots continue to insist on unilateral drilling activities then we will also authorize companies for drilling. We have reached this final stage. If the Greek Cypriot side continues to insist on unilateral hydrocarbon activities, then the Turkish Cypriot side will start its own drilling process, in cooperation with Turkey, through the Turkish Petroleum Corporation. This is not in the distant future." See "TRNC" Deputy Prime Ministry and Ministry of Foreign Affairs, *Press Release*, 21 March 2018, <mfa.gov.ct.tr/ozersay-reached-full-agreement-turkey-regarding-future-cyprus-problem-maritime-jurisdiction-hydrocarbon-issue/>, visited on 25 March 2018.

134 *Guyana v. Suriname*, 17 September 2007, Permanent Court of Arbitration- Arbitral Tribunal, Decision, paras. 433-439, 445, <pcacases.com/web/sendAttach/902>, visited on 19 May 2017.

135 'Turkish Warships Block Drilling Rig Near Cyprus', *supra* note 133.

recourse, if necessary, to the International Court of Justice. The EU urges Turkey to avoid any kind of threat or action directed against a Member State, or source of friction or actions, which damage good neighbourly relations and the peaceful settlement of disputes. The EU has repeatedly underlined that negative statements that damage good neighbourly relations should be avoided.[136]

Turkey's provocative statements including verbal and military threats against international oil and gas companies that are taking part in international tenders for hydrocarbon exploration and exploitation in Cypriot EEZ have been repeatedly condemned by the RoC and the EU.[137] It should be noted that the EU has repeatedly called for the normalisation of the relations between Turkey and the RoC and has urged Turkey to avoid threatening acts against the sovereignty of the RoC.[138] Nevertheless, throughout 2018 Turkey issued several NAVTEXs "declaring its intention to hold military exercises, taking place partially in the Cypriot airspace and EEZ".[139]

---

136 *See* President Juncker, *Parliamentary Questions-Answers*, 30 January 2018, <www.europarl.europa.eu/sides/getAllAnswers.do?reference=E-2017-006460&language=EN>, visited on 24 June 2018; General Affairs Council, *Conclusions*, 13 December 2016 <www.consilium.europa.eu/media/21524/st15536en16.pdf>, visited on 24 June 2018.

137 *See* Letter dated 5 August 2016 from the Permanent Representative of Cyprus to the United Nations addressed to the Secretary-General, A/70/1008, 5 August 2016, <undocs.org/A/70/1008> , visited on 24 June 2018; Letter dated 7 April 2016 from the Permanent Representative of Cyprus to the United Nations addressed to the Secretary-General, A/70/825–S/2016/329, 12 April 2016, <undocs.org/A/70/825>, visited on 24 June 2018; Letter dated 12 November 2013 from the Permanent Representative of Cyprus to the United Nations addressed to the Secretary-General, A/68/593–S/2013/662, 13 November 2013, <undocs.org/S/2013/662>, visited on 24 June 2018; E. Maurice, "EU Warns Turkey over "Threat" to Cyprus", *EU Observer*, 12 February 2018, <euobserver.com/foreign/140954> visited on 24 June 2018.

138 *See* General Affairs Council, *Conclusions*, 16 December 2014, <www.consilium.europa.eu/uedocs/cms_data/docs/pressdata/EN/genaff/146326.pdf>, visited on 24 June 2018; General Affairs Council, *Outcome of Proceedings*,15 December 2015, <data.consilium.europa.eu/doc/document/ST-15356-2015-INIT/en/pdf>,visited on 24 June 2018; EU Commission Staff Working Report, *Turkey 2014 Progress Report*, 8 December 2014, <ec.europa.eu/neighbourhood-enlargement/sites/near/files/pdf/key_documents/2014/20141008-turkey-progress-report_en.pdf>, visited on 24 June 2018.

139 *See* 'Turkey-Greece-Cyprus dispute over Mediterranean hydrocarbons risks disruption to shipping routes and localised naval incidents in 2018', *IHS Markit*, 19 January 2018, <ihsmarkit.com/country-industry-forecasting.html?ID=10659123035>, visited

Finally, the RoC's sovereign rights over the continental shelf have been once again breached by Turkey with the laying of the underwater pipeline and the underwater electricity cable. The UNCLOS recognises that coastal States enjoy specific rights over such activities.[140] According to Article 79 of the UNCLOS, which also reflects customary international law:

1. All States are entitled to lay submarine cables and pipelines on the continental shelf, in accordance with the provisions of this article.
2. Subject to its right to take reasonable measures for the exploration of the continental shelf, the exploitation of its natural resources and the prevention, reduction and control of pollution from pipelines, the coastal State may not impede the laying or maintenance of such cables or pipelines.
3. The delineation of the course for the laying of such pipelines on the continental shelf is subject to the consent of the coastal State.[141]

The consent of the RoC has never been sought by Turkey or granted for the laying of pipelines on Cyprus' continental shelf pursuant to Article 79(3) of the UNCLOS. To the contrary, the two agreements between the "TRNC" and Turkey concerning the water supply pipeline and the underwater electricity cable omit the significant fact that the cable and pipeline will be situated in the continental shelf of the RoC. Further, they

---

on 24 July 2018, where a risk of escalation in the Eastern Mediterranean was identified: "Further NAVTEXs covering other blocks where exploration and drilling are due to begin, such as Block 10 (Exxon Mobil/ Qatar Petroleum), would signal Turkish intent to use its military to interfere with operations, even in areas of Cyprus's EEZ to which it does not stake a claim. This is likely to cause disruption to shipping routes passing near the island. Moreover, there is a risk of Turkish harassment targeting vessels travelling between the drilling sites and onshore support bases in Larnaca and Limassol, including arbitrary inspections of vessels, potentially resulting in temporary detention of the vessels and their crews. There is an elevated risk that companies that have won offshore exploration licences from Cyprus will see cancellations of any existing contracts that they have in Turkey, as well as being blacklisted from future tenders. These include Italy's ENI, the US's Exxon Mobil, France's Total, and South Korea's KOGAS."

140   R. R. Churchill and A.V. Lowe, *The Law of the Sea*, 3rd ed. (Juris Publishing, Manchester, 1999) p. 156.
141   Convention on the Law of the Sea, *supra* note 44.

omit to acknowledge that an environmental impact assessment needs to be carried out on the impact of the cable and pipeline on the seabed before the projects take place. The latter is standard practice for pipeline laying and it is part of the licensing process. This is in line with Article 206 of the UNCLOS, which places an obligation on States to carry out environmental impact assessments "if they have reasonable grounds for believing that planned activities under their jurisdiction or control may cause substantial pollution of or significant and harmful changes to the marine environment".[142]

It should be noted that the licensing procedure for the laying of cables and pipelines entails that the coastal State will have to consent *a priori* to the deconstruction plan of the said pipelines as well. Furthermore, a lawful laying of cables can only be carried out on the condition that the coastal State has expressed its consent in writing, which will be then annexed to the cable laying plan and which must also include dispute resolution terms. Under the UNCLOS, the consent of the coastal State to pipeline laying is not expected to be given within a reasonable time; it may be the case that the coastal State is in fact denying the laying of the pipeline. The exercise of the sovereign rights of the coastal State will not be impeded should it not consent to the laying of the pipeline. In this case, Turkey's laying of the underwater pipeline and the underwater electricity cable has violated the Republic of Cyprus' sovereign rights and jurisdiction on the continental shelf and the EEZ.

Nonetheless, the RoC's sovereign rights over the laying of pipelines are not suspended even after their unlawful laying by Turkey; the RoC is still entitled to object on reasonable grounds as to their operation, *i.e.* to prevent, reduce, and control pollution. It should be noted that until now it is not clear what the environmental impact of the said pipelines could be.[143] This matter falls within EU interests as well given the rich EU environmental protection regulations. Hence, the EU might step in to provide political support to the RoC in preventing the environmental impact of

---

142   Ibid.
143   See EU, *Directive 2004/35/CE of the European Parliament and of the Council of 21 April 2004 On Environmental Liability With Regard To The Prevention And Remedying Of Environmental Damage*, 30 April 2004, OJ L 143, pp. 56–75.

the pipeline.[144] In any case, the unlawful laying of the pipeline and cable by Turkey adds to the RoC's claims against Turkey.[145]

5 Conclusion

The above analysis identifies the numerous violations committed by Turkey and asserts the rights of the occupied sovereign State, the RoC, under the law of the sea, international humanitarian law and occupation law, and general public international law.[146] The water and electricity supply projects aimed at consolidating Turkey's political and economic control over the occupied part of Cyprus, along with the conclusion of an agreement between the "TRNC" and Turkey, providing for the delimitation of maritime boundaries which is legally a European Union area, are illegal under international law. However, even though the violations have been established as a matter of fact and law, whether they will be addressed before the competent international legal mechanisms is a matter of politics.[147]

---

144 M. Bryza, 'Cyprus energy – averting a US-Turkey crisis', *Euractiv*, 18 May 2018, <www.euractiv.com/section/global-europe/opinion/cyprus-energy-averting-a-us-turkey-crisis/>, visited on 19 May 2018.

145 *See* for example Article 297 of the UNCLOS, *supra* note 44; Art 20 of the Statute of the International Tribunal for the Law of the Sea, <www.itlos.org/fileadmin/itlos/documents/basic_texts/statute_en.pdf>, visited on 25 March 2018.

146 In his 2018 report the UN Secretary General noted that Turkey has been increasingly committing military violations in the buffer zone too, for example with the overmanning of military positions and the installation of closed-circuit television equipment. See UN Secretary General, *Report of the Secretary General United Nations Operation in Cyprus*, S/2018/676, 6 July 2018, para. 16, <https://unficyp.unmissions.org/sites/default/files/sg_report_july_2018.pdf>, visited on 29 August 2018, where it is stated that "since my previous report, and despite objections by UNFICYP, there have been 17 new military violations involving the installation of CCTV equipment at Turkish forces positions along the buffer zone without evidence of accompanying unmanning of those positions. The investment in solar panels to power the cameras and in a networked microwave communications system to transmit information to local headquarters, along with the installation of water pipes at the positions, as observed by UNFICYP, are indications of the envisaged permanence of those cameras and of the positions themselves".

147 'Cyprus should seek maritime arbitration to nullify EEZ claims', *Cyprus Mail Online*, 23 July 2017, <cyprus-mail.com/2017/07/23/cyprus-seek-maritime-arbitration-nullify-turkish-eez-claims/>, visited on 23 July 2017.

Turkey is following, it seems, an expansionist policy[148] and, presently has troops stationed in three of its neighbouring countries (Cyprus, Syria, and Iraq) violating thus numerous important norms and rules of international law. This policy's implementation started with Cyprus in 1974 and is best described by Ahmet Davutoglu, Turkey's former Minister of Foreign Affairs and Prime Minister: "even if there was not one Muslim Turk there, Turkey had to maintain a Cyprus issue. No country can stay indifferent towards such an island, located in the heart of its very own vital space".[149] Given the above policy, it would be a tremendous surprise to see, for example, Turkey accepting generally or *ad hoc* the competence of the ICJ or another international arbitral court, enabling the RoC, or any other neighbour, to bring a case to court. Perhaps, one way around this would be for the Security Council to step in and adopt a Resolution on the matter; after all, the Security Council remains seized of the matter.

In contrast, the RoC is a small state trying to reverse Turkey's invasion and its unwanted consequences.[150] The RoC is denouncing Turkey's aggressive behaviour in international *fora* or bringing the dispute to relevant international jurisdictional instances, such as the two European Courts. Yet, deciding to bring the dispute the court is a matter of politics, as such a decision needs to be taken within a specific international context, and according to the State's priorities and limitations (that the State may face) in the domestic and international political setting.

Independently of these policy considerations, however, what should be of concern is that Turkey's settlement activities in the occupied territory is not only a blatant act of defiance of international law but also deepens the existing division on the island and creates new *faits accomplis* on the ground. And the overall question is: do politics trump international law in such circumstances? Can international law offer any protection to occupied territories and their sovereign States? In this case, international organisations have condemned the illegal activities of Turkey in the occupied territory of Cyprus again and again. Nevertheless, the end of Cyprus' occupation is far from materialising any time soon and Turkey's activities in the occupied territory are setting a dangerous prec-

---

148   I. Kouskouvelis, 'The Problem with Turkey's "Zero Problems", *Middle East Quarterly,* (2013), pp. 47-56.
149   A. Davutoğlu, *Stratejik Derinlik. Türkiye'nin Uluslararası Konumu,* 24th ed. (Küre Yayınları, Istanbul, 2008) p. 179.
150   I. Kouskouvelis, "'Smart' Leadership In A Small State: The Case Of Cyprus', in S. N. Litsas & A. Tziampiris (eds.), *The Eastern Mediterranean in Transition: Multipolarity, Power and Politics* (Ashgate Publishing, 2015, London) pp. 93-117.

edent for the non-compliance with and non-enforcement of international law. Furthermore, perpetrating unlawful acts without any hindrance or cost spreads the message that might makes right or that Thucydides' Athenian generals in Melos were ever since right when stating arrogantly that law matters among equals in power. Such a message certainly undermines the principles of the post-WWII international order and encourages further various international actors to not abide by the UN Charter and other rules of international law that have been established since then.

3 Putting the Nail in the Coffin: Isn't it Time to Let the European Consensus Doctrine Put an End to the Use of the Death Penalty in the United States?

*Rebecca Huertas**

Abstract

The European Court of Human Rights employs the consensus doctrine to analyse the merits of claims. The consensus doctrine requires a comparative analysis of the domestic laws of the 47 Member States to identify jurisprudential trends. The European Convention on Human Rights is considered a living instrument that may be interpreted broadly and in new ways in accordance with 'present-day conditions', and the Court seeks to harmonise the protection of human rights across Europe by applying the consensus doctrine to its case-law. The United States Supreme Court is likewise often obliged to analyse and compare the state laws of the 50 separate US states with an eye to ensuring compliance with the United States Constitution. Some Supreme Court Justices prefer to stay 'within the four corners' of the Constitution in their efforts to interpret its meaning, while others argue that they must look to evolving standards of decency that mark the progress of a maturing society. This article proposes that the US should use the European consensus doctrine in its death penalty jurisprudence, both by identifying trends within the 50 states and by looking at international law and the treaties to which the US is a party.

---

* Juris Doctor Candidate, 2019, Suffolk University Law School, Boston, Massachusetts. The author would like to thank Russell G. Murphy, Professor of Law, Suffolk University Law School, for inspiring this research into death penalty jurisprudence, and Daniel Rietiker, PhD, Senior Attorney, European Court of Human Rights, and Professor of Law at the University of Lausanne and Suffolk University Law School, for unveiling the intricacies of the European consensus doctrine.

1 Introduction

The Council of Europe (COE) is an intergovernmental organization with 47 Member States governing approximately 820 million Europeans.[1] The COE was created in 1949 upon the conclusion of World War II to promote peace and unity and to ensure that the atrocities of WWII would not be repeated.[2] The principal purpose of the COE was then, and continues to be, the defence of human rights and democracy in Europe.[3] The European Court of Human Rights ('ECtHR') is one of several European Institutions within the COE, and it is responsible for ensuring Member State compliance with the European Convention of Human Rights and its Protocols (together, 'the ECHR', or 'the Convention').[4] The ECtHR is considered to be the judicial arm of the COE, and in response to applications from citizens, it examines whether Member States have violated duties or obligations under the Convention.[5] The Court's principal task is to ensure that the human rights of Europeans are protected and enforced.[6]

When individuals complain that Member States have violated a right or duty under the Convention, the ECtHR uses several methods of judicial interpretation to analyse the meaning of the Convention as it bears on the dispute. This paper focuses on the ECtHR's use of the consensus doc-

---

1 *Institutions Under the Authority of the Council of Europe,* <en.strasbourg-europe.eu/council-of-europe,2090,en.html>, visited on 11 August, 2018, describing the intergovernmental organisation of Europe.
2 *Statute of the Council of Europe,* 5 May 1949, 87 U.N.T.S., 103 E.T.S. 1, <rmcoe.int/1680306052 [perma.cc/6QML-QMK7]>, describing the founding purpose, primary goals and aspirations of the COE, visited on 17 July 2018.
3 *Ibid.*
4 *European Convention for the Protection of Human Rights and Fundamental Freedoms,* Nov. 4, 1950, 213 U.N.T.S. 222. The ECHR was drafted in 1950 and entered into force in 1953. The ECtHR was established in 1959 to implement the ECHR.
5 Institutions, *supra* note 1. *See also* Rules of Court for the ECtHR, < www.echr.coe.int/Documents/Rules_Court_ENG.pdf>, last visited on 11 August 2018. The procedures for accepting and examining applications to the Court are described in the ECtHR's Admissibility Guide, which explains the process that individuals must use to submit applications, the procedures for determining whether an application is admissible or not, and how an application moves forward once it is found to be admissible < www.echr.coe.int/Documents/Admissibility_guide_ENG.pdf>, visited on August 11, 2018.
6 *See* preamble to the Convention, describing the overarching mission of the Convention, note 5.

trine in its broadest sense,[7] and argues that this interpretive technique could beneficially be used by the US in its death penalty jurisprudence.

The language used in the United States Constitution regarding punishment is similar to the Convention language on the same matter. Article 3 of the Convention (Article 3) provides, "No one shall be subjected to torture or to inhuman or degrading treatment or punishment". The Eighth Amendment of the Constitution ('the Eighth Amendment') states, "Excessive bail shall not be required, nor excessive fines imposed, nor cruel and unusual punishments inflicted."[8] The similarities in language between Article 3 and the Eighth Amendment, the development of case-law in the US related to the Eighth Amendment, the development of case-law in the ECtHR respecting Article 3,[9] and the parallel goals of the ECtHR and the United States Supreme Court ('Supreme Court') to ensure uniform application of laws across vast geographic regions all provide a foundation for recommending the use of the consensus doctrine in the US – particularly with respect to its death penalty jurisprudence.

Part 2 of this paper looks at the ECtHR's consensus doctrine with particular regard to how this doctrine is weighed against a State's 'margin of appreciation' in the Court's deliberations. The author considers how the consensus doctrine has been used, discusses the Convention Articles that do not lend themselves to the consensus analysis, and raises some of the complexities and benefits of this form of judicial analysis by reviewing two landmark cases.

Part 3 traces the United States' acknowledgement and acceptance of obligations under international law, including both customary international law and multilateral treaties. This Part includes a discussion of

---

[7] Arguably, the broadest interpretation of the consensus doctrine is that described by Dzehtsiarou. He lists four elements of the consensus doctrine to which the Court frequently turns, including comparative analysis of the laws of the Member States, international treaties, internal consensus in the respondent Member State, and expert consensus on the issue. K. Dzehtsiarou, 'Does Consensus Matter? Legitimacy of European Consensus in the Case Law of the European Court', 3 *Public Law* (2011) pp. 548-549.

[8] U.S. Const. amend. VIII (1789).

[9] *Overview of the Case-Law of the European Court of Human Rights*. Each year, the ECtHR publishes an overview of its key case law during that calendar year keyed to the Articles of the Convention. To trace the evolution of law under Article 3, one can look at this publication over several years, including, for example, the discussion of Article 3 jurisprudence for 2017 <www.echr.coe.int/Documents/Short_Survey_2017_ENG.pdf>, pp. 22-27, and for 2016 <www.echr.coe.int/Documents/Short_Survey_2016_ENG.pdf>, pp 22-37, both visited on 11 August 2018.

pertinent jurisprudence. Part 4 looks at evolving case-law, legislative changes at the State level, and statistical trends in the US regarding use of the death penalty.

Part 5 considers two US Supreme Court cases. In *Stanford* v. *Kentucky*,[10] the majority found that use of the death penalty was acceptable even in cases of crimes committed by juveniles, and the author discusses a dissenting opinion. In *Glossip* v. *Gross*,[11] the majority approved a particular drug protocol as a method of execution. The paper describes two dissenting opinions in the case analysing the constitutionality of the death penalty generally, and this method of execution particularly. The first dissent, regarding the death penalty generally, relied in part on the consensus doctrine, without using that term.

Part 6 concludes by suggesting that based on the consideration of five factors (the jurisprudential function of the ECtHR's interpretive doctrine of consensus; the periodic use of a similar method of interpretation by individual Supreme Court justices, including looking to jurisprudence outside US borders; long-standing US acceptance of the law of nations, customary international law, and treaties; the evolution of European and international human rights law; and long-voiced concerns in the US about use of the death penalty and incarceration on death row), it behooves the Supreme Court to adopt the European consensus doctrine for use in its ongoing death penalty jurisprudence.

2 The Consensus Doctrine at the ECtHR

2.1 *The Consensus Doctrine Generally*

The ECtHR has a remarkable and unique responsibility. In addition to enforcing compliance by States with human rights that have been bestowed upon 820 million individuals, the Court must ensure that the Convention is truly effective in 47 different countries with 47 different histories and cultures.[12] The Court needs to affirm the predictability and reliability of

---

10   *Stanford* v. *Kentucky*, 1989, United States Supreme Court, 492 U.S. 361.
11   *Glossip* v. *Gross*, 2015, United States Supreme Court, 576 U.S., dissenting opinions by Justices S. Breyer and S. Sotomayor.
12   In 'Establishment of the post of Jurisconsult,' the Court reiterates the December 2011 position of the Steering Committee for Human Rights as follows, "Clarity and consistency of the Court's case-law are essential for the full assumption by Contracting Parties and national courts of their role as guarantors of human rights and for the effectiveness of the subsidiarity principle ... Principles established in pre-

its own judgments; enable individuals to exercise their rights by seeking redress against Member States; ensure that its rulings are viewed as legitimate and neutral; and facilitate the development of human rights in a way that serves the needs of a growing and changing European community.[13] In other words, it must foster its own legitimacy, allow the 47 Member States to inhabit their own moral and judicial frameworks, and integrate their citizens into an increasingly harmonised European community.[14]

Working with a single document, the Convention, the ECtHR accomplishes these enormous goals chiefly by examining applications from individuals against States (rarely State claims against other States) using two principal interpretive tools that allow it to identify the meaning of a Convention term and apply it to disputes: European consensus doctrine and margin of appreciation analysis.[15] This paper discusses both methods because they are often balanced against one another in the Court's assessment of the law.[16]

Consensus doctrine refers to the Court's continuous study of the legal frameworks of all 47 Member States to identify uniformity or the emergence of a new European approach to a current issue.[17] The consensus doctrine invites the Court to examine trends, compare legal frameworks, and study international law and supranational jurisprudence in regional

---

vious judgments should be followed by the Court in subsequent cases. National authorities, including courts, and applicants should be able to have confidence that the principles established in the Court's case-law will be consistently applied." <Jurisconsult, DM ref: 5246919, 8/12/2015>, last visited 11 August 2018. *See also The ECtHR in 50 Questions,* (Public Relations, Council of Europe, February 2014), pp. 3-12, *and The Conscience of Europe, 50 Years of the European Court of Human Rights,* (Council of Europe, Editorial Board, 10 October 2010), pp. 16-105 and 162-181. These latter two COE publications contain a comprehensive discussion of the ECtHR's obligations across 47 countries.

13   S. Williams, 'Human Rights in Europe', in S. Power and G. Allison (eds.) *Realizing Human Rights* (St. Martin's Press, New York, 2000) pp. 82 87.
14   S. Greer, *The Margin of Appreciation: Interpretation and Discretion Under the European Convention of Human Rights,* Council of Europe Publishing, Strasbourg (2000) p. 19, describing how the Court's autonomy in interpreting Convention terms independently of how Convention terms are understood by Member States still leaves room for national variation in State interpretations of their Convention obligations.
15   *Interpretive Mechanisms of ECHR Case-law: the concept of European Consensus,* Human Rights Education for Legal Professionals, Council of Europe, p. 1, <www.coe.int/en/web/help/article-echr-case-law>, visited on 17 July 2018.
16   *Ibid.,* p. 2.
17   *Ibid.*

tribunals to ensure that the Convention is interpreted in a meaningful, effective manner so that it is capable of responding to current issues. This sometimes requires a more expansive interpretation of terms to address issues that did not exist at the time of the drafting of the Convention, for example, artificial fertilisation and same-sex marriage.[18]

Dzehtsiarou cleverly describes the consensus doctrine as a rebuttable presumption in favour of "the solution adopted by the majority of the Contracting Parties".[19] Use of consensus enables the Court to meet its goals of ensuring judicial harmony across all 47 Member States while furthering a Europe-wide embrace of human rights via the Convention.[20]

Margin of appreciation analysis, on the other hand, refers to the amount of discretion granted to States to interpret the meaning of Convention terms. Typically, the greater the European consensus on a given issue, the narrower the State's room to choose a different path. Where there is little consensus and many countries are taking different approaches to a given human rights issue (for example, religious apparel), the margin of appreciation granted to a State will be broader. Because consensus is typically balanced against a State's margin of appreciation, the Court necessarily remains attuned to emerging trends.[21]

---

18 Section 2.2 of this chapter discusses the ECtHR's *Bayatyan* v. *Armenia* case, 23459/03, 7 July 2011, as an example of the Court's recurring need to examine new human rights issues that were not recognized as such in 1949: in this case, the status of conscientious objectors. In addition to handling new human rights issues as they arise in applications, the ECtHR also is concerned with how new issues are addressed by domestic courts across Europe long before such issues arrive at the ECtHR. The ECtHR's Steering Committee for Human Rights considers the interplay between domestic courts, national parliaments, the COE and the ECtHR as new issues arise, and focuses on the interpretive authority of the ECtHR to identify and define new rights. Working documents and agenda items from the Steering Committee are updated and available at the following site <www.coe.int/en/web/human-rights-intergovernmental-cooperation/echr-system/future-of-convention-system>.

19 K. Dzehtsiarou, *European Consensus and the Evolutive Interpretation of the European Convention on Human Rights,* German Law Journal: Developments in German, European, and International Jurisprudence, 12 German Law Journal, No. 10 (2011) pg 1730, <static1.squarespace.com/static/56330ad3e4b0733dcc0c8495/t/56b718d36 2cd94dc824ac88l/1454840020402/GLJ_Vol_12_No_10_Dzehtsiarou2.pdf>, visited on 11 August 2018.

20 Greer, *supra* note 14.

21 The Court is not an appeals court for domestic law decisions. The Court's role is to supervise the decisions that domestic courts make to ensure that their decisions are compatible with the Convention. Domestic courts must ensure that any restrictions on rights are in accordance with the domestic law (and that law is foresee-

2.2 A Landmark Case Illustrating the Power of the Consensus Doctrine: Bayatyan v. Armenia

The case of *Bayatyan* v. *Armenia*[22] concerned a conscientious objector who was convicted and sentenced to two and a half years in jail for having requested permission to perform alternative civilian service rather than military service based on his religious beliefs.[23] The Court noted that it had never looked at the applicability of Article 9 (freedom of thought, conscience and religion) with respect to conscientious objectors,[24] so it performed a detailed consensus analysis, beginning with an affirmation of the ECtHR's underlying philosophy that the Convention is a living instrument subject to 'evolutive' interpretation as conditions change:

> The Court reiterates ... that the Convention is a living instrument which must be interpreted in the light of present-day conditions and of the ideas prevailing in democratic societies today. Since it is first and foremost a system for the protection of human rights, the Court must have regard to the changing conditions in Contracting States and respond, for example, to any emerging consensus as to the standards to be achieved. Furthermore, in defining the meaning of terms and notions in the text of the Convention, the Court can and must take into account elements of international law other than the Convention and the interpretation of such elements by competent organs. The consensus emerging from specialised international instruments may constitute a relevant consideration for the Court when it interprets the provisions of the Convention in specific cases [internal citations omitted].[25]

The Court then went on to perform a meticulous consensus analysis evaluating the trend among European countries in recognising the rights of conscientious objectors, including statistical data on States and their respective positions over time. This involved a search for any new laws, judicial approaches, or legal frameworks regarding conscientious objec-

---

      able and accessible), done for a legitimate purpose, and necessary to achieve that purpose. The Court lastly considers whether the restriction was proportionate to the purpose, thus assuring that the domestic court struck a fair balance between competing interests. See Greer, *supra* note 14.

22   *Bayatyan* case, *supra* note 18.
23   *Ibid.*, para. 37.
24   *Ibid.*, para. 99.
25   *Ibid.*, para. 102.

tors.[26] The Court next analysed interpretations of Articles 8 and 18 of the International Covenant on Civil and Political Rights ('ICCPR')[27] by the United Nations Human Rights Commission ('UNHRC'), developments in UNHRC case-law, and European developments including statements by the Parliamentary Assembly and the Committee of Ministers.[28] The Court also searched for newer interpretations of the Charter of Fundamental Rights of the European Union respecting conscientious objectors.[29] Notably, the Court considered all these sources not only worthy of analysis, but important for arriving at a conclusion as to the applicability and interpretation of a Convention Article with respect to a new issue.

In this illustrative case of how the consensus doctrine is meant to work, the Court described its supervisory responsibilities as follows:

> According to its settled case-law, the Court leaves to States Parties to the Convention a certain margin of appreciation in deciding whether and to what extent an interference is necessary. This margin of appreciation goes hand-in-hand with European supervision embracing both the law and the decisions applying to it. The Court's task is to determine whether the measures taken at national level were justified in principle and proportionate.[30]

The Court then summarised its assessment of all the factors, which included the prevailing national (Armenian), supranational (European), and international consensus, and reached its conclusions:

> In the Court's opinion, such a system (the then-existing Armenian system of mandatory military service) failed to strike a fair balance between the interests of society as a whole and those of the applicant. It therefore considers that the imposition of a penalty on the applicant, in circumstances where no allowances were made for the exigencies of his conscience and beliefs, could not be considered a measure necessary in a democratic society. Still less can it be seen as necessary taking into account that there existed viable and effective alternatives capable of accommodating competing interests,

---

26   *Ibid.*, paras. 102-109.
27   International Covenant on Civil and Political Rights, GA Res. 2200 (Dec. 16, 1966).
28   *Institutions Under the Authority of the Council of Europe, supra* note 1.
29   *Bayatyan* case, *supra* note 18, paras. 102-109.
30   *Ibid.*, para. 121.

as demonstrated by the overwhelming majority of the European States.[31]

The Court's judgment in *Bayatyan* is a stellar example of the subtle yet convincing power of the consensus doctrine as an interpretive tool.

2.3 Using the Consensus Doctrine to Expand an Absolute Right: Soering v. United Kingdom

In another case, the ECtHR also looked at emerging trends, and based on its evaluation of those trends, the Court was able to broaden the meaning of an absolute Convention right. The Articles of the Convention include (i) absolute rights that may not be restricted and do not lend themselves to consensus or margin of appreciation analysis, (ii) qualified rights that may be restricted under certain circumstances, and (iii) Article 15, which broadly addresses derogation in times of emergency or war.

Absolute rights, also referred to as unqualified rights, categorical rights, or fundamental rights, are those that are non-derogable and not subject to any restriction. Given this, the Court does not apply a proportionality analysis to complaints that such rights have been breached, so they are not generally subject to the consensus doctrine or the margin of appreciation analysis. Traditionally, three Articles have been considered to contain absolute rights. These are Article 3 ("No one shall be subjected to torture or to other inhuman or degrading treatment or punishment"), Article 4 § 1 ("No one shall be held in slavery or servitude"), and Article 7 ("No punishment without law").[32] Dzehtsiarou notes, "[t]he unconditional nature of the rights protected by certain Articles … does not leave much scope for the Court to assess European consensus in relation to them."[33]

Other Convention Articles contain qualified rights that may be restricted at times by States for certain prescribed reasons. Thus, any restrictions on an individual's rights, and the basis for them, are subject to the Court's examination in the event of a claim against a State. The Court assesses whether the restriction was in accordance with domestic law, whether the restriction met a legitimate purpose of the State, and

---

31   *Ibid*, para. 124.
32   *Absolute Rights Notes,* Oxbridge Notes (2015), <www.oxbridgenotes.co.uk/revision_notes/law-european-human-rights-law/samples/absolute-rights>, visited on 17 July 2018.
33   Dzehtsiarou, *supra* note 7, p. 546.

whether it was necessary in a democratic society in order to accomplish that legitimate aim. In other words, did the State, when it restricted an individual's rights, strike a fair balance between the competing interests? It is in this examination that the Court routinely uses the consensus doctrine and the margin of appreciation analysis.[34]

The qualified rights that may be subject to restriction by a State for prescribed reasons include Article 8 ("Right to respect for private and family life"), Article 9 ("Freedom of thought, conscience and religion"), Article 10 ("Freedom of expression"), and Article 11 ("Freedom of assembly and association"). In each case, the second paragraph of the Article contains the prescribed reasons that would potentially allow a State to restrict the right.[35]

In addition to prescribing exactly when a State may restrict qualified rights, the Convention also includes Article 15 (derogation in time of emergency) which generally affects most provisions of the Convention. Article 15 states, "[i]n time of war or other public emergency threatening the life of a nation any High Contracting Party may take measures derogating from its obligations under this Convention to the extent strictly required by the exigencies of the situation, provided that such measures are not inconsistent with its other obligations under international law." This broad empowerment is narrowed by the Article's second paragraph,

---

[34] See Greer, supra note 14, for a discussion of the Court's supervisory role in the regard.

[35] The rights under Article 8 may be restricted by a state "in accordance with the law and (where) ... necessary in a democratic society in the interests of national security, public safety or the economic well-being of the country, for the protection of health and morals, or for the protections of the rights and freedoms of others." The rights under Article 9 may be restricted "as ... prescribed by law and ... necessary in a democratic society in the interests of public safety, for the protection of public order, health or morals, or for the protections of the rights and freedoms of others." Exercise of the rights of expression under Article 10 is considered to involve "duties and responsibilities". Therefore, such rights may be restricted for a fairly broad spectrum of reasons, where they are "prescribed by law and ... necessary in a democratic society in the interests of national security, territorial integrity or public safety, for the prevention of disorder or crime, for the protection of health or morals, for preventing the disclosure of information received in confidence, or for maintaining the authority and impartiality of the judiciary." The rights under Article 11 may be restricted where "prescribed by law and ... necessary in a democratic society in the interests of national security or public safety, for the prevention of disorder or crime, for the protection of health or morals or for the protection of the rights and freedoms of others." All these potential restrictions of rights are quoted from the second paragraphs of Articles 8, 9, 10, and 11 of the ECHR.

which states that "[n]o derogation from Article 2, except in respect of deaths resulting from lawful acts of war, or from Articles 3, 4 (paragraph 1) and 7 shall be made under this provision." Ultimately, Articles 3, 4 § 1, and 7 contain non-derogable, absolute rights, and those rights may never be eroded, not even in time of war or emergency.[36]

Soering v. *UK*,[37] concerned a German national who had committed two murders in the US and then fled to the UK to avoid prosecution. The US requested his extradition to the State of Virginia. Soering filed several actions in the UK to avoid extradition, and ultimately an application to the ECtHR under Article 3, arguing that if he were to be found guilty and placed on death row in the US, the death row experience would be inhuman and degrading.[38] Soering thus applied to the Court under an absolute right ("No one shall be subjected to torture or to other inhuman or degrading treatment or punishment").

Because Article 3 is an absolute right, the balancing test that weighs consensus against a State's margin of appreciation, as illustrated by *Bayatyan,* was not done. Instead, the Court traced and evaluated an expanding international consensus as to the meaning of the terms 'inhuman' and 'degrading', and an emerging scientific consensus as to the impact on individuals of certain incarceration regimes.[39] Relying on both trends, the Court was able to extend the meaning of Article 3's absolute proscription against "torture or other inhuman or degrading treatment or punishment" by including the experience of being on death row in a US prison.[40] The Court was thus also able to extend the reach of the newly broadened meaning of Article 3 by preventing certain extraditions. Sig-

36 *Guide on Article 15 of the European Convention on Human Rights* (2018), <www.echr.coe.int/Documents/Guide_Art_15_ENG.pdf>, visited on 17 July 2018. The Guide contains a detailed discussion of how and when Article 15 might apply, and discusses the impact on absolute rights as illustrated in the Court's jurisprudence.
37 *Soering* v. *UK, 7 July 1989, ECtHR, no.* 14038/88.
38 *Ibid.*, para. 76.
39 See *Soering* case, *supra* note 37, paras. 86–91 as to evolving international legal consensus, and paras. 56, 81, 99 and 106 as to the death row phenomenon. *See also* S. Grassian, 'Psychopathological Effects of Solitary Confinement', 140:11 *American Journal of Psychiatry* (1983) pp. 1450-1454. This research was published shortly before the Soering murders. Dr. Grassian coined the phrase "death row phenomenon".
40 *Soering* case, *supra* note 37, para. 88, in which the Court noted that case law and treaties already precluded the extradition to a State where he might foreseeably undergo torture, and added, "[i]n the Court's view, this inherent obligation not to extradite also extends to cases in which the fugitive would be faced … by a real risk of exposure to inhuman or degrading treatment or punishment proscribed by Article 3".

natory States could no longer extradite individuals charged with capital murder into States where those individuals might foreseeably be subject to death row phenomenon.[41] *Soering* is commonly viewed as a fine example of how the Court can use consensus doctrine in its broadest sense to expand rights by interpretation.[42]

Some argued that *Soering* was an alarming extraterritorial judicial over-reach since it meant the Court was effectively ruling on the conduct of non-Convention States.[43] The Court explained:

> In interpreting the Convention regard must be had to its special character as a treaty for the collective enforcement of human rights and fundamental freedoms. Thus, the object and purpose of the Convention as an instrument for the protection of individual human beings require that its provisions be interpreted and applied so as to make its safeguards practical and effective. In addition, any interpretation of the rights and freedoms guaranteed has to be consistent with 'the general spirit' of the Convention, an instrument designed to maintain and promote the ideals and values of a democratic society ... [internal citations omitted][44]

By emphasising collective enforcement, the Court suggested that the Convention as a whole, and certainly Article 3, implies protections for all. The Court concluded:

> Article 3 makes no provisions for exceptions and no derogation from it is permissible ... This absolute prohibition of torture and inhuman or degrading treatment or punishment under the terms of the Convention show that Article 3 enshrines one of the fundamental values of the democratic societies making up the Council of Europe. It is also to be found in similar terms in other international agreements such as the 1966 International Covenant on Civil

---

41 *Soering* case, *supra* note 37.
42 Dzehtsiarou, *supra* note 7.
43 S. Miller, 'Revisiting extraterritorial Jurisdiction: A Territorial Justification for Extraterritorial Jurisdiction under the European Convention', 20:4 *The European Journal of International Law* (2010), no. 4. Miller notes, "[y]et, the Commission concluded, 'These considerations cannot, however, absolve the Contracting Parties from responsibility under Article 3 for any and all foreseeable consequences of extradition suffered outside their jurisdiction.'"
44 *Soering* case, *supra* note 37, para. 87.

and Political Rights (ICCPR) and the 1969 American Convention on Human Rights and is generally recognized as an internationally accepted standard.[45]

In effect, the Court banned extradition into States where Article 3 violations were foreseeable, thus substantially extending the reach of the protections afforded by Article 3, and it did so in part by relying on an emerging international and scientific consensus as to the meaning of inhuman and degrading.

3 US Acceptance of Customary International Law and Human Rights Treaties: From the Constitution to Case-Law to International Agreements

Broadly, the US is somewhat like Europe. The US has 50 states (and the District of Columbia) to Europe's 47, but it has a relatively sparse population of 330 million when compared against Europe's 820 million. Nonetheless, to the US Supreme Court falls a task similar to that of the ECtHR: to maintain its legitimacy in the eyes of the people, to recognise 51 different jurisdictions and regional cultures, and to be able to take a single document, the Constitution, and apply its terms to seemingly unending cases in controversy so that one framework, one document, can be made to work for all.[46] Just as the ECtHR defines and shapes the contours of the Convention's rights, the Supreme Court works with its supreme law, the Constitution, to keep that document's meaning and purpose alive in 51 different jurisdictions. And like the ECtHR, the Supreme Court sometimes expands the meaning of those rights by interpretation as society changes.[47]

---

45 *Ibid.*, para. 88.
46 E. Chemerinsky, *Constitutional Law, Principles and Policies,* Aspen Treatise Series, 3rd edition (Aspen Publishers, Maryland, 2006) pp. 1-6; 15-28.
47 Perhaps most famously, Supreme Court Justice William O. Douglas described the unenumerated rights that must exist in order to support the enumerated ones as follows, "The foregoing cases suggest that specific guarantees in the Bill of Rights have penumbras, formed by emanation from those guarantees that help give them life and substance." From those penumbras and emanations, he inferred a right to privacy without which many rights could not truly be enjoyed. *Griswold* v. *Connecticut, 1965, United States Supreme Court, 181 U.S. 479. Griswold* turned on a Connecticut law that prohibited the furnishing of information about, and access, to contraception and birth control for married couples. After finding a Constitutional

The US has a poor reputation for its commitment to, and compliance with, international human rights conventions, treaties, and protocols.[48] This is partly based on its decision to withdraw from the International Court of Justice (ICJ) following an adverse decision by that court,[49] and partly based on its exceptions and reservations to several protocols, and the signing but not ratifying of several treaties.[50] Setting that reputation

---

right to marital privacy, even though such a right was not mentioned in the Constitution, the Supreme Court invalidated the Connecticut law on the grounds that it violated the newly found right to privacy. The Court noted that individuals had a right to protection from government intrusion into their privacy.

48 *See, for instance,* M. Wilkin, 'US Aversion to International Human Right Treaties,' 22 June 2017, Global Justice Center Blog, <www.globaljusticecenter.net/blog/773-u-s-aversion-to-international-human-rights-treaties>, visited on 17 July 2018.

49 The ICJ is the judicial organ of the UN pursuant to Article 92 of the UN Charter, which the US ratified in 1945 (59 Stat 1033, 1945). Member States may consent to general jurisdiction of the ICJ, or to categorical jurisdiction over certain types of cases. In *Military and Paramilitary Activities in and against Nicaragua (Nicaragua v. United States of America)*, 27 June 1986, ICJ, Jurisdiction and Admissibility, *I.C.J. Reports 1986*, p.14,

the ICJ examined US military and paramilitary activity in Nicaragua, including clandestine action by the US-funded 'Contras' against the established government. The ICJ ruled in favour of Nicaragua and awarded reparations. The US refused to participate in the proceedings after the Court rejected its argument that the ICJ lacked jurisdiction, and the US blocked enforcement of the judgment by using its veto power in the UN Security Council thereby preventing Nicaragua from obtaining any compensation. Almost 20 years later, another ICJ-US disagreement arose. This case involved death penalties that had been imposed on 54 Mexican nationals who had been condemned to death in Texas. México argued that the men had been tried and sentenced to death without having been notified of their right to consular support under Article 36 of the Vienna Convention on Consular Relations. (*Case Concerning Avena and Other Mexican Nationals v. United States of America,*), commonly called the *Avena* case, 31 March 2004, ICJ, *I.C.J. Reports 2004*, 2 General List, 128.) The ICJ ruled in favor of México stating that the 54 men were entitled to a review and reconsideration of their convictions and sentences. The next year, one of the 51 men (the number of men changed from case to the next due to citizenship questions) filed suit in a US court essentially asking the court to enforce the ICJ ruling (*Medellín v. Texas*, 2008, United States Supreme Court, 552 U.S. 49). The case moved up to the Supreme Court, which ruled that the US Congress had never adopted implementing legislation providing for redress for violations of the Vienna Convention so the Supreme Court determined that it could take no action. Medellín was executed. To this day, the US does not recognise the general jurisdiction of the ICJ.

50 A detailed account of the status of ratifications and reservations appears in "US Ratification of International Human Rights Treaties," <www.hrw.org/news/2009/07/24/united-states-ratification-international-human-rights-treaties, 24 July 2009>, visited on 17 July 2018.

aside for purposes of this article, the author will focus on areas where the US founding documents and case-law have supported international law, customary international law, and many substantive human rights treaties. This positive line of authority will be the basis for arguing in Part 6 that there is a jurisprudential basis for the US to move forward in the arena of human rights protection, and a sound basis for adopting the European consensus doctrine as a method of informing its death penalty jurisprudence.

This section lists and briefly describes key national laws, court decisions, and treaty obligations. Where appropriate, the article also describes the legal reasoning of various courts and the precedents created by their rulings. Together these laws, decisions, and obligations form a basis on which the Supreme Court could elect to adopt a more outwardly looking consensus-based death penalty approach.

The judicial powers of the US government are contained in Article III of the Constitution, which states that US law shall be comprised of "this Constitution, the Laws of the United States, and Treaties made, under this Authority".[51] Notably, international treaties were included in the Constitution in 1789 as being the equivalent of federal law – as comprising the supreme law of the land.

A series of important court decisions followed, based on, and extending this constitutional foundation. One particularly important case was *The Paquete Habana*,[52] in which the Supreme Court explicitly adopted international law as "part of our law", and went on to adopt the principles of customary international law as well. The court reasoned, "[i]nternational law is part of our law, and must be ascertained and administered by the courts of justice ... For this purpose, where there is no treaty, and no controlling executive or legislative act or judicial decision, resort must be had to the customs and usages of civilized nations". Accordingly, both

---

51   U.S. Const. Art. III, para. 2 [1] (1789).

52   *The Paquete Habana* v. *United States*, 1 January 1900, United States Supreme Court, 175 U.S. 677. In this case, two fishing vessels were captured as prizes by US merchant seamen as part of a blockade of Habana Harbor during the Spanish-American War. The ships were taken to Florida and sold. The owners of the vessels filed a claim for the loss, which ultimately was heard by the US Supreme Court. The Court cited laws, legal traditions and customs going back to 1403 that protected fishing vessels from capture in times of war, laws that had long been considered part of customary international law, and the Supreme Court considered part of customary international law with which all nations were meant to comply. The Court ordered that the proceeds of the sale of the illegally taken vessels be returned to the owners, with damages and costs.

international law and customary law were viewed jurisprudentially as part of US law, and as something to be complied with.

More cases followed along this line, including another important and fairly recent case, *Filártiga* v. *Peña-Irala*.[53] In this case, a young man had been tortured to death under a military dictatorship in Paraguay. Years later the torturer, a Paraguayan police officer, and the family of the victim, found themselves living in the US. The young man's sister and father filed a claim in New York against the police officer for the death and torture in Paraguay relying on the United States' Alien Tort Statute, 28 USC § 1350. The Supreme Court began:

> Upon ratification of the Constitution, the thirteen former colonies were fused into a single nation, one which, in its relations with foreign states, is bound both to observe and construe the accepted norms of international law, formerly known as the law of nations … [In 1789] the law of nations became preeminently a federal concern. [Construing the Judiciary Act of 1789, Ch. 20, §9(b), 1 Stat. 73, 77] We hold that deliberate torture perpetrated under color of official authority violates universally accepted norms of the international law of human rights, regardless of the nationality of the parties.

The court then analysed international human rights laws and treaties, offered a detailed discussion of the universal repugnance for the use of torture, and concluded:

> The treaties and accords cited above, as well as the express foreign policy of our own government, all make it clear that international law confers fundamental rights upon all people vis-á-vis their own governments. While the ultimate scope of these rights will be a subject for continuing refinement and elaboration, we hold that the right to be free from torture is now among them … Indeed … the torturer has become – like the pirate and slave trader before him – *hostis humani generis*, an enemy of all mankind.[54]

---

53   *Filártiga* v. *Peña Irala*, 1980, United States Supreme Court, 630 F. 2d 876 (2d Cir. 1980).

54   It is worth noting more of the court's reasoning here as the author will rely on this line of argumentation in Part 6. The court reasoned: "The United Nations Charter (a treaty of the United States, 59 Stat 1033 (1945)) makes it clear that in the modern age a state's treatment of its own citizens is a matter of international concern … Although there is no universal agreement as to the precise extent of the 'hu-

This is a powerful testament to the expectation that all people should be free from torture. It is still good law and considered US precedent even though the ruling was subsequently narrowed by the Supreme Court with respect to extraterritorial applications in *Kiobel* v. *Royal Dutch Petroleum Company*.[55]

Finally, in addition to Article III of the US Constitution and the judicial precedents described above, the US is party to almost all of the major human rights treaties and declarations. These are listed and cited together in the footnote.[56]

---

man rights and fundamental freedoms' guaranteed to all by the Charter, there is at present no dissent from the view that the guaranties include, at a bare minimum, the right to be free from torture. This prohibition has become part of customary international law, as evidenced and defined by the Universal Declaration of Human Rights, General Assembly Resolution 217(III)(A) (Dec, 10, 1948) which states, in the plainest terms, no one shall be subjected to torture. Particularly relevant is the Declaration on the Protection of All Persons from being subjected to Torture, General Assembly Resolution 3452, 30 U.N. GAOR Supp. (No. 34) 91, U.N.Doc A/1034 (1975) ... which provides that where it is proved that an act of torture or other cruel, inhuman or degrading treatment or punishment has been committed by or at the instigation of a public official, the victim shall be afforded redress and compensation, in accordance with national law ... Several commentators have concluded that the Universal Declaration has become, *in toto*, a part of binding, customary international law."

55 *Kiobel* v. *Royal Dutch Petroleum Company*, 2013, United States Supreme Court, 569 U.S. In this case, the plaintiffs were citizens of Nigeria claiming in US courts that Dutch, British and Nigerian oil exploration firms had brutally crushed peaceful protests against the oil exploration in Nigeria. The Supreme Court requested additional briefs to consider whether the Alien Tort Statute (ATS) (28 USC § 1350) would recognize a cause of action for violations of the law of nations occurring within the territory of a sovereign other than the US. The Court held that there would be no presumption of extraterritorial application of the ATS, but the presumption could be displaced when the claims "touch and concern the territory of the US with sufficient force."

56 United Nations *Charter*; United Nations *General Assembly Resolution* 217 (III) A; United Nations *Universal Declaration of Human Rights* (10 December 1948); United Nations *General Assembly Resolution* 3452; United Nations *Declaration on the Protection of All Persons from Being Subjected to Torture* (9 December 1975); Inter-American Commission on Human Rights, *American Declaration on the Rights and Duties of Man* (2 May 1948); United Nations *General Assembly Resolution* 39/46, *Convention Against Torture and Other Cruel, Inhuman or Degrading Treatment or Punishment* (10 December 1984); United Nations *General Assembly Resolution* 2200A (XXI), *International Covenant on Civil and Political Rights* (16 December 1966); United Nations *General Assembly Resolution* 2200, *International Covenant on Economic, Social and Cultural Rights* (16 December 1966); United Nations *General Assembly Resolution* 1904, *International Covenant on Elimination of All Forms*

Separately, per Article 18 of the Vienna Convention on the Law of Treaties,[57] once a State signs a treaty but prior to its ratification, that State may not act in any way to defeat the purpose and object of the treaty. The US has also signed three major treaties that have not yet been ratified but, by virtue of having signed them, the US has committed to not undermining their purpose and object. These are listed and cited together in the footnote.[58]

The US has engaged in almost all the major international human rights treaties and protocols, was a charter signatory to most, and has had an outwardly looking comprehension of law dating back to the Constitution. Notably, since the days of the Universal Declaration, the US has also had a significant role in the *travaux préparatoires* of the majority of these treaties despite sometimes being reluctant later to ratify agreements that it had a major hand in writing, a phenomenon well described in the Moravcsik article on unilateralism.[59] Overall, there is a substantial constitutional and jurisprudential foundation for use of the consensus doctrine by the Supreme Court.

---

of Racial Discrimination (20 November 1963); United Nations *Resolution General Assembly Resolution* A/RES/54/263, *Optional Protocol to the Convention on Rights of the Child on the Involvement of Children in Armed Conflict* (25 May 2000); United Nations *General Assembly Resolution* A/RES/54/263, *Optional Protocol to the Convention on Rights of the Child on the Sale of Children, Child Prostitution, and Child Pornography* (25 May 2000); United Nations *General Assembly Resolution* 260, *Convention on Prevention and Punishment of the Crime of Genocide* (9 December 1948).

57 United Nations *Vienna Convention of the Law of Treaties*, 1155 U.N.T.S. 331, art. 18 (1969).

58 United Nations General *Assembly Resolution* 34/180, *Convention on the Elimination of All Forms of Discrimination against Women* (18 December 1979); United Nations *General Assembly Resolution* 61/106, *Convention on the Rights of Persons with Disabilities* (24 January 2007); United Nationals *General Assembly Resolution* 44/25, *Convention on the Rights of the Child* (20 November 1989).

59 A. Moravcsik, 'Why is US human Rights Policy so Unilateralist?', <https://www.princeton.edu/~amoravcs/library/unilateralism.pdf>, discussing the US role in promoting and establishing human rights instruments while later being reluctant to adopt them into domestic law. *See also* T. Evans, 'United States Hegemony and the Project of Human Rights', DOI 10.1057/9780230380103, pp. 48-71 (1996) looking at the US role in creating the foundational 'idea' of human rights.

4 Statistical Death Penalty Trends and Legislative Changes in the US

To provide context for the discussion of two specific cases in Part 5, it is worth looking at statistical trends in the US regarding application of the death penalty today. If the Supreme Court were to use the consensus doctrine, it would need to have an understanding of these trends as part of its tool-kit for interpreting the meaning of the Eighth Amendment in the light of evolving standards. As noted in the Introduction, the amendment states, "Excessive bail shall not be required, nor excessive fines imposed, nor cruel and unusual punishments inflicted."

A Gallup Poll in 2017 showed that 55 per cent of those polled support the death penalty for convicted murderers, the lowest level of support since 1972.[60] Significantly, when people are given other penalty options to choose from, 61 per cent do not choose death, preferring instead life with parole, life without parole, or life without parole plus restitution.[61] As of today, 27 US states permit the death penalty and 23 do not, although only eight out of 50 States have executed anyone in the last two years.[62] Seven of those eight states are in the south, except Ohio. From 1977 to 2017, the percentages of those executed, by race, are as follows: 59.7 per cent white, 34.3 per cent black, 8.3 per cent Hispanic, 1.6 per cent other.[63] [The statistics included in this paragraph and the next come from the DPIC data and statistical information listed in footnotes 60 and 61.]

In 2017, 39 people in the US were executed, the second lowest number since 1972.[64] Two States (Texas and Arkansas) accounted for 48 per cent of those deaths.[65] Since 1973, 161 prisoners on death row have been exonerated and declared innocent of the charges against them based on new evidence produced through their judicial appeals.[66] The number of prisoners on death row declined in 2017 for the 17th consecutive year.[67]

Lastly, four important judicial decisions have affected and will continue to affect the use of the death penalty. In 2002, the Supreme Court ruled

---

60   Death Penalty Information Center (DPIC), last updated on 28 June 28 2018, <deathpenaltyinfo.org/documents/FactSheet.pdf.>, visited on 17 July 2018.
61   Lake Research Partners poll, 2010, visited on June 25, 2018.
62   DPIC, *supra* note 60.
63   *Ibid.*
64   *Ibid.*
65   *Ibid.*
66   *Ibid.*
67   *Ibid.*

in *Atkins* v. *Virginia*[68] that executing individuals with intellectual disabilities was unconstitutional. In 2005, in *Roper* v. *Simmons*,[69] the Supreme Court struck down as unconstitutional the execution of individuals who committed crimes as juveniles under the age of 18. In 2017, Florida abolished non-unanimous jury recommendations of a sentence of death.[70] And also in 2017, Alabama abolished its use of judicial override whereby the Alabama Supreme Court had been permitted to overturn a jury's sentencing recommendation of life in prison and instead order the prisoner to be executed.[71]

No matter how one analyses these statistics and judicial decisions, it is clear that the individual States and the US as a whole are moving away from acceptance of the death penalty. From an initial 50 states with this punishment on the books, there are now only 27. Of these, only eight States have applied the punishment in the last two years and those States are in one region of the country. In each of the last 18 years, the number of prisoners being ordered to death row has declined, and 61 per cent of polling subjects prefer other punishments to death.

If the Supreme Court were to use consensus doctrine as the ECtHR did in *Soering* to identify and analyse judicial and penological trends, the weight would necessarily fall toward abolition of this penalty as violating the Eighth Amendment given "evolving standards of decency".[72]

5 Two Supreme Court Cases: *Stanford* v. *Kentucky* and *Glossip* v. *Gross*

As noted, the US Supreme Court has a long line of authority supporting an outward looking jurisprudence. It also has shown a willingness to allow its interpretation of the Constitution to evolve so as to be capable of being applied to newer social circumstances as they arise.[73] As early as

---

68   *Atkins* v. *Virginia*, 2002, United States Supreme Court, 536 U.S. 304.
69   *Roper* v. *Simmons,* 2005, United States Supreme Court, 543 U.S. 551.
70   DPIC, *supra* note 60.
71   *Ibid.*
72   A simple compilation and consolidation of the statistical and judicial findings by the DPIC would probably suffice for this purpose. *See* footnotes 60 and 61.
73   In addition to the *Griswold* case cited in note 47, finding a constitutional right to marital privacy where no such right existed explicitly in the Constitution, two other examples are noteworthy. In *Brown* v. *Board of Education,* 1954, United States Supreme Court, 347 U.S. 483, the Supreme Court banned the use of separate educational facilities for students of different races on the determination that "sepa-

1958, in *Trop* v. *Dulles*,[74] Chief Justice Warren discussed the Court's "willingness in *Weems* v. *US* to give the meaning of the Eighth Amendment a dynamic interpretation". Warren noted: "The Court recognized in that case that the words of the Amendment are not precise, and that their scope is not static. The Amendment must draw its meaning on the evolving standards of decency that mark the progress of a maturing society",[75] a phrase very like the ECtHR's description of the Convention as a "living instrument" designed to meet "present-day conditions".[76]

The tension between imposing a majority view on a recalcitrant minority lies at the heart of the death penalty debate in the US.[77] In the US, most aspects of criminal law and criminal procedure have traditionally been left to the 50 States, with the important exception of several constitutional Amendments related to criminal matters that apply to all States.[78] Assuming States abide by these constitutional principles, they are largely free to establish their own criminal law and procedure, and all 50 States have their own penal codes.[79] Hence the situation today where

---

rate was inherently unequal" under the Constitution even where no such limitation could explicitly be found within the Constitution. In *Loving* v. *Virginia,* 1967, United States Supreme Court, 388 U.S. 1, the Supreme Court barred States from preventing inter-racial marriage as being an unconstitutional infringement on the freedom to marry the person of one's choice even though no explicit right to marry whomever one wanted could explicitly be found within the Constitution.

74   *Trop* v. *Dulles*, 1958, United States Supreme Court, 356 U.S. 86.
75   *Ibid.,* p. 356.
76   *Tyrer* v. *United Kingdom*, 25 April 1978, ECtHR, 5856/72, para. 31. The ECtHR notes, "The Court must also recall that the Convention is a living instrument which, as the Commission rightly stressed, must be interpreted in the light of present-day conditions. In the case now before it the Court cannot but be influenced by the developments and commonly accepted standards in the penal policy of the member States of the Council of Europe in this field.
77   J. Marriott, 'Walking the Eighth Amendment Tightrope: "Time Served" in the US Supreme Court', in J. Yorke, *Against the Death Penalty* (Ashgate, Surrey and Vermont, 2008). Marriot analyses the remaining retentionist US States, and compares 'evolving standards' with foreign norms to illustrate the tension between their differing jurisprudence.
78   These include the Fourth Amendment's prohibition against unreasonable searches and seizures, the Sixth Amendment's requirement of fair and speedy trials and the ability to confront witnesses, the Eighth Amendment's prohibition of cruel and unusual punishment and the Fifth and Fourteenth Amendment provisions respecting the right to due process.
79   There are a number of federal criminal statutes governing particular classes of crime, often arising from agencies of the federal government. These include tax evasion, racketeering, federal hate crimes, kidnapping, counterfeiting, human trafficking, credit card fraud, and certain weapons violations, among others. In some

some States have the death penalty on their books but do not sentence people to death, a few States actually use the death penalty, and several others have abolished it altogether.

The ECtHR's long-standing method of contending with such tensions and variations among its 47 Member States by balancing consensus against a State's margin of appreciation has proved to be effective and could be effective in the US as well.[80] Like the ECtHR, the Supreme Court is in a position to consider the emerging consensus among the 50 US States regarding the Eighth Amendment. Such analysis by certain Justices is not uncommon, and the Justices are likewise free to look beyond the borders of US jurisprudence. In addition to the three dissents by Brennan, Breyer, and Sotomayor discussed in the section, it is worth noting that Justice O'Connor also often discussed trends and legal decisions from outside the US, and she became somewhat notorious in this regard. She was frequently rebuked by Justice Scalia for looking beyond the 'four corners' of the US Constituion.[81] The dissents in *Stanford* v. *Kentucky* (1989) and *Glossip* v. *Gross* (2015) discussed here are important because, among other things, they provide an additional basis, beyond those mentioned in Part 3, for using the consensus doctrine in the US. In both cases, the dissenting Justices not only looked explicitly at evolving standards and practices within the 50 States, but also to existing and evolving standards and practices outside the US.[82]

---

areas, there are both federal and State criminal codes. For a detailed discussion, see N. Abrams and S. Beale, *Federal Criminal Law and its Enforcement, 6th ed.* (West Academic Publishing, Minnesota, 2015).

80   *Bayatyan* case, *supra* note 18, paras. 121-124, carefully balancing consensus against the margin of appreciation.

81   In a speech at the Southern Center for International Studies, Justice O'Connor proclaimed quite forthrightly, "There is talk today about the 'internationalization of legal relations'. We are already seeing this in American courts, and should see it increasingly in the future... Conclusions reached by other countries and by the international community, although not formally binding upon our decisions, should at times constitute persuasive authority in American courts – what is sometimes called 'transjudicialism.'" <www.webcitation.org/5nAlaoWHe?url=http://www.southerncenter.org/OConnor_transcript.pdf.>, visited on 17 July 2018.

82   In the US, one of the values of dissenting opinions is that they often lead the way to a new direction in law, and provide persuasive authority for subsequent decisions overruling or modifying existing precedent. For a collection and analysis of significant dissents and the jurisprudential role they played, see M. Tushnet, *I Dissent: Great Opposing Opinions in Landmark Supreme Court Cases* (Beacon Press, Boston, 2008).

In *Stanford* v. *Kentucky*, two young men had, separately, been sentenced to death for crimes and murders committed at ages 16 and 17, respectively.[83] The Supreme Court narrowly held (5 to 4) that execution of anyone whose crimes were committed at age 16 or older was not unconstitutional and did not violate the ban on cruel and unusual punishment. (This decision was later overruled.[84]) The *Stanford* dissent by Justice William Brennan is significant because his line of reasoning closely parallels the ECtHR's use of consensus, in stark contrast to Justice Scalia's majority opinion refusing to look beyond the four corners of the Constitution. Justice Brennan reasoned as follows (all citations omitted, and reducing his 26-page dissent to the following paragraph):

> We begin the task of deciding ... whether our Nation has set its face against a punishment to an extent that it can be concluded that the punishment offends our 'evolving standards of decency'. Our cases recognize that objective indicators of contemporary standards of decency in the form of legislation in other countries is also of relevance to Eighth Amendment analysis ... Many countries, of course – over 50, including nearly all in Western Europe – have formally abolished the death penalty, or have limited its use to exceptional crimes such as treason ... In addition to national laws, three leading human rights treaties ratified by the United States explicitly prohibit juvenile death penalties. Within the world community, the imposition of the death penalty for juvenile crimes appears to be overwhelmingly disapproved. Together, the rejection of the death penalty for juveniles by a majority of the States, the rarity of the sentence for juveniles ... the decisions of respected organizations in relevant fields that this punishment is unacceptable, and its rejection generally throughout the world, provide to my mind a strong grounding for the view that it is not constitutionally tolerable that certain States persist in authorizing the execution of adolescent offenders.

Brennan's discussion of international human rights treaties ratified by the US is noteworthy in and of itself, and he included a footnote to that discussion citing with great particularity each of those treaty obliga-

---

83   *Stanford* case, *supra* note 10, p. 492.
84   In 2005, *Roper* v. *Simmons* abolished the death penalty for crimes committed by individuals under age 18, *supra* note 69.

tions.[85] Brennan not only considered legislative actions within the 50 States, but he also looked outside the US to help identify and understand civilized norms and trends regarding the imposition of the death penalty. He assumed that such knowledge should inform US jurisprudence and help determine what is constitutionally tolerable. He also noted that only a small number of States "persist" in imposing this penalty.

The *Stanford* v. *Kentucky and Soering* v. *UK* cases were both decided in 1989, and it is very insightful, and rather touching, to look at an exchange of letters between ECtHR Judge Brian Walsh and Supreme Court Justice Brennan in 1989 regarding the *Soering* and *Stanford* cases. Walsh and Brennan over the years had become friends, and they conducted a 34-year correspondence, much of it to do with the cases they were working on. The letters have not been published, but are kept in the US Library of Congress.

ECtHR Judge Walsh wrote to Justice Brennan regarding *Soering* on August 25, 1989, as follows (omitting major portions of his letter):

> Many thanks for your letter concerning our judgment in Strasbourg in the *Capital Punishment* case ... As you will appreciate the combination of factors in the case, namely, youth, mental capacity and other matters is not likely to recur very frequently. Therefore while all these matters were taken into account by the judgment the judgment is not dependent upon that particular combination. You will have noticed that ... the factors set out include 'the manner and method of its ... execution.' That is a most important matter ... I had written a separate concurring opinion dealing almost exclusively with the electric chair method, which I believed constituted a breach of Article 3. Personally, I would regard the gas chamber and the electric chair as being so gruesome as to amount to inhuman and degrading treatment.

Justice Brennan responded as follows on September 7, 1989:

> It was a particular pleasure to have your good letter of August 25. I feel much informed about the problem of juvenile executions. I was also very interested in your discussion of executions by the electric chair method. I don't remember if I had told you, I myself had written an opinion taking the position that execution by electrocu-

---

85   *Stanford* case, *supra* note 10, footnote 10 of Brennan dissent.

tion violates the Eighth Amendment. I'm enclosing a copy of that opinion. The only colleague who joined it was Justice Marshall, and I don't foresee its acceptance generally, at least in the near future. But, there are some signs of real concern again with the death penalty itself....[86]

The second US death penalty case meriting consideration is *Glossip* v. *Gross*,[87] decided by the Supreme Court in 2015, 26 years after Justice Brennan's dissent in *Stanford* v. *Kentucky*. The majority upheld Oklahoma's use of a particular drug protocol to execute people, finding that the method did not constitute cruel and unusual punishment. The larger issue of the constitutionality of the death penalty was not at issue; instead the court looked at a particular means of execution. The dissents by Justices Breyer and Sotomayor are important because Breyer invited a full reconsideration of the death penalty partly based on evolving standards and international consensus, and Sotomayor urged a fresh look at the meaning of the foundational words 'cruel' and 'unusual', arguing that certain methods of execution were inherently barbarous and akin to long-prohibited methods of punishment.

In his 27-page dissent, Justice Breyer provided a detailed description of his conclusions after working on "thousands" of death penalty appeals over 20 years, noting that the death penalty fails on all penological fronts: it does not rehabilitate, it does not deter, it does not provide retribution, and it is not rationally or consistently applied – making it essentially random. He argued as follows (all citations omitted, and reducing the opinion to one paragraph focusing on his line of reasoning):

> Rather than try to patch up the death penalty's wounds one at a time, I would ask for a full briefing on a more basic question: whether the death penalty violates the Constitution. Almost 40 years of studies, surveys, and experience strongly indicate that ... today's administration of the death penalty involves three fundamental defects: (1) serious unreliability, (2) arbitrariness in application, and (3) unconscionably long delays. Perhaps as a result, most places in the United States have abandoned its use. [This] has led me to believe that the death penalty, in and of itself, now likely constitutes a

---

86   US Library of Congress, William J. Brennan papers, file folder Walsh, Brian, LCCN mm 82052266.
87   *Glossip* case, *supra* note 11.

> legally prohibited 'cruel and unusual punishment.' ... The arbitrary imposition of punishment is the antithesis of law ... The Eighth and Fourteenth Amendments cannot tolerate the infliction of a sentence of death under legal systems that permit this unique penalty to be so wantonly and so freakishly imposed ... I note ... that many nations, indeed 95 of the 193 members of the United Nations have formally abolished the death penalty and an additional 42 have abolished it in practice ... I believe it highly likely that the death penalty violates the Eighth Amendment.[88]

In his full discussion of "many nations", Justice Breyer mentioned the *Soering* case among others. For her part, Justice Sotomayor threw down the gauntlet to those fellow Justices who are most comfortable staying within the four corners of the Constitution. Sotomayor turned directly to the words 'cruel' and 'unusual', and looked at what those words meant in 1789, how they have subsequently been defined in case-law, and what they mean today. She argued as follows (with most, but not all, citations omitted, and reducing her dissent to one paragraph):

> This Court has long recognized that certain methods of execution are categorically off-limits. The Court first confronted an Eighth Amendment challenge to a method of execution in *Wilkerson v. Utah* (1879) ... The Court made clear that 'public dissection,' 'burning alive,' and other 'punishments of torture' ... in the same line of unnecessary cruelty, are forbidden by the Eighth Amendments ... 'Nor has there been any question that the Amendment *categorically* prohibits the infliction of cruel and unusual punishments.' 'Nor has there been any question that the Amendment prohibits such 'inherently barbaric punishments *under all circumstances.*' A method of execution that is 'barbarous,' (*Rhodes*) or 'involves torture or a lingering death,' (*Kemmler*), does not become less so just because it is the only method currently available to a State ... 'By protecting even those convicted of heinous crimes, the Eighth Amendment reaffirms the duty of the government to respect the dignity of all persons (*Roper*).'[89]

---

88   *Glossip* case, *supra* note 11. Breyer dissent pp. 1-41.
89   *Glossip* case, *supra* note 11. Sotomayor dissent pp. 1-31, reference to *Roper*, pg. 31.

Sotomayor focused on the precise meaning of the words 'cruel' and 'unusual' in a way that might satisfy even jurists who wish to stay within the four corners.[90] Moreover, she was comfortable relying on the evolution of the meaning of those words over time, as society matures and social conditions change, in order to find ways to expand the protections provided by the Eighth Amendment. This is much like the reasoning of the ECtHR in *Soering*. She would have the Court include certain execution methods by definition as cruel and unusual, just as the ECtHR chose to include death penalty phenomenon within the meaning of Article 3. Killingley has argued that the most effective way for the US to accomplish abolition of the death penalty may be by "strict confinement of the penalty through imaginative application of the Eighth Amendment".[91] Sotomayor's dissent moved in this direction.

These important dissents demonstrate a willingness on the part of some Supreme Court Justices to look beyond the four corners of the Constitution, and a concern about the fact that the US position on the death penalty has become increasingly isolated. It is fitting to close this discussion of death penalty jurisprudence with a common-sense approach to this distinctly uncommon problem expressed by Justice Stevens writing for the majority in *Thompson v. Oklahoma*.[92] The Court was deciding whether the execution of 15-years olds was compatible with the Eighth Amendment. In saying no, Stevens voiced what we might call a 'Common Man' vote for consensus:

> Our capital punishment jurisprudence has consistently recognized that contemporary standards, as reflected by the actions of legis-

---

90   In the US, three types of constitutional interpretation are commonly used by the Justices. 'Originalism', or 'original intent', looks to what the words meant when they were written. What did the framers intend? No interpretation of the words in light of social change or contemporary meaning is allowed. 'Textualism' involves interpreting the law in accordance with its ordinary meaning today. Nothing is added, and no flourishes about ancient meanings are allowed. 'Pragmatism' is sometimes called 'living document interpretation'. This method views the Constitution as a contemporary document primarily designed to solve problems. For a detailed view of these, and several other methods of interpretation, see Brando J. Morrill, Modes of Constitutional Research, Congress Research Service, 15 March 2018 <fas.org/sgp/crs/misc/R45129.pdf.>, visited on 17 July 2018.

91   J. Killingley, 'Constraining America's Death Penalty: The Eighth Amendment and Excessive Punishment', in J. Yorke (ed.), *Against the Death Penalty* (Ashgate, Surrey UK, 2008) p. 127.

92   *Thompson v. Oklahoma*, 1988, United States Supreme Court, 487 U.S. 815.

latures and juries, provide an important measure of whether the death penalty is 'cruel and unusual'. Part of the rationale for this index of constitutional value lies in the very language of the constitutional clause: whether an action is 'unusual' depends, in common usage, upon the frequency of its occurrence or the magnitude of its acceptance.[93]

A brief look today at international consensus on the use of the death penalty, and consensus within the 50 States would no doubt reveal that the execution of prisoners is indeed 'unusual'. On this point alone, a legal analysis using the consensus doctrine might quickly establish that the death penalty is incompatible with the Eighth Amendment.

6 Conclusion

Based on consideration of the foregoing material, it is strikingly clear that it behoves the US Supreme Court to adopt the European consensus doctrine in its broadest sense for use in its death penalty jurisprudence. Six key factors support this view.

First, the consensus doctrine allows the ECtHR to foster uniformity across 47 Member States in their efforts to comply with their Convention obligations. The consensus doctrine allows the Court to take the measure of evolving standards and trends and to ensure that the meaning of the Convention follows closely upon, and is interpreted consistently with, these trends. It also allows the Court to nudge Member States into alignment with evolving standards over time by carefully balancing the margin of appreciation analysis with the consensus doctrine. The US Supreme Court similarly aspires to ensure consistency in State compliance with the Constitution. Regional variations persist in State conduct under the Eighth Amendment, and the consensus doctrine could help achieve greater uniformity.

Second, as the dissents in *Stanford* v. *Kentucky* and *Glossip* v. *Gross* demonstrate, Justices of the Supreme Court are perfectly adept at using a version of the consensus doctrine, both by analysing evolving standards within the 50 States, and also evolving standards across the globe. There is no reason why the Supreme Court's traditional desire to stay within the four corners of the Constitution should mean that no other information

---

93 Ibid.

is tolerated or welcome. Justice Sotomayor has also shown in her *Glossip* dissent that, in some ways, one need not look beyond the four corners of the Constitution to find words that may readily be interpreted to comport with international interpretations of those same words as they appear in international treaties and the Convention.

Third, the US has accepted the law of nations from the beginning. That is considered "our law".[94] The Constitution's Supremacy Clause places the Constitution, federal law, and international treaties on the same plane as the supreme law of the land. The US has ratified a significant number of human rights treaties, including all the major ones, and signed many others. US jurisprudence is full of cases adjudicated in the light of these judicial obligations and frameworks. Applying the consensus doctrine to ensure consideration of these laws and commitments would foster predictability and world-wide harmonisation. Consensus and harmonisation are also fostered by judicial dialogue like that between Judge Walsh and Justice Brennan. What was, in 1989, an exchange of letters between two jurists has now become a global conversation among jurisdictions, and this conversation contributes to consensus.[95] It behoves the US to be part of this conversation, rather than marginalized from it by a narrow focus on remaining within the four corners of the Constitution.

Fourth, imposition of the death penalty becomes more disfavoured as a punishment each year. All 47 States of the COE have adopted Protocol 13 to the Convention abolishing the death penalty. The United Nations has been working consistently to abolish the death penalty in an ongoing effort that will affect its Member States, including the US.[96] Views on

---

94   *The Paquete Habana case, supra* note 52, particularly the text in Part 3 following footnote 52.

95   See C. Cheeseman, 'The death penalty as addressed by regional and international human rights bodies: exploring jurisprudential cross-fertilisation and harmonisation,' in C. Buckley et al (eds.) *Towards Convergence in Human Rights Law: Approaches of Regional and International Systems* (Koninklijke Brill NV, Leiden, 2017). See also A. H. de Wolf and D. H. Wallace, 'The Overseas Exchange of Human Rights Jurisprudences: the US Supreme Court in the European Court of Human Rights', 19 *International Criminal Justice Review* (2009) pp. 287-288, and T. L. Grove, 'The International Judicial Dialogue: When Domestic Constitutional Courts Join the Conversation', 114 *Harvard Law Review* (2001) pp. 2050-2972.

96   Former UN Secretary-General Ban Ki-moon noted that more and more Member States acknowledge that the death penalty undermines human dignity, and that its abolition contributes to the enhancement and progressive development of human rights. He noted, "[m]ore than 160 Members States of the United Nations with a variety of legal systems, traditions, cultures and religious backgrounds, have either abolished the death penalty or do not practice it." In 1989, the UN General

human dignity change, standards of decency evolve; Europe is not what it was in 1949 when the COE was established, nor is the US what it was then. This process will never stop, and it benefits the international judicial community to have governing instruments that are capable of more encompassing interpretation when warranted. The US judiciary would likewise benefit from using consensus as an interpretive tool to identify and measure change.

Lastly, few scholars and fewer citizens are comfortable with the US continuing use of the death penalty. The penalty itself and the methods involved in applying it are outside the bounds of acceptable penological norms. It is increasingly intolerable to have a handful of States applying a punishment that most Americans view as abhorrent. Use of the consensus doctrine would allow the Supreme Court to raise the profile of domestic statistical trends among the 50 States to the forefront of its decision-making to ensure that outlier states are nudged, or forcefully directed, to come into conformance with the majority of the States. In closing, the author urges the US Supreme Court to add the European consensus doctrine to its interpretive tool-kit.

Assembly adopted the Second Optional Protocol to the ICCPR. Member States that became parties to the Protocol agreed not to execute anyone within their jurisdictions. In 2014, the General Assembly adopted a resolution calling for a moratorium on use of the death penalty. 117 Member States voted in favour. <ohchr.org/EN/Issues/DeathPenalty/Pages/DPIndex.aspx>, visited on 17 July 2018.

4 The Application of Bilateral Investment Treaties in Annexed Territories: Whose BITs are Applicable in Crimea after its Annexation?

*Katharina Wende**

Abstract

This article analyses the applicability of bilateral investment treaties (BITs) in Crimea after the events of 2014, when the latter was annexed by the Russian Federation. More precisely, it is trying to answer the question whether Ukrainian or Russian BITs are to be applied as of the date of annexation. At first sight, it seems as if the annexation of Crimea resulted in a legal vacuum, in which investments on the peninsula are left unprotected. This is because States are not allowed to recognise the applicability of Russian BITs in Crimea as a consequence of the duty of non-recognition and Ukrainian BITs do not offer effective protection as any violations of BIT standards could not be attributed to Ukraine. Nevertheless, as this article will show, the law of treaties as well as the law of occupation may offer a way out of this legal vacuum with the result that not only Russian but also Ukrainian BITs may be applicable in the annexed territory of Crimea.

1 Introduction

Crimea's annexation into the Russian Federation in 2014 has been condemned by the majority of States and Russia has faced economic and political sanctions ever since. Meanwhile, the interstate territorial dispute persists. While Russia is claiming that Crimea constitutes Russian territory, the duty of non-recognition calls upon all States not to recognise any shift in the territorial sovereignty over Crimea. However, it is difficult to deny that in fact Crimea has been incorporated into Russia, as Ukraine

---

* LL.M. Graduate in International Laws, University of Maastricht; Bachelor of Arts in International Relations, University of Geneva.

does not exercise any effective control over the territory and Russia has gradually introduced its laws and administration into the area.[1] This situation leads to a conflict between law and fact in Crimea, which is likely to continue for an extended period of time. While legal scholars concerned with the events in Crimea have primarily focused on the consequences under public international law,[2] the annexation of Crimea has also triggered questions concerning international investment law. Today's international investment law is based above all on a system of bilateral investment treaties (BITs) protecting investors on the basis of bilateral treaties between the host State and their home State. These treaties generally provide for a certain standard of investment protection and for a possibility to have recourse to international arbitration in case of a violation of the treaties' provisions.

As of August 2017, Ukrainian investors have filed at least seven claims over alleged breaches of their investment against Russia under the Russia-Ukraine BIT[3] in so-called investor-State arbitration.[4] This raises important questions as to the applicability of BITs in the territory of Crimea following its annexation and occupation. It seems that in order to decide upon the merits in the above-mentioned disputes arbitral tribunals

---

1 Федеральный конституционный закон от 21 марта 2014 N 6-ФКЗ (ред. от 29 июля 2017) "О принятии в Российскую Федерацию Республики Крым и образовании в составе Российской Федерации новых субъектов – Республики Крым и города федерального значения Севастополя."

2 B. R. Roth, 'The Virtues of Bright Lines: Self-Determination, Secession, and External Intervention', 16 *German Law Journal* (2015); M. Fabry, 'How to Uphold the Territorial Integrity of Ukraine', 16 *German Law Journal* (2015); A. Catala, 'Secession and Annexation: The Case of Crimea', 16 *German Law Journal* (2015).

3 Agreement between the Government of the Russian Federation and the Cabinet of Ministers of Ukraine on the Encouragement and Mutual Protection of Investments (Russia-Ukraine) (adopted 27 November 1998, entered into force 27 January 2000), <http://investmentpolicyhub.unctad.org/IIA/mostRecent/treaty/2859>, visited on 15 September 2017.

4 *Aeroport Belbek LLC and Mr Igor Valerievich Kolomoisky* v. *The Russian Federation*, PCA Case No 2015-07 (Pending); *PJSC CB PrivatBank and Finance Company Finilon LLC* v. *The Russian Federation*, PCA Case No AA 568 (Pending); *PJSC Ukrnafta (Ukraine)* v. *The Russian Federation*, PCA Case No 2015-34 (Pending); *Stabil LLC, Rubenor LLC, Rustel LLC, Novel-Estate LLC, PII Kirovograd-Nafta LLC, Crimea-Petrol LLC, Pirsan LLC, Trade-Trust LLC, Elefteria LLC, VKF Satek LLC, Stemv Group LLC* v. *The Russian Federation*, PCA Case No 2015-35 (Pending); *Everest Estate LLC et al* v. *The Russian Federation*, PCA Case No AA 577 (Pending); *Limited Liability Company Lugzor, Limited Liability Company Libset, Limited Liability Company Ukrinterinvest, Public Joint Stock Company DniproAzot, Limited Liability Company Aberon Ltd* v. *The Russian Federation*, PCA Case No 2015-29 (Pending).

must come to the conclusion that Crimea constitutes Russian territory. However, this is difficult to affirm as annexation cannot give right to a valid legal title over territory, which, *prima facie*, would exclude the application of Russian BITs in Crimea. On the other hand, even if Ukrainian treaties are applicable, it is unlikely that any breach of a BIT could be attributable to Ukraine, as the latter does not exercise any effective control over the territory. In that case, investors would find themselves in a legal vacuum with the result that these investors and their investments would be left unprotected. This would not only harm investors having invested in Crimea but also harm the future economic development in Crimea as investors would have one more reason to avoid the peninsula. Last but not least, the existence of this legal vacuum would ultimately undermine the principle of the prohibition of the law of force as it would create a situation favourable to Russia even though the latter has acted against that principle when annexing Crimea.

This article provides an analysis of the territorial application of BITs in Crimea under the law of treaties and the law of occupation to determine whether Russian or Ukrainian BITs are applicable in the territory of Crimea. First of all, it gives an overview of the problems raised by Crimea's annexation for the applicability of BITs in Crimea. It follows an analysis of the legal consequences of Crimea's annexation under public international law paying special attention to the duty of non-recognition and the Namibia exception. Further, it examines to what extent Russia's BITs may be applicable to Crimea under the law of treaties. At last, it shall be established whether Russia may have a duty under the law of occupation to respect the application of Ukrainian BITs in Crimea. Finally, this article concludes that instead of being the victims of a legal vacuum, investors benefit from double protection under the law of treaties and the law of occupation.

2   Consequences of Crimea's Annexation for Investment Protection in Crimea

2.1   *The Role of Bilateral Investment Treaties*

BITs are the most commonly used and most important legal instruments in contemporary international investment law. As of today, around 2900

BITs are in force worldwide.[5] Ukraine has signed 77 BITs, 57 of which are in force.[6] Russia has signed 85 BITs, 65 of which are in force.[7] BITs provide for protection of investments and investors from one of the Contracting States in the territory of the other Contracting State. They usually consist of three parts: a first part containing definitions, a second part consisting of substantive standards for the protection of investments and investors and a third part concerning dispute settlement.[8] Furthermore, most BITs start with a preamble stating the aim of the treaty, which is usually the creation and maintenance of favourable conditions for mutual investments and the promotion of trade and economic cooperation.[9]

The dispute resolution clauses contained in BITs offer investors direct access to effective international remedies, which is a great advantage for them as they do not have to rely on traditional and less effective methods of dispute resolution such as diplomatic protection and actions in domestic courts.[10] By inserting a dispute resolution clause into the BIT the State parties to the treaty consent to international arbitration by means of a standing offer to arbitrate.[11] In case of violation of a substantive standard contained in a BIT, investors may accept the host State's offer through the filing of an arbitral claim and thus can benefit from easy access to a remedy.[12] However, international arbitral tribunals as all other tribunals have the competence to decide their own jurisdiction (*competence-competence*).[13] This means that in certain cases they may declare themselves incompetent if they decide that they do not have the

---

5   United Nations, 'World investment Report: Investing in the SDGs: An Action Plan' (2014), <http://unctad.org/en/pages/PublicationWebflyer.aspx?publication id=937>, visited on 15 September 2017.

6   Investment Policy Hub, International Investment Agreements Navigator, Ukraine, <http://investmentpolicyhub.unctad.org/IIA/CountryBits/219>, visited on 30 August 2017.

7   Investment Policy Hub, International Investment Agreements Navigator, Russian Federation, <http://investmentpolicyhub.unctad.org/IIA/CountryBits/175>, visited on 30 August 2017.

8   R. Dolzer and C. Schreuer, *Principles of international investment law* (Oxford University Press, Oxford, 2014) p. 13.

9   *See for example* the preamble of the Russia-Ukraine BIT, *supra* note 3.

10   Dolzer, *supra* note 8, p. 236.

11   S. Wuschka, 'Das Investitionsschutzrecht: Rechtssicherheit für deutsche Investoren auf der Krim?' (2016), p. 3, <http://www.ostinstitut.de/documents/Wuschka_Das_Investitionsschutzrecht_Rechtssicherheit_fr_deutsche_Investoren_auf_der_Krim_OL_3_2016.pdf>, visited on 1 September 2017.

12   *Ibid.*

13   A. Kawharu, 'Arbitral Jurisdiction', 23:2 *New Zealand Law Review* (2008) p. 238.

competence to determine the issue brought before them. This is the main problem that arose in the arbitration proceedings in relation to the expropriation claims brought by Ukrainian investors against Russia.

2.2 The Investment Arbitration Proceedings against Russia

As of today, Ukrainian investors have brought at least seven expropriation claims before international arbitral tribunals against the Russian Federation under the UNCITRAL Arbitration Rules 1976 pursuant to the Russia-Ukraine BIT.[14] These claims may serve as a starting point as they illustrate certain problems relating to the applicability of BITs in Crimea in the aftermath of its annexation. The immediate issue is whether the arbitral tribunals seized have jurisdiction to decide upon the merits, which is the case only if the Russia-Ukraine BIT applies to the territory of Crimea. Curiously, all parties to the dispute have an interest in convincing the tribunal that Crimea constitutes Russian territory.[15] This is because Russia is claiming that Crimea has been legally integrated into the Russian Federation and because Ukrainian investors seem to be able to claim damages only if Russian BITs apply in Crimea. Nonetheless, as will be demonstrated, it is indisputable that Crimea does not legally form part of the Russian Federation.

In February 2017, an arbitral tribunal administered by the Permanent Court of Arbitration (PCA) at The Hague issued an interim award, in which it declared its competence to decide upon the merits in the expropriation cases brought by Kolomoisky and Aeroport Belbek LLC, and PrivatBank.[16] The interim award has not been published yet but the defending party noted that the award constituted the first decision by an international tribunal "to apply a BIT to the occupying power in control of

---

14 M. Davletbaev, 'The applicability of Russia-Ukraine BIT treaty to investments in Crimea: current status and future developments', 21 *Across the EUniverse: A simple tool to enhance our understanding of EU Law* (2017) p. 15.

15 P. Tzeng, 'Sovereignty over Crimea: A Case for State-to-State Investment Arbitration', 41:2 *Yale Journal of International Law* (2016) p. 460.

16 'Hughes Hubbard Wins Jurisdiction Decisions in Crimea Arbitration', 1 March 2017, <https://www.hugheshubbard.com/news/breaking-news-hughes-hubbard-secures-first-award-holding-russia-responsible-in-crimea>, visited on 30 August 2017; L. E. Peterson, 'In Jurisdiction Ruling, Arbitrators rule that Russia is obliged under BIT to protect Ukrainian Investors in Crimea following Annexation', *Investment Arbitration Reporter*, 9 March 2017, <https://www.iareporter.com/articles/in-jurisdiction-ruling-arbitrators-rule-that-russia-is-obliged-under-bit-to-protect-ukrainian-investors-in-crimea-following-annexation/>, visited on 30 August 2017.

territory in defiance of international law".[17] This may be surprising since a strict application of the duty of non-recognition would seem to oblige tribunals to interpret the territorial application of BITs in a restrictive way and thus to negate its jurisdiction.[18]

2.3   Uncertainties in the Aftermath of Crimea's Annexation

In order to be able to rely on the dispute resolution clause of a certain BIT, investors need to prove that they have made an investment in the territory of the host State. This may be difficult as at the time of investment foreign investors made their investment in the territory of the *de jure* sovereign Ukraine. Moreover, as neither annexation nor occupation can give right to a valid legal title to land, it is unlikely that a tribunal would determine that Crimea has become Russian territory and that therefore Russian BITs apply. Such a finding would be contrary to the duty of non-recognition.

On the other hand, it would be complicated to bring a claim against Ukraine, as any violation of a BIT standard, having occurred after Ukraine had lost control over the territory, could hardly be attributed to Ukraine. According to Article 2 of the Draft Articles on State Responsibility there is an internationally wrongful act of a State only if the State conduct constituting the breach of an international obligation is attributable to that State.[19] Articles 4 to 11 of the Draft Articles regulate the attributability of State conduct in more detail.[20] Pursuant to these Articles, in order for any conduct to be attributable to Ukraine it must be the conduct of either (1) a Ukrainian State organ,[21] or (2) a person or entity empowered by the law of Ukraine to exercise elements of governmental authority or exercise such elements of governmental authority *de facto*,[22] or (3) an organ that is placed at the disposal of Russia by Ukraine,[23] or (4) a person or group of persons acting on the instructions of, or under the direction or control

---

17   *Ibid.*
18   S. Wuschka, 'Erste Krim-Investitionsschiedsklagen nehmen die Zuständigkeitshürde', 493 D *Bofaxe* (2017), <http://www.ifhv.de/documents/bofaxe/bofaxe2017/493d.pdf>, visited on 1 September 2017.
19   International Law Commission, *Draft Articles on Responsibility of States for Internationally Wrongful Acts, with commentaries*, 2001 (U.N. Doc. A/56/10), Art.2, <http://legal.un.org/ilc/texts/instruments/english/commentaries/9_6_2001.pdf>, visited on 29 November 2011.
20   *Ibid.*, Art. 4-11.
21   *Ibid.*, Art.4.
22   *Ibid.*, Art.5 and 9.
23   *Ibid.*, Art.6.

of that State.²⁴ Lastly, State conduct could be attributed to Ukraine if it acknowledged and adopted the conduct as its own.²⁵

Since Crimea's integration into the Russian Federation, the peninsula continues to form *de facto* part of Russia. Ukraine has lost effective control over the territory. It is unlikely that Ukraine has control over any organs, entities or persons acting in the territory of Crimea. It is also improbable that Ukraine would place organs at the disposal of Russia. Moreover, it is highly unlikely that Ukraine would acknowledge and adopt any conduct constituting a breach of a BIT as its own. It results that any violation of a BIT could not be attributed to Ukraine.

Investors might thus find themselves in a legal vacuum, in which their investment is left unprotected and Russia is the party ultimately benefiting from its illegal actions.²⁶ Nevertheless, there seem to be two ways for investors to escape this legal vacuum. Firstly, it may be possible that Russian BITs apply extraterritorially to Crimea as a consequence of it exercising effective control over the territory. And secondly, the law of occupation may impose a duty on the Russian Federation to respect Ukrainian BITs in Crimea as the laws in force in the occupied territory. However, before analysing whether investors and their investments are protected by virtue of extraterritorial application or under the law of occupation, it is necessary to examine more deeply the legal consequences of Crimea's annexation having special regard to the duty of non-recognition and the latter's exception as spelled out by the International Court of Justice (ICJ) in the *Namibia Advisory Opinion*.²⁷

3   Legal Consequences of Crimea's Annexation

3.1   *Crimea's Illegal Annexation*

It is uncontested that Crimea's incorporation into the Russian Federation by way of an incorporation treaty²⁸ constitutes an illegal annexation of the peninsula by Russia. This is due to the latter's military involvement in

---

24   *Ibid.*, Art.8.
25   *Ibid.*, Art.11.
26   Wuschka, *supra* note 11, p. 5.
27   *Legal Consequences for States of the Continued Presence of South Africa in Namibia (South West Africa) notwithstanding Security Council Resolution 276*, 21 June 1971, ICJ, Advisory Opinion, I.C.J. Reports 1971.
28   Договор между Российской Федерацией и Республикой Крым о принятии в Российскую Федерацию Республики Крым и образовании в составе Российской Фе-

the events accompanying Crimea's declaration of independence[29] and the treaty's signature. Even though international law is in general neutral as regards to the legality of declarations of independence, any such declaration will be illegal if it is connected with the unlawful use of force.[30] The international community predominantly concurs that the incorporation of Crimea into the Russian Federation is a case of such illegal annexation.[31]

Annexation in international law is defined as a "domestic legal act of a State purporting to extend sovereignty over a piece of territory over which it has gained effective control through non-consensual, forcible means".[32] As annexation is the result of the unlawful use of force in violation of Article 2(4) of the Charter of the United Nations (UN Charter),[33] an illegal annexation cannot serve as the basis of a valid title to territory.[34] It therefore does not produce any international legal effects. This was confirmed in Security Council Resolution 662 concerning the annexation of Kuwait, which had "no legal validity, and [was] considered null and void".[35] Thus, even though Russia is claiming to be the *de jure* sovereign over the territory of Crimea, this claim proves to be wrong considering international law. As an illegal annexation does not change the legal status of the annexed territory, Ukraine is still to be considered the *de jure* sovereign. Nonetheless, it cannot be denied that Russia exercises *de facto* authority over Crimea.

дерации новых субъектов (18 mars 2014), <http://www.kremlin.ru/news/20605>, visited on 7 September 2017.

29 Государственный Совет Республики Крым, Декларация о независимости Автономной Республики Крым и города Севастополя (11 mars 2014), <http://www.rada.crimea.ua/app/2988>, visited on 7 September 2017.

30 *Accordance with International Law of the Unilateral Declaration of Independence in Respect of Kosovo*, 22 July 2010, ICJ, Advisory Opinion, I.C.J. Reports 2010, para. 81.

31 M. Herdegen, *Völkerrecht* (C. H. Beck, München, 2015) p. 194; S. Hobe and O. Kimminich, *Einführung in das Völkerrecht* (UTB, Stuttgart, 2008) p. 85.

32 D. Costelloe, 'Treaty succession in annexed territory', 65 *International and Comparative Law Quarterly* (2016), p. 353.

33 The Charter of the United Nations (San Francisco, 26 June 1945), ATS 1 / 59 Stat. 1031; TS 993; 3 Bevans 1153, entered into force 24 October 1945, Art. 2(4); *see also* UN General Assembly, *Declaration on Principles of International Law Concerning Friendly Relations and Cooperation Among States in Accordance with the Charter of the United Nations*, 24 October 1970, G.A. Res. 2625 (XXV), 25 UN GAOR Supp. 18 122; 65 AJIL 243 (1971).

34 Herdegen, *supra* note 31, p. 194.

35 UN Security Council, *Security Council resolution 662 (1990) [Iraq-Kuwait]* (S/RES/662).

3.2 The Duty of Non-Recognition

In light of the principle *ex injuria jus non oritur,* Article 41(2) of the ILC Draft Articles on State Responsibility establishes a duty not to recognise as lawful a situation created by a serious breach of an obligation arising under a peremptory norm of general international law, nor render aid or assistance in maintaining such situation.[36] This duty of non-recognition is an *erga omnes* obligation anchored in international customary law.[37] The term recognition is used as a concept of international law and is not related with recognition of statehood. The duty of non-recognition includes not only a duty to withhold explicit recognition but also a duty not to implicitly recognise the consequences of the annexation.[38] Moreover, the obligation to abstain from rendering aid or assistance in maintaining a situation created by means of a serious breach of a peremptory norm has an extended scope of application as it includes acts which may not imply recognition.[39]

Only four States worldwide have recognised Crimea's integration into the Russian Federation.[40] In the aftermath of the referendum leading to Crimea's declaration of independence, the UN General Assembly (GA) issued a resolution calling upon "all States, international organizations and specialized agencies not to recognize any alteration of the status of the Autonomous Republic of Crimea and the city of Sevastopol on the basis of the [...] referendum and to refrain from any action or dealing that might be interpreted as recognizing any such altered status".[41] Non-recognition means that the purported change of the legal status of Crimea must be treated as non-existing,[42] which confirms that despite Russia's

---

36   *Draft Articles on State Responsibility, supra* note 19, Art. 41.
37   *Military and Paramilitary Activities in and against Nicaragua (Nicaragua v. United States of America)*, 27 June 1986, ICJ, Judgement, I.C.J. Reports 1984, para. 188. The ICJ confirms that Article 1 of the 1970 Declaration on Friendly Relations represents international customary law. According to Art. 1 "[t]he territory of a State shall not be the object of acquisition by another State resulting from the threat or use of force. No territorial acquisition resulting from the threat or use of force shall be recognized as legal."
38   Report of the International Law Commission, GAOR, 56th Session, Suppl. No.10 A/56/10 (2001) 287, para. 5; *ILC Draft Articles on State Responsibility, supra* note 19, commentary to Art. 41.
39   *Ibid.*
40   Afghanistan, Nicaragua, Cuba and Venezuela.
41   UN General Assembly, *Territorial Integrity of Ukraine: resolution adopted by the General Assembly* (A/RES/68/262), para. 6.
42   M. Bothe, 'The Current Status of Crimea: Russian Territory, Occupied Territory or What?', 53 *Military L. & L. War Rev.* (2014) p. 101.

exercise of *de facto* authority over Crimea, the latter remains Ukrainian territory.

The annexation of Crimea is not the first situation which has required States to withhold recognition. Other examples are the illegal continuation of South Africa's presence in Namibia[43] or Turkey's occupation of Northern Cyprus following its purported separation from the Republic of Cyprus.[44] In the context of South Africa's illegal presence in Namibia, the ICJ analysed the implications of the duty of non-recognition on treaty relations between an illegally occupying power and other States.[45]

According to the ICJ in the *Namibia Advisory Opinion*, States are under an obligation not to enter into treaty relations with an illegal regime, when the latter purports to act on behalf of the territory.[46] With respect to existing bilateral treaties, States must abstain from invoking or applying those treaties or provisions of treaties concluded by the illegal regime on behalf of or concerning the occupied territory which involve active intergovernmental co-operation.[47] However, multilateral treaties may continue to apply if their non-performance may adversely affect the people of the occupied territory.[48] The Court further established a general exception, known as the Namibia exception, clarifying that "the non-recognition of South Africa's administration of the territory should not result in depriving the people of Namibia of any advantages derived from international co-operation".[49]

3.3 *The Namibia Exception*

The Namibia exception was formulated by the ICJ in its *Namibia Advisory Opinion* as an exception to the duty of non-recognition. In 2004, the ICJ confirmed its position in its Advisory Opinion on the *Consequences of the Construction of a Wall (Wall Advisory Opinion)*.[50] The principle *ex injuria jus non oritur* is balanced by the principle *ex factis jus oritur*. While the

---

43 See *Namibia Advisory Opinion*, supra note 27.
44 See *Cyprus* v. *Turkey*, 10 May 2001, ECHR, no. 25781/94 paras. 13-16, <http://hudoc.echr.coe.int/eng?i=001-59454>, visited on 27 November 2017; *Loizidou* v. *Turkey*, 18 December 1996, ECHR, no. 15318/89, para. 16, <http://hudoc.echr.coe.int/eng?i=001-58007>, visited on 27 November 2017.
45 See *Namibia Advisory Opinion*, supra note 27.
46 *Ibid.*, para. 122.
47 *Ibid.*
48 *Ibid.*
49 *Ibid.*, para. 125.
50 *Legal Consequences of the Construction of a Wall in the Occupied Palestinian Territory*, 9 July 2004, ICJ, Advisory Opinion, I.C.J. Reports 2004.

emphasis of the first principle is the invalidity of the acts of the illegal regime, the second and opposite principle mandates that acts of the illegal regime may carry legal consequences in the view that facts create law in certain circumstances.[51] Thus, while the duty of non-recognition requires States to treat any purported change of the legal status of Crimea as non-existing, it is clear that they must not ignore Russia's *de facto* control over the territory.[52]

According to the exception, an occupying power is under an obligation to perform certain administrative tasks to guarantee a proper administration of the social life of the population in the occupied territory.[53] The ICJ stated that:

> [i]n general, the non-recognition of South Africa's administration of the Territory should not result in depriving the people of Namibia of any advantages derived from international co-operation. In particular, while official acts performed by the Government of South Africa on behalf of or concerning Namibia ... are illegal and invalid, this invalidity cannot be extended to those acts, such as, for instances, the registration of births, deaths and marriages, the effects of which can be ignored only to the detriment of the inhabitants of the Territory.[54]

The main rationale of the Namibia exception is the well-being of the local population, in the sense that strict compliance with the duty of non-recognition should not go as far as to being detrimental to the inhabitants of the occupied territory. It may therefore be possible that BITs could be covered by the Namibia exception with the result that States would not be under an obligation to abstain from invoking or applying these treaties.

The Namibia exception concerns internal acts of the illegal regime.[55] It is possible to give exceptional recognition to certain internal acts of the illegal regime, if doing otherwise would be harmful for the well-being of

---

51   J. Crawford, *The Creation of States* (Oxford University Press, Oxford, 2006) pp. 166-167.
52   Bothe, *supra* note 42, p. 109.
53   J. Vidmar, 'Territorial Entitlement and Exit Scenarios', in M. Nicolini *et al.* (eds), *Law, Territory and Conflict Resolution* (Brill Nijhoff, Leiden, 2016) p. 115.
54   *Namibia Advisory Opinion, supra* note 27, para. 125.
55   Y. Ronen, *Transition from Illegal Regimes under International Law* (Cambridge University Press, Cambridge, 2011) p. 83.

the population.⁵⁶ Which internal acts fall under the exception has been subject to numerous interpretations.

In his separate opinion in the *Namibia Advisory Opinion*, Judge de Castro suggested that there must be a distinction between the private and the public sector.⁵⁷ While acts of the illegal regime concerning the rights of private persons must be regarded as valid, public acts should not.⁵⁸

A second interpretation was given by Judge Onyeama, who affirmed that the duty of non-recognition concerns only acts aimed at or being capable of entrenching the illegal regime.⁵⁹ This means that any act, regardless of its purpose or form, which is capable of advancing the aim of establishing sovereignty by the occupant, is not to be recognised.⁶⁰

A third possibility is applying a literal interpretation of the exception, which is based on a case-by-case examination of whether a certain act would be detrimental for the inhabitants of the territory.⁶¹ This is also in line with paragraph 122 of the *Namibia Advisory Opinion*, in which the Court stated that multilateral conventions may be applied if their non-performance would be detrimental to the people of the occupied territory.⁶² This interpretation is based on a wide interpretation of the prohibition and its exception with the result that otherwise illegal acts may be recognised for the sake of the protection of the population and shall serve as a basis for the following analysis.

When interpreting the expression "inhabitants of the territory" literally, the beneficiaries of the exception are the individuals and the population as a whole living in the annexed or occupied territory.⁶³ Nevertheless, the exception can also be interpreted more expansively as including

---

56   Ibid.
57   *Legal Consequences for States of the Continued Presence of South Africa in Namibia (South West Africa) notwithstanding Security Council Resolution 276*, 21 June 1971, ICJ, Advisory Opinion, I.C.J., Separate Opinion of Judge de Castro, pp. 218-219, <http://www.icj-cij.org/files/case-related/53/053-19710621-ADV-01-07-EN.pdf>, visited on 26 November 2017.
58   Ibid.
59   *Legal Consequences for States of the Continued Presence of South Africa in Namibia (South West Africa) notwithstanding Security Council Resolution 276*, 21 June 1971, ICJ, Advisory Opinion, Separate Opinion of Judge Onyeama, p. 149, <http://www.icj-cij.org/files/case-related/53/053-19710621-ADV-01-05-EN.pdf>, visited on 26 November 2017.
60   Ronen, *supra* note 55, p. 87.
61   *Namibia Advisory Opinion*, *supra* note 27, paras. 99-100.
62   Ibid., para. 122.
63   Ronen, *supra* note 55, p. 98.

the interests of any person affected by the occupation or annexation even if that person is outside the occupied or annexed territory.[64] This was confirmed by the European Court of Human Rights (ECtHR) in its jurisprudence concerning the illegal regime in Northern Cyprus.[65] Such interpretation would allow the inclusion of investors, having invested in the territory, into the scope of the exception. If this is the case, it could be possible for other States to acknowledge the applicability of Russia's BITs on behalf of the territory of Crimea without acting contrary to the duty of non-recognition. This would allow for an extraterritorial application of Russian BITs. However, it is not quite clear whether a duty for Russia to apply its BITs in Crimea can be deducted from the Namibia exception. The exception seems to be intended as an *ex post facto* rule, which governs the internal acts of the illegal regime, while the prohibition to apply bilateral treaties is the *ex ante* control of the international conduct with the aim of preventing the illegal regime from consolidating its control.[66]

The ICJ excluded from the suspension of treaties multilateral conventions if their non-application would deprive the people of Namibia of any advantages resulting from international co-operation. Does this mean that the Court explicitly excluded the recognition of bilateral treaties even if their suspension would have the same consequences?

It follows from the exception that any internal act by an illegal regime in accordance with a bilateral treaty aimed at the protection of the population or other persons affected by the regime can be recognised. Benvenisti argues that the exception applies also to bilateral and regional treaties such as for example free trade areas, as these are beneficial to the population of the occupied territory.[67] The Namibia exception thus allows States to recognise the application of Russian BITs by Russia in Crimea and especially because BITs do not involve active inter-governmental co-operation but provide a set of rules addressed to investors.

---

64   Ibid.
65   *Demopoulos and Others* v. *Turkey*, 1 March 2010, ECHR, nos. 46113/99, 3843/02, 13751/02, 13466/03, 10200/04, 14163/04, 19993/04, 21819/04, <http://hudoc.echr.coe.int/eng?i=001-97649>, visited on 27 November 2017; *Cyprus* v. *Turkey*, 12 May 2014, ECHR, no. 25781/94, <http://hudoc.echr.coe.int/eng?i=001-144151>, visited on 27 November 2017; *Xenides-Arestis* v. *Turkey*, 22 December 2005, ECHR, no. 46347/99, <http://hudoc.echr.coe.int/eng?i=001-71800>, visited on 27 November 2017.
66   Ronen, *supra* note 55, p. 83.
67   E. Benvenisti, *The International Law of Occupation* (Oxford University Press, Oxford, 2013) p. 85.

Nevertheless, a positive duty for the Russian Federation to apply its BITs to Crimea cannot be derived from the exception.

Such a positive duty has been established by the ECtHR in regards to the European Convention of Human Rights (ECHR); the ECtHR concluded that the Convention applied extraterritorially in Northern Cyprus. Similar to the events in Crimea, Northern Cyprus had also issued an illegal declaration of independence after significant involvement of and occupation by Turkish military forces.[68] Whether there is a similar duty for the Russian Federation to apply its BITs extraterritorially shall be determined below.

4 Applicability of BITs under the Law of Treaties

The extraterritorial application of treaties forms part of the law of treaties. The law of treaties is of importance in situations involving legal or illegal attempts in changing a title to land.

As mentioned above it may be possible that Russian BITs apply in Crimea extraterritorially. However, in order to determine whether this is the case, it is necessary to start by defining the general territorial scope of treaties.

4.1 Defining Territory

The most important instrument for treaty interpretation is the 1969 Vienna Convention on the Law of Treaties (VCLT).[69] However, no definition of the meaning of territory can be found in the VCLT. Other than that, territory is usually defined as "all the land, internal waters and territorial sea, and the airspace above them, over which a party has sovereignty".[70] Article 29 VCLT stipulates that "unless a different intention appears from the treaty or is otherwise established, a treaty is binding upon each party in respect of its entire territory".[71] This means that the concluding parties of a treaty are free to provide, either explicitly or implicitly, for the extraterritorial application of their treaty. Furthermore, it is widely accepted that

---

68   *See* UN Security Council, *Security Council resolution 541 (1983)* [*Cyprus*] (S/RES/541); Herdegen, *supra* note 31, p. 82.

69   Vienna Convention on the Law of Treaties, UN Doc. A/Conf.39/27; 1155 UNTS 331; 8 ILM 679 (1969); 63 AJIL 875 (1969), entered into force 27 January 1980.

70   A. Aust, *Modern Treaty law and Practice* (Cambridge University Press, Cambridge, 2000) p. 162.

71   VCLT, *supra* note 69, Art. 29.

Article 29 VCLT implies the so-called moving treaty frontiers rule, which automatically extends the application of a treaty to newly acquired territory.[72] The moving-treaty frontiers rule is enshrined in Article 15 of the Vienna Convention on Succession of States in respect of Treaties (VCST).[73]

4.2 The Moving Treaty-Frontiers Rule

The moving treaty-frontiers rule forms part of the law of State succession. Any situation of State succession triggers a wide range of legal issues on the domestic and international level. One of these issues is the fate of treaties in such situations. While Crimea is still legally part of Ukraine, it is clear that, *de facto,* it has been integrated into the Russian Federation. Therefore, it is necessary to examine whether the law of State succession in respect of treaties allows one to draw conclusions concerning the application of BITs in Crimea after its annexation.

In this context, the VCST offers some insights. While it is disputed whether the VCST in its entirety reflects international customary law,[74] it appears that the relevant article to the present case, Article 15 VCST, is indeed a codification of pre-existing customary law.[75] The VCST divides situations of State succession into three categories, the third of which is the one of interest as regards to Crimea. While the first and second categories are concerned with newly independent States and the secession and dissolution of States not emerging from colonisation, Article 15 VCST embraces succession in part of the territory stipulating that when part of the territory of a State becomes part of the territory of another existing State, then the treaties of the predecessor State cease to be in force in that territory and the treaties of the successor State apply as of the date of succession.[76] This so-called moving treaty-frontiers rule is to be regarded as a

---

72 R. Happ and S. Wuschka, 'Horror Vacui: Or Why Investment Treaties Should Apply to Illegally Annexed Territories', 33:3 *Journal of International Arbitration,* Kluwer Law International (2016) p. 5.

73 Vienna Convention on Succession of States in Respect of Treaties, 1946 UNTS 3; 17 ILM 1488 (1978); 72 AJIL 971 (1978), entered into force 6 November 1996, Art. 15.

74 Herdegen, *supra* note 31, p. 223; Hobe, *supra* note 31, p. 105; M. Krajewski, *Völkerrecht* (Nomos, Baden-Baden, 2016) p. 73.

75 Costelloe, *supra* note 32, p. 344; *Sanum Investments Ltd* v. *The Government of the Lao People's Democratic Republic,* Award on Jurisdiction, 13 December 2013, UNCITRAL, PCA Case No 2013-13, para. 270; UN Office of Legal Affairs, *Final Clauses of Multilateral Treaties: Handbook* (United Nations Publication, 2003) p. 78.

76 VCST, *supra* note 73, Art. 15.

special expression of Article 29 VCLT.[77] Similarly, Article 15 VCST applies only if it does not "appear from the treaty or is otherwise established that the application of the treaty to that territory would be incompatible with the object and purpose of the treaty or would radically change the conditions for its operation".[78]

The arbitral decision *Sanum* v. *Laos,* in which the arbitral tribunal extended the China-Laos BIT to the Macao,[79] provides an illustration of the moving-treaty frontiers rule in relation to the object and purpose of BITs. Macao had been under the administration of Portugal until 1999, when it was transferred to the People's Republic of China.[80] The tribunal held that

> The purpose [of the BIT in question] is twofold: to protect the investor and develop economic cooperation. The Tribunal does not find ... that the extension of the PRC/Laos BIT could be contrary to such a dual purpose. In fact, the larger scope the Treaty has, the better fulfilled the purposes of the Treaty are in this case: more investors – who could not otherwise be protected – are internationally protected, and the economic cooperation benefits a larger territory that would otherwise not receive such benefit."[81]

While under international law previous decisions are not authoritative and therefore do not bind other arbitral tribunals,[82] the *Sanum* v. *Laos,* nevertheless, gives important insights into the effects of the moving-treaty frontiers rule. However, in the case of Macao the transfer of title was lawful and executed by means of a treaty.[83] This constitutes a fundamen-

---

[77] Vienna Convention on Succession of States in Respect of Treaties, with Commentaries, Art. 14(1)-(2), <http://legal.un.org/ilc/texts/instruments/english/commentaries/3_2_1974.pdf>, visited on 27 November 2017; VCLT, *supra* note 69, Art. 29.

[78] VCST, *supra* note 73, Art. 15.

[79] *Sanum* v. *Laos, supra* note 75.

[80] Joint Declaration of the Government of the Portuguese Republic and the Government of the People's Republic of China on the Question of Macao (with annexes) (People's Republic of China–Portuguese Republic) (signed 13 April 1987, entered into force 15 January 1988) 1498 UNTS 228.

[81] *Sanum* v. *Laos, supra* note 75, para. 240.

[82] Dolzer, *supra* note 8, p. 33.

[83] Joint Declaration of the Government of the Portuguese Republic and the Government of the People's Republic of China on the Question of Macao, *supra* note 80, Art. 1.

tal difference with the present situation involving annexation. An important limitation to the scope of the Convention is enshrined in Article 6 VCST, which confines the application of the Convention to "the effects of a succession of States occurring in conformity with international law and, in particular, the principles of international law embodied in the Charter of the United Nations".[84] The term 'territory' of Article 15 VCST and Article 29 VCLT is thus to be regarded as referring only to the *de jure* territory of a State and not to territory over which a State exercises effective control by virtue of an illegal annexation. Therefore, one would conclude that because the annexation of Crimea was contrary to the obligation to refrain from the use of force enshrined in Article 2(4) UN Charter, Russia's BITs cannot apply to Crimea by virtue of the moving treaty-frontiers rule. Nevertheless, as it is disputed whether the VCST as a whole reflects international customary law, it could be conceivable that customary law provides a possibility to apply the moving treaty-frontier rule to situations of annexation. However, there exists no evidence in State practice that would affirm the existence of such a customary rule.

4.3 Le Fait Accompli

It may be conceivable that the moving-treaty frontiers rule becomes applicable as time elapses. In international law, there is no clear distinguishing line between occupation and annexation. Even though it is widely accepted that annexation cannot result in a legal title to territory because the acquisition of territory by means of the use of force is prohibited under public international law, one may argue that over time acquiescence can legalise such a transfer in territory.[85] Moreover, occupation is primarily seen as a temporary status. Is it thus possible that time may 'cure' the illegality of occupation or annexation?

Since the opposing voices against Crimea's integration into the Russian Federation seem to be fading, it may be possible that such resignation (or even acceptance) points towards the creation of a legal title.[86] Consequently, even an illegal transfer of territory, when enduring over a significant period of time, may eventually be regarded as a *fait accompli*,

---

84   VCST, *supra* note 73, Art. 6; VCST, with Commentaries, *supra* note 77, commentary to Art. 6 and Art. 14.
85   J. Klabbers, *International Law* (Cambridge University Press, Cambridge, 2013) p. 83.
86   Ibid.

if a return to the *status quo ante* is not in sight.[87] An example of such a *fait accompli* is the occupation by Indonesia of the territory of East Timor.[88]

Some authors have argued that the duty of non-recognition of illegal annexations cannot amount to a duty of insulation of the territory.[89] This would especially be the case during a long-term occupation, when the occupying power should be able to conclude treaties on behalf of and concerning the territory as the legitimate sovereign is no longer able to do so.[90] This could be justified by a necessity not to harm the local population or by pure pragmatism. As regards to the Occupied Palestinian Territory, many States have entered into certain practical arrangements with Israel in order to guarantee diplomatic and consular protection on the territory even though this is contrary to the duty of non-recognition.[91]

However, it seems that the vast majority of States are not ready to forget about the illegality of Crimea's annexation which crystalizes in the adoption and prolongation of political and economic sanctions.[92] Sanctions as well as the duty of non-recognition must be seen as a decentralised enforcement mechanism,[93] which aim at forcing the perpetrating party to undo its violation of international law. The international community has thus not acquiesced to the annexation of Crimea and a general application of the moving-treaty frontiers rule has to be ruled out. Nevertheless, there may be another possibility to acknowledge to applicability of Russian BITs to Crimea by way of extraterritorial application.

4.4 *Extraterritorial Application*

While Article 15 VCST and Article 29 VCLT establish the *prima facie* application of treaties in the entire *de jure* territory of a State, they do not necessarily confine the application of treaties to that territory only.[94] The doctrine of extraterritorial application proves this point. Concerning extraterritorial application, the main question is to what extent Russia's BITs may be binding on the territory of Crimea, over which it exercises effective control. The extraterritorial application of treaties may be re-

---

87 Costelloe, *supra* note 32, p. 347.
88 Ibid.
89 Bothe, *supra* note 42, p. 109.
90 Ibid.
91 Ibid.; *Namibia Advisory Opinion*, *supra* note 27, para. 122.
92 S. Secrieru, *Russia under Sanctions: Assessing the Damage, Scrutinising Adaptation and Evasion* (PISM, Warsaw, 2015) pp. 19-25.
93 Costelloe, *supra* note 32, p. 356.
94 Ibid., p. 349.

garded as a sort of exception to the impossibility to apply the moving frontiers-treaty rule to annexed or occupied territories. Article 29 VCLT can be interpreted to contain a general presumption against the extraterritorial application of treaties.[95] This presumption can be overcome by means of a specific provision contained in a treaty.[96] Or, it can be established otherwise that the parties intended the treaty to have extraterritorial effect.[97]

4.4.1　Extraterritorial Application of BITs by Means of Treaty Provision

In conformity with Article 29 VCLT, the concluding parties of a treaty are free to agree on the extraterritorial application of BITs by virtue of a treaty provision included into the BITs themselves. In that case, the question is one of treaty interpretation according to Article 31 VCLT.[98] Like most BITs, Russian and Ukrainian BITs refer to territory only in general terms. Despite that fact, BITs regulate State conduct in respect of a certain territory. BITs define the terms of investor and investment with reference to the parties' territory and thus limit the substantive protection of the BITs geographically. What is more, many treaties, as in the Russia-Ukraine BIT, explicitly refer to territory 'in accordance with international law', which could even be interpreted as excluding territories acquired by internationally illegal means.[99] However, treaties must not only be interpreted literally but also with a reference to their object and purposes, which may allow to expand their territorial scope and allow for their extraterritorial application.

4.4.2　The Extraterritorial Application of Human Rights Treaties

In general, extraterritorial application primarily concerns treaties meant to govern State conduct in general and not with respect to a certain territory, as their object and purpose goes beyond the regulation of State conduct exclusively on its territory.[100] Treaties of armed conflict and human rights treaties are a prominent example of treaties governing State con-

---

95　N. Burke, 'A Change in Perspectives: Looking at Occupation through the Lens of the Law of Treaties', 41:1 *New York University Journal of International Law and Politics* (2008-2009) p. 122.
96　VCLT, *supra* note 69, Art. 29.
97　*Ibid.*
98　*Ibid.*, Art. 31.
99　Russia-Ukraine BIT, *supra* note 3, Art. 1(4).
100　Costelloe, *supra* note 32, p. 361.

duct in general. In the case of human rights treaties, it seems that these may also apply extraterritorially by virtue of their object and purpose, which is the protection of rights and interests of natural and legal persons. Thus, human rights treaties create obligations for the State towards individuals, not towards other States.[101]

Extraterritorial application certainly occurs for treaties that apply extraterritorially by definition, such as treaties of armed conflict.[102] However, in opposition to treaties pertaining to the law of armed conflict, there is no rule in international law calling for an extraterritorial application of human rights treaties in all cases, with the result that a case-by-case analysis will be necessary.[103]

Certain scholars are of the opinion that occupied territory can be considered *de facto* territory of the occupying power with the effect that certain obligations, and especially human rights obligations of the occupying power apply in the occupied territory.[104] The ICJ confirmed the extraterritorial application of the International Covenant on Civil and Political Rights (ICCPR),[105] and the International Covenant on Economic, Social and Cultural Rights (ICESCR)[106] in its *Wall Advisory Opinion*.[107] In the advisory opinion the ICJ held that the construction of the wall in Palestine is tantamount to a *de facto* annexation of the Palestinian ter-

---

101   Burke, *supra* note 95, p. 123.
102   *For example* Convention (IV) Respecting the Laws and Customs of War on Land and its Annex: Regulation concerning the Laws and Customs of War on Land (1907 Hague Convention IV) 187 CTS 227; 1 Bevans 631 entered into force 26 January 1910; 1949 Geneva Convention (I) for the Amelioration of the Condition of the Wounded and Sick in Armed Forces in the Field 75 UNTS 31/ [1958] ATS No 21 entered into force 21 October 1950; 1949 Geneva Convention (II) for the Amelioration of the Condition of Wounded, Sick and Shipwrecked Members of Armed Forces at Sea 75 UNTS 85/ [1958] ATS No 21 entered into force 21 October 1950; 1949 Geneva Convention (III) Relative to the Treatment of Prisoners of War 75 UNTS 135/ [1958] ATS No 21 entered into force 21 October 1950; 1949 Geneva Convention (IV) Relative to the Protection of Civilian Persons in Time of War 75 UNTS 287/ 1958 ATS No 21 entered into force 21 October 1950.
103   Costelloe, *supra* note 32, p. 362.
104   Burke, *supra* note 95, p. 120.
105   International Covenant on Civil and Political Rights (ICCPR), 999 UNTS 171 and 1057 UNTS 407 / [1980] ATS 23 / 6 ILM 368 (1967) entered into force 23 March 1976.
106   International Covenant on Economic, Social and Cultural Rights (ICESCR), 993 UNTS 3 / [1976] ATS 5 / 6 ILM 360 (1967) entered into force 3 January 1976.
107   The ICJ affirmed that "it is not excluded that [the Covenant] applies both to territories over which a State party has sovereignty and to those over which that State exercises territorial jurisdiction" (*Legal Consequences of the Construction of a Wall, supra* note 50, para. 112).

ritories.¹⁰⁸ Therefore, these territories could be said to constitute part of the territory of Israel for the purpose of the application of these Conventions. Furthermore, the Court held that the ICCPR was applicable to acts done by a State "in exercise of its jurisdiction outside its own territory."¹⁰⁹ Similarly, in its *Armed Activities Decision*, the ICJ held that multilateral human rights treaties apply "in respect of acts done by a State in the exercise of its jurisdiction outside its own territory, *particularly in occupied territories*".¹¹⁰

Moreover, the ECtHR has addressed the issue of extraterritorial application as regards to the applicability of the European Convention on Human Rights (ECHR) in Cyprus.¹¹¹ The Court concluded that due to the influence of the Turkish military and other support provided by the Turkish government to the local administration, Turkey can be held responsible for acts of that administration.¹¹² In that sense, the Court extended Turkey's jurisdiction to the territory of Northern Cyprus, over which it exercises effective control.¹¹³ The Court thus established a positive duty for Turkey to comply with the ECHR on the territory of Northern Cyprus.

Another leading case on the extraterritorial application of the ECHR is *Loizidou*, in which the ECtHR considered that a violation of the property rights of a Greek Cypriot in the territory of Northern Cyprus was attributable to Turkey, since the latter exercised effective control over the territory, affirming that such effective control constituted jurisdiction within the meaning of Article 1 ECHR.¹¹⁴ It follows that the jurisdiction under Article 1 ECHR is not restricted to the national territory of the contracting parties but includes the territory which is under the effective control of a contracting party.

Thus, both the ICJ and the ECtHR refer to jurisdiction when ruling on the extraterritorial application of the treaties in question. As many human rights treaties define the obligations of States towards individuals

---

108 *Ibid.*, para. 121.
109 *Ibid.*, para. 111.
110 *Armed Activities on the Territory of the Congo (Democratic Republic of the Congo v. Uganda)*, 19 December 2005, ICJ, Judgment, I.C.J. Reports, para. 216.
111 *Cyprus v. Turkey, supra* note 44, para. 77.
112 *Ibid.*
113 *Ibid.*
114 *Loizidou v. Turkey, supra* note 44, para. 62; European Convention for the Protection of Human Rights and Fundamental Freedoms, as amended by Protocols Nos. 11 and 14 (ECHR) ETS 5; 213 UNTS 221 entered into force 3 March 1953. Art. 1: "The High Contracting Parties shall secure to everyone within their jurisdiction the rights and freedoms defined in Section I of this Convention."

under their jurisdiction and not with reference to territory,[115] this may indicate that the parties intended to apply these treaties extraterritorially. The usage of the term jurisdiction instead of territory can indeed be interpreted as pointing towards the parties' intention to apply these treaties extraterritorially in compliance with the 'otherwise established' language of Article 29 VCLT.[116]

4.4.3 The Extraterritorial Application of BITs

While BITs do not fall under the category of treaties that by definition are to be applied extraterritorially and they are not human rights treaties. Furthermore, BITs are not meant to regulate State conduct in general. Instead they make specific reference to territory and are applicable only when the investment is made in the territory of the host State. In opposition to Article 1 ECHR, bilateral treaties do not refer to jurisdiction but to territory, which could point towards the necessity to interpret the territorial scope of BITs in a restrictive manner excluding their extraterritorial application.

Moreover, in contrast to human rights treaties, BITs are not multilateral but bilateral treaties, which might put States under the obligation not to recognise the application of Russian BITs in Crimea as a consequence of the duty of non-recognition. This is because the application of Russia's BITs in the territory of Crimea, which does still constitute Ukrainian territory, could be interpreted as a violation of Ukraine's sovereignty.[117] Despite all this, it may still be possible to apply the doctrine of extraterritorial application by analogy. Since Russia exercises effective control over the territory of Crimea, which it has annexed, Crimea should be regarded as Russia's territory for the purposes of BITs. This is because BITs essentially have the same object and purpose as human rights treaties which is the protection of the rights and interests of natural and legal persons.[118]

This is reaffirmed by the rationale of the Namibia exception. It results from the exception that the interests of the sovereign must be balanced against the needs of the local population. Thus, if the non-application of BITs caused unnecessary hardship to the local population this could be a reason to opt for extraterritorial application of a treaty.[119]

---

115   Burke, *supra* note 95, p. 124.
116   Costelloe, note 32, p. 372.
117   T. Meron, 'Applicability of Multilateral Conventions to Occupied Territories', 72 American Journal International Law (1978), p. 550.
118   *Sanum v. Laos, supra* note 75, para. 240.
119   *Ibid.*

Even though BITs are not multilateral treaties, their suspension would nonetheless deprive the investors of the advantages established by the system of BITs. In investment law, multilateral treaties are scarce; instead, investment protection is largely based on an extensive net of BITs. This particularity of international investment protection should not deprive investors of their protection in situations of occupation or annexation. Therefore, this extensive net of BITs should be treated in the same manner as any multilateral treaty. In that sense, it should be noted that at the time the Court pronounced the *Namibia Advisory Opinion*, the proliferation of BITs had just started, which makes it unlikely that the Court meant to explicitly exclude such treaties from the scope of the exception.

Ultimately, States should not be able to benefit from any illegal transfer of territory and should also not be able to escape obligations, which would be the case if Russian BITs would not be applicable in Crimea. Such a result would be contrary to the object and purpose of BITs, which is the furthering and maintenance of economic development through effective investment protection.

Therefore, it should be concluded that Russia has a duty to apply its BITs in Crimea by way of extraterritorial application. This seems to be in line with the conclusion made by the arbitral tribunal in its interim award in February 2017, in which the tribunal decided to apply the Russia-Ukraine to the occupying power of an illegally occupied territory. Nevertheless, this raises some issues regarding the temporal scope of these BITs, which will be treated below.

4.4.4   The Temporal Scope of BITs

Even if the annexing State's treaties apply with respect to the territory of Crimea, the principle of non-retroactivity, enshrined in Article 28 VCLT,[120] still governs. According to Article 28 VCLT, any treaty's provisions do not bind a party in relation to any act or fact which took place or any situation which ceased to exist before the date of the entry into force of the treaty with respect to that party, unless a different intention appears from the treaty or is otherwise established.[121] Moreover, Article 13 of the ILC's Draft Articles on State Responsibility confirms that "an act of a State does not constitute a breach of an international obligation un-

---

120   VCLT, *supra* note 69, Art. 28.
121   *Ibid.*

less the State is bound by the obligation in question at the time the act occurs".[122]

In this context, a problem may arise as regards to investments made in Crimea before its annexation, since these investments were made under Ukrainian and not Russian BITs. An additional issue arises for Ukrainian investors and their investments in Crimea. As the purported investments have been made in Crimea prior to its annexation by Russia in February 2014, these were domestic investments as they were made on domestic territory according to domestic law. BITs, however, were never intended to protect domestic but only foreign investment made on the territory of the other contracting party. It is thus questionable whether Russia can be held responsible for breaches of investments that were initially made as foreign investments under Ukrainian BITs or as domestic investments under Ukrainian law. This is only the case if it can be established that Russia was under the obligation to apply its BITs to these investments at the time of occurrence of such breach.

In the case of Crimea, the critical date is not the date of entry into force of Russia's BITs but the date as of which Russia's BITs apply extraterritorially to Crimea. Russia's BITs should apply to Crimea from the moment the Russian Federation took effective control over Crimea. While it is difficult to determine an exact date, it is likely that effective control can be established as early as the date of the referendum or at the latest, as of the date of the signature of the integration treaty.

Many investment treaties provide that their substantive protection shall apply to all investments, regardless of whether they were made before or after their entry into force.[123] In this case, it should be established by analogy that the extraterritorial application of Russian BITs providing for such a clause should extend to existing investments, both by international and Ukrainian investors.

Nevertheless, the absence of such a clause does not necessarily mean that a treaty applies only to investments made after its entry into force.[124] The Russia-Ukraine BIT is an example of a treaty that is silent on this question.[125] However, if Russia's duty to apply its BITs to investments in Crimea were confined to investments made after taking effective control over the territory, this would certainly be detrimental for those affected

---

122   *ILC Draft Articles on State Responsibility*, *supra* note 19, Art. 13.
123   Dolzer, *supra* note 8, p. 41.
124   *Ibid.*
125   Russia-Ukraine BIT, *supra* note 3, Art. 14.

by the occupation. In that case, the extraterritorial application of Russia's BITs would be deprived from any actual effect. Therefore, Russia's duty to apply the substantive provisions of its BITs extraterritorially should be interpreted as including existing investments, if these are not explicitly excluded in the treaty.

4.5   Conclusion on the Applicability of Russia's BITs in Crimea

It has been established above that Russia's BITs apply in the territory of Crimea by way of extraterritorial application. This is the result of an interpretation of the object and purposes of BITs in light of the core principle of the Namibia exception. Many would certainly not agree with such a wide interpretation of the territorial scope of BITs. Nevertheless, this seems to be in line with the argumentation adopted by the arbitral tribunal administered by the PCA, when it decided that BITs apply to the occupying power of an illegally occupied territory. Awaiting the publishing of the interim award, only the future will show whether this assumption is correct.

5   Applicability of BITs under the Law of Belligerent Occupation

5.1   The Applicability of the Law of Belligerent Occupation

In addition to the law of treaties, the law of occupation may be instructive as regards to the applicability of BITs in Crimea. However, before turning to an analysis of the impact the law of occupation may have on the applicability of BITs in Crimea, it shall be determined whether Crimea is indeed to be regarded as a territory under belligerent occupation.

The concept of belligerent occupation is an integral part of war and as such is governed by the law of armed conflict.[126] As a part of the law of armed conflict, the law of occupation was codified in the 1907 Hague Regulations, the 1949 Geneva Conventions and the First Additional Protocol to the Geneva Conventions.[127] With the exception of the First Additional Protocol it is commonly accepted that these instruments reflect

---

126   P. Daillier et al., Droit international public (L.G.D.J., Paris, 2009) p. 1080.
127   1907 Hague Convention IV, supra note 102; 1949 Geneva Convention (I), supra note 102; 1949 Geneva Convention (II), supra note 102; 1949 Geneva Convention (III), supra note 102; 1949 Geneva Convention (IV), supra note 102; 1977 Protocol Additional to the Geneva Conventions of 12 August 1949, and relating to the Protection of Victims of International Armed Conflicts (Protocol I) 1125 UNTS 3/ 1991 ATS No 29/ 16 ILM 1391 (1977) entered into force 7 December 1978.

international customary law.[128] These sources focus on the protection of the interests of mainly three actors: the population of the occupied territory, the occupying power and the displaced sovereign.[129] In this sense, the law of occupation regulates how the occupied territory and the local population must be administered.[130] Moreover, one of the goals of the law of occupation is minimizing the economic loss to civilians.[131]

Regarding the material scope of the application of the law of occupation as part of the law of armed conflict, a distinction must be drawn between the occurrence of occupation in the course of an armed conflict and an occupation met with no armed resistance. The applicability of the law of occupation for situations falling under the first category is enshrined in §1 of common Article 2 of the Geneva Conventions, according to which "the Convention shall apply to all cases of declared war or of any other armed conflict which may arise between two or more High Contracting Parties, even if the state of war is not recognised by one of them."[132] For the second category, §2 of common Article 2 stipulates that the law of armed conflict, and more specifically the law of occupation, shall apply "to all cases of partial or total occupation of the territory of a High Contracting Party, even if the said occupation meets with no armed resistance".[133] However, it is important to note that this distinction does not bear any consequences for the application of the law of occupation, in the sense that there would be different rules depending on which type of occupation exists in a certain territory.

In the case of Crimea, the presence of Russian military started with the appearance of soldiers in uniform without any marks of nationality after the removal of the former president of Ukraine Yanukovych in February 2014.[134] While, at that time, Russia claimed that these were Ukrainian self-defence units, it appears that it later admitted these were in fact Rus-

---

128　J. D'Aspremont and J. de Hemptinne, *Droit international humanitaire* (Pédone, Paris, 2012) p. 42.
129　Bothe, *supra* note 42, p. 103.
130　Burke, *supra* note 95, p. 109.
131　O. J. Mayorga, 'Occupants, Beware of BITs: Applicability of Investment Treaties to Occupied Territories', XIX *Palestine Yearbook of International Law* (Forthcoming) (2016) p.2, <https://ssrn.com/abstract=2890281>, visited on 2 September 2017.
132　Geneva Conventions, *supra* note 102, common Art. 2(1).
133　*Ibid.*
134　Ministry of Foreign Affairs, 'On Violations of Ukraine's Laws in Force and of Ukrainian-Russian Agreements by Military Units of the Black Sea Fleet of the Russian Federation in the Territory of Ukraine', 3 March 2014, <http://mfa.gov.ua/en/newsfeeds/foreign-offices-news/18622-shhodo-porusheny-chinnogo-zakonodavstva-

sian soldiers.[135] In March 2014, the Russian Duma issued an authorisation for the Russian Army to operate in Ukraine and following Crimea's declaration of independence, Russian soldiers were stationed in Crimea.[136] Thus, while some military involvement from Russia's side has been observed in Crimea prior and after the integration of the peninsula into the Russian Federation, there has not been any actual fighting. Therefore, the Russia's military presence does not meet the threshold of an armed conflict.[137] Neither has there been a declaration of war.[138]

Nevertheless, it is probable that Crimea's territory is under hostile occupation without armed resistance. Some have argued that annexation, by definition, is the result of military occupation and as such governed by the rules of belligerent occupation.[139] Occupation is defined in Article 42 of the 1907 Hague Regulations as "territory ... actually placed under the authority of the hostile army".[140] This means that the occupying power must exercise effective control on the occupied territory absent the consent of the *de jure* sovereign[141] and that during that time the authority of the *de jure* sovereign is suspended.[142]

Effective control can be exercised directly or indirectly. Indirect occupation occurs when the occupying power is in control of the territory through the control of a subordinate administration.[143] It follows that the temporal and the spatial scope of applicability of the law of occupation depends on a factual determination of the occupying power's effective control over the territory.[144] In general, there are three criteria for the de-

---

ukrajini-ta-ukrajinsyko-rosijsykih-ugod-vijsykovimi-formuvannyami-chf-rf-na-teritoriji-ukrajini>, visited on 10 September 2017.

135 'Шойгу: действия Минобороны РФ в Крыму были вызваны угрозой жизни мирного населения', *Итар-тасс : Информационное телеграфное агентство России*', 4 April 2014, <http://itar-tass.com/politika/1097051>, visited on 5 September 2017.

136 'Direct Line with Vladimir Putin', *Kremlin,* 17 April 2014, <http://eng.kremlin.ru/news/7034>, visited on 10 September 2017.

137 For more details *see* R. Kolb, *Advanced introduction to international humanitarian law* (Edward Elgar Pub, Cheltenham, 2015) pp. 96-101.

138 *Ibid.,* pp. 100-101.

139 *See* R. Hofmann, 'Annexation', *Max Planck Encyclopedia of Public International Law* (2013) 28.1, <http://www.mpepi.com>, visited on 10 September 2017.

140 1907 Hague Regulations, *supra* note 102, Art. 42.

141 E. Wilmshurst, *International Law and the Classification of Conflicts* (Oxford University Press, Oxford, 2012) 44; Burke, *supra* note 95, p. 108.

142 Klabbers, *supra* note 85, p. 214.

143 *Ibid.*

144 Benvenisti, *supra* note 67, p. 43.

termination of effective control.¹⁴⁵ Firstly, the military forces of the occupying power must be physically present in the territory of the occupied State without the consent of the local government. Secondly, the local government is, since the moment of invasion, incapable or can be rendered incapable of exercising its authority as a consequence of the occupation. And thirdly, the occupying power has substituted or is capable of substituting its authority over the authority of the local government.¹⁴⁶

Since the issuing of the declaration of independence, there is continued presence of Russian military in Crimea. The Ukrainian government has not given its consent to such military presence.¹⁴⁷ Furthermore, it is also clear that the Ukrainian government is not capable of exercising its authority in the territory of Crimea since the latter's annexation, since Russia has gradually introduced its laws and established its institutions in Crimea. This also means that the third criterion is fulfilled. Therefore, it can be concluded that Crimea constitutes territory under hostile occupation without armed resistance and the law of occupation is applicable in the entire territory of Crimea, which is under Russia's effective control.¹⁴⁸ The temporal scope of the law of occupation entails that occupation begins as soon as effective control has been established and ends when the occupying power's armed forces cease to control the occupied territory.¹⁴⁹

It is important to note that the fact that Russia is claiming sovereignty over Crimea does not change this conclusion. According to Article 47 of the Geneva Convention VI, the question of title is not relevant to the ap-

---

145   T. Ferraro, 'Comment déterminer le début et la fin d'une occupation au sens du droit international humanitaire', 94:1 Revue Internationale de la Croix-Rouge (2012) p. 74.

146   *Ibid*, p. 91.

147   It has been argued that Russian military forces have been invited by the then ousted president Yanukovych. In a letter, Yanukovych had asked for Russian military assistance in order to face the chaos and anarchy in Ukraine at that time. However, this letter has never been published and, at the time the letter was written, Yanukovych had already been voted out of office by the parliament and had flown to Russia. An interim president had been put into office. Yanukovych had thus no effective control over Ukraine at the moment when he wrote the purported letter. Therefore, he could not legitimately consent to the military intervention of the Russian armed forces.

148   For more details on the spatial scope of application of the law of armed conflicts see R. Kolb and R. Hyde, *An introduction to the international law of armed conflicts* (Hart Publishing, Oxford, 2008) p. 94; 1907 Hague Regulations, *supra* note 102, Art. 42.

149   Benvenisti, *supra* note 67, pp. 55-56.

plication of the law of occupation.[150] Otherwise, it would suffice to claim title over an occupied territory (for example by means of annexation), in order to undermine the application of the law of occupation.[151] This would be contrary to the aim of the law of armed conflict: to ensure the greatest amount of effective protection.[152] Moreover, similarly to the effects annexation, military occupation does not affect the legal status of the territory in question.[153]

5.2 The Status of BITs in Occupied Territories

5.2.1 Termination or Suspension of BITs in Times of Occupation

Having concluded that the law of occupation is applicable to the situation of Crimea, the effects of that law on the operation of BITs need to be examined. In the first half of the 20th century, it was commonly accepted that treaties between opposing States were automatically terminated with the outbreak of war.[154] This view is not valid anymore. Instead, the continuity of a treaty will depend on the nature of the treaty and of the conflict.[155] Below, it will be analysed whether occupation leads to the automatic termination or suspension of BITs.

While the VCLT does not explicitly mention situations of armed conflict,[156] the International Law Commission's Draft Articles on the Effects of Armed Conflict on Treaties (AREAC)[157] address exactly these questions. However, the AREAC does not make an explicit distinction between situations of armed conflict and situations of occupation since the law of occupation developed as a part of the law of armed conflict.[158] The VCLT is a complementary instrument to the AREAC meaning that the rules of interpretation enshrined in the VCLT apply alongside the AREAC.[159] The Draft Articles aim at codifying customary international

---

150   Ibid.; Geneva Convention (IV), *supra* note 102, Art. 47.
151   Kolb, *supra* note 137, p. 103.
152   Ibid.
153   Ibid.
154   A. Pronto, 'The Effect of War on Law – What Happens to Their Treaties When States Go to War?', 2:2 *Cambridge Journal of International and Comparative Law* (2013) p. 230.
155   Ibid.
156   VCLT, *supra* note 69, Art. 73.
157   International Law Commission, *Draft Articles on the Effects of Armed Conflict on Treaties, with Commentaries* (AREAC) (U.N. Doc. A/66/10).
158   Burke, *supra* note 95, p. 103.
159   AREAC, *supra* note 157, Art. 5.

law.¹⁶⁰ Nevertheless, since the AREAC has been drafted quite recently, it is not yet possible to make a clear statement concerning the question of whether or not it constitutes a proper reflection of international customary law. Nevertheless, for the purposes of this article the AREAC shall serve as a starting point for analysing the applicability of BITs in times of occupation.

Article 2 AREAC provides a general rule: the continued application of treaties in armed conflict.¹⁶¹ However, the general principle can be rebutted. This is the case if treaties explicitly provide for their termination in situations of armed conflict.¹⁶² This is generally not the case for BITs.¹⁶³ Instead, BITs normally operate for a certain period of time, which is extended automatically, unless the parties to the treaty agree otherwise.¹⁶⁴ Other than the possibility to terminate or suspend a treaty by means of express provision, Article 5 points to the application of general international law on treaty interpretation in order to determine whether a treaty may be terminated or suspended.¹⁶⁵ Article 6 provides for a two limb test requiring the analysis of (a) the nature of the treaty and (b) the characteristics of the armed conflict.¹⁶⁶ Thus, while there may be grounds that permit the termination or suspension of a treaty in the case of armed conflicts, there is no rule leading to an automatic termination of treaties.

As neither Ukraine nor Russia have made any advances in the direction of termination or suspension of their BITs, it results that these are still in force. In this context, it is important to note that BITs usually include a sunset clause, which extends their application in case of termination to those investments made prior to the termination for a certain period of time.¹⁶⁷ This means that even in the case that a BIT is terminated uni-

---

160   AREAC, *supra* note 157, Art. 1; *see also* O.G. Repousis and J. Fry, 'Armed Conflict and state succession in investor-state arbitration', 22 *Columbia Journal of European Law* (2016) p. 421.
161   *Ibid.*, Art. 2: "The existence of an armed conflict does not ipso facto terminate or suspend the operation of treaties: (a) as between States parties to the conflict; (b) as between a party to the conflict and a State that is not."
162   *Ibid.*, Art. 4.
163   Repousis, *supra* note 160, p. 427.
164   *Ibid.*
165   AREAC, *supra* note 157, Art. 5.
166   *Ibid.*, Art. 6.
167   T. Voon and A.D. Mitchell, 'Denunciation, Termination and Survival: The Interplay of Treaty Law and International Investment Law' 31/2 *ICSID Review – Foreign Investment Law Journal* (2016) pp. 420-430.

laterally this would not immediately affect the protection of investment existing prior to the date of termination.

Furthermore, Article 7 AREAC contains an indicative list of treaties, the nature of which implies continued operation during armed conflict.[168] While BITs are not explicitly enumerated, one may argue that they fall under the scope of treaties of friendship, commerce and navigation.[169] If this is the case, the substantive and procedural private rights granted to foreign individuals in BITs survive in situations of armed conflict.[170] This is strengthened by the fact that BITs often include 'war clauses', which provide for compensation for losses in a situation of armed conflict.[171] Both Ukrainian and Russian BITs generally contain such a war clause,[172] which strongly points towards the assumption that these BITs continue to apply in times of armed conflict and during occupation.

5.2.2 The Duty to Respect BITs as Laws in Force in the Occupied Territory

One of the main duties arising from the law of occupation is the obligation of the occupying power to maintain, as far as possible, the *status quo* in the occupied territory.[173] This a logical consequence from the fact that the law of occupation does not only aim at protecting the interests of the inhabitants of the occupied territory, but also those of the displaced sovereign.

Therefore, Article 43 of the 1907 Hague Regulations stipulates that the Occupying Power "shall take all the measures in his power to restore, and ensure, as far as possible, public order and safety, while respecting, unless absolutely prevented, the laws in force in the country".[174] Thus, even though the occupying power may in certain circumstances depart from applying the laws in force in the occupied territory, it must, if not absolutely prevented, respect the legal *status quo ante*.[175] An important aspect

---

168 AREAC, *supra* note 157, Art. 7.
169 For a detailed analysis *see* Repousis, *supra* note 160, p. 430.
170 AREAC, *supra* note 157, commentary to the indicative list, category (e).
171 *See for example* the Russia-Ukraine BIT, *supra* note 3, Art. 6.
172 For Russian BITs *see* Investment Policy Hub, International Investment Agreements Navigator, Russian Federation, <http://investmentpolicyhub.unctad.org/IIA/CountryBits/175>, visited on 30 August 2017; for Ukrainian BITs *see* Investment Policy Hub, International Investment Agreements Navigator, Ukraine, <http://investmentpolicyhub.unctad.org/IIA/CountryBits/219>, visited on 30 August 2017.
173 Kolb, *supra* note 148, p. 231.
174 1907 Hague Regulation, *supra* note 102, Art. 43.
175 Burke, *supra* note 95, p. 111.

of this obligation is the prohibition of altering the status of the occupied territory, for instance, by annexation.[176]

Article 43 of the 1907 Hague Regulations was concretised in Article 64 of the Geneva Convention VI according to which

> [t]he penal laws of the occupied territory shall remain in force, with the exception that they may be repealed or suspended by the Occupying Power in cases where they constitute a threat to its security or an obstacle to the application of the present Convention. ... The Occupying Power may ... subject the population of the occupied territory to provisions which are essential to enable the Occupying Power to fulfil its obligations under the present Convention, to maintain the orderly government of the territory, and to ensure the security of the Occupying Power, of the members and property of the occupying forces or administration, and likewise of the establishments and lines of communication used by them.[177]

The main objective of Article 64 is thus to allow the introduction of measures to fulfil obligations of the occupying power towards the population.[178] The occupant has the authority to change the laws in place in the occupied territory in order to restore and ensure public order and civil life.[179] However, by the same token, it may be argued that according to Articles 43 of the 1907 Hague Regulations and 64 of the Geneva Convention VI, an occupying power is under the obligation, unless absolutely prevented, to respect the international obligations of the occupied territory – such as multilateral and bilateral treaties.[180] This is especially true if the constitution of the occupied State grants such treaties the status of domestic law as does the Ukrainian constitution.[181] This is because the

---

176 Kolb, *supra* note 148, p. 232.
177 It is commonly accepted that although Article 64 mentions only penal law, the entire legal system of the territory under occupation is meant by this rule. *See also* R. Kolb and S. Vité, *Le droit de l'occupation militaire: perspectives historiques et enjeux juridiques actuels* (Emile Bruylant, Bruxelles, 2009) pp. 192-194.
178 *Ibid.*
179 Benvenisti, *supra* note 67, p. 83.
180 *Ibid.*, p. 115.
181 Mayorga, *supra* note 131, p. 7; Constitution of Ukraine, adopted at the Fifth Session of the Verkhovna Rada of Ukraine on 28 June 1996, Art. 9 "International treaties that are in force, agreed to be binding by the Verkhovna Rada of Ukraine, are part of the national legislation of Ukraine.", <http://www.coe.int/t/dghl/cooperation/ccpe/profiles/ukraineConstitution_en.asp>, visited on 9 September 2017.

expression 'laws in force in the occupied territory' should be interpreted as including every component of the domestic legal system of the occupied State.[182] In this vein, the International Committee of the Red Cross (ICRC) in its Commentary on the 1949 Geneva Convention confirmed that Article 64 applied to the whole of the law in the occupied territory.[183] In this scenario, the occupying State's consent to comply with the treaties in force in the occupied territory is given indirectly through its consent to the application of the law of occupation.[184]

Under such circumstances, the Russian Federation has a duty to respect Ukraine's BITs in the occupied territory of Crimea. This also means that foreign investors can bring investment claims against Russia on the basis of the BITs of the *de jure* sovereign Ukraine as it can be assumed that the occupant has given its consent to arbitrate indirectly through Article 43 of The Hague Regulations.[185] However, under Ukrainian BITs Ukrainian investors cannot qualify as foreign investors as they are not nationals of another country. They will thus be deprived of the possibility of invoking BITs to claim damages for acts that took place in Ukraine because they are Ukrainian nationals. This is the case despite the fact that Crimea is under effective control of the Russian Federation.

Nevertheless, there is an exception to the occupying power's duty to apply the laws in force in the occupied territory. This is the case if the occupying power is absolutely prevented from respecting the laws in force. In this sense, the occupying power may depart from applying local laws in order to secure the safety of its armed forces.[186] Moreover, in certain cases the occupant may have the obligation to abrogate or change the laws in force. Such obligation arises, for example, if the laws in force in the occupied territories contain rules that are contrary to international human rights standards or the Geneva Convention IV or if a change in the legislation is necessary to ensure public order and safety in the occupied territory.[187]

In casu, it is clear that the application of the *de jure* sovereign's BITs is not contrary to international human rights standards or the Geneva

---

182   Mayorga, *supra* note 131, p. 24; Benvenisti, *supra* note 67, p. 94.
183   International Committee of the Red Cross (ICRC), *Commentary on the Geneva Conventions of August 12 1949*, Volume I, 1952.
184   Mayorga, *supra* note 131, p. 9; C. F Amerasinghe, *Jurisdiction of International Tribunals* (Kluwer Law International, The Hague, 2003) p. 89.
185   Mayorga, *supra* note 131, p. 33.
186   Kolb, *supra* note 148, p. 232; Geneva Convention (IV), *supra* note 102 Art. 64(2).
187   *Ibid.*

Convention IV, as BITs do not touch upon these topics. BITs are instruments used to protect investors and their investments in foreign countries, not to harm them. It is therefore unlikely that it will be necessary for the Russian Federation to withhold applying these BITs to ensure public order and safety. On the contrary, the effective protection of investment in Crimea is even necessary to ensure public order as investment is an important element of the functioning of the economy and the maintenance of international commercial relations.

Lastly, Russia could argue that the application of Ukraine's BITs is harmful to the safety of its armed forces. The object and purpose of BITs is the establishment and maintenance of economic prosperity and international trade relations. This is to be achieved through the protection of investors and their investment. *Prima facie*, such protection does not compromise the military purposes of the occupation. At least, it could not be upheld that BITs as a whole are contrary to such military purposes. If Russia still wanted to argue that certain guarantees contained in BITs have such a compromising effect, this would have to be analysed case-by-case. Moreover, Russia would have to comply with the principle of proportionality.[188]

It is commonly accepted that military necessity demands that members of occupying forces cannot be subject to the laws and jurisdiction of the occupied State since this would threaten the military purpose of the occupation.[189] However, investment arbitration claims are not directed towards the occupant's military forces but towards the occupant itself. Mostly, arbitration awards result in a duty of the wrong-doing State to stop its illegal actions and to pay damages to the injured party. Such duties do not threaten the military purposes of the occupation as the military personnel of the occupant is not touched by the award.[190] Therefore, an occupant cannot enjoy immunity from arbitral jurisdiction on the basis of the argument that this would compromise the military purposes of the occupation.

In conclusion, Russia is under an obligation to respect Ukraine's BITs according to Articles 43 of the 1907 Hague Regulations and 64 of the Geneva Convention VI, unless it proves that it cannot do so on the basis of military necessity.

---

188 Klabbers, *supra* note 85, pp. 208-209.
189 Mayorga, *supra* note 131, p. 35.
190 *Ibid.*, pp. 34-44.

5.2.3 The Law of Occupation as *Lex Specialis*

It is important to note that the law of occupation is the *lex specialis* in occupied territories, which may render certain rules stemming from other areas of law inapplicable. The *lex specialis* principle as a rule of interpretation applies only if two provisions of international law deal with the same subject matter and there exists some actual inconsistency between these provisions.[191] This means that the *lex specialis* rule comes into play if there exists a conflict of norms relating to the same subject matter. Therefore, even though the law of occupation is the *lex specialis* applicable in occupied territory, this does not entail that the law of occupation is to be applied to the exclusion of any other area of law. Thus, BITs applicable in the occupied territory of Crimea coexist with the law of occupation as long as a conflict of norms does not arise. Nevertheless, the *lex specialis* character of the law of occupation leads to an important limitation of the personal scope of the applicability of BITs.

The personal scope of BITs relates to the definition of who constitutes an investor under the BIT, since it is only their investments that are protected under the treaty and who thus may bring investment claims. To give an example, the Russia-Ukraine BIT defines investors as "any natural person, who is a citizen of the state of a Contracting Party, and who is legally capable under its respective legislation to carry out investments on the territory of the other Contracting Party"[192] or "any legal entity, set up or instituted in conformity with the legislation prevailing on the territory of the given Contracting Party, under the condition that the said legal entity is legally capable, under the legislation of its respective Contracting Party, to carry out investments on the territory of the other Contracting Party".[193]

The personal scope of the Geneva Convention IV is limited to protected persons. These are persons, "who, at a given moment and in any manner whatsoever, find themselves, in case of a conflict or occupation, in the hands of a Party to the conflict or Occupying Power of which they are not nationals".[194] Article 4 further excludes four categories of persons from the protection of the Convention: nationals of the occupier, nationals of a co-belligerent, if their home country maintains normal diplomatic rela-

---

191 *Draft Articles on State Responsibility*, *supra* note 19, commentary to Art. 55.
192 Russia-Ukraine BIT, *supra* note 3, Art. 1(2)a.
193 *Ibid.*, Art. 1(2)b.
194 Geneva Convention IV, *supra* note 102, Art. 4.

tions with the occupier, persons protected by Geneva Conventions I to III and nationals of a State not bound by the Convention.[195]

It is thus possible that a conflict of norms arises between the rules defining the personal scope in the Ukrainian BIT and the personal scope of the law of occupation. While Russian investors in Crimea are protected under the BIT, they are not protected under the Geneva Convention IV, since they are nationals of the occupying power. As Ukrainian BITs are applicable by virtue of Article 43 of The Hague Regulations, which is a part of the *lex specialis* law of occupation, it follows that the personal scope of the law of occupation is applicable to the situation even though it limits the personal scope of Ukrainian BITs. Concerning the personal scope of the law of occupation, the Geneva Convention IV has replaced The Hague Regulations, which renders Article 4 applicable to the whole body of the law of occupation.[196]

As a result, Russian investors in Crimea are not protected under the Russia-Ukraine BIT in times of occupation. Therefore, Russian investors are deprived of their right to invoke an investment claim under the BIT.

5.2.4   Long-Term Occupation

As the occupation lingers, it may be possible that the occupant's prescriptive powers change. As occupation continues across time, it becomes more and more difficult to maintain the *status quo ante,* especially since this could prove detrimental to the local population. It would be wrong to leave the legal situation unchanged and thus prevent necessary adaptations to new situations.[197]

In this context, the Israeli Supreme Court held that where an initial short-term occupation becomes a long-term occupation, the occupant's powers are extended because "[l]ife does not stand still, and no ... [occupation administration] ... can fulfil its duties with respect to the population if it refrains from legislating and from adapting the legal situation to the exigencies of modern times".[198] This could serve as a basis for the occupying power to change laws in place in the occupied territory as occupation endures over time. This could also have consequences for the applicability of BITs in the occupied territory. The occupant could argue

---

195   *Ibid.*
196   Mayorga, *supra* note 131, p. 48.
197   Benvenisti, *supra* note 67, p. 246.
198   *HCJ 337/71 The Christian Society for the Sacred Places* v. *Minister of Defense,* 26(1) PD 574, 582 (1971).

that it is not under an obligation to apply the ousted sovereign's BITs. This could be used as an argument in favour for the application of the occupant's BITs or for the conclusion of new BITs by the occupant on behalf of the territory.

However, legal scholars generally tend to negate that the occupant's prescriptive powers are widened in long-term occupation. Instead they suggest that the occupant should be under an obligation to encourage the participation of the ousted government and the local population in order to guarantee that the body of law is adapted to the necessities of new circumstances.[199] Moreover, if the occupying power accepts its duty to assume obligations under the *de jure* sovereign's BITs, there is no *prima facie* necessity to even change the regime of investment treaties in the occupied territory even in cases of long-term occupation especially since this would clearly be a disproportional interference into the authority of the ousted sovereign.

5.3 Conclusion on the Applicability of BITs in Occupied Territories

Russia is under an obligation to respect Ukraine's BITs as the laws in force in the occupied territory according to Articles 43 of the 1907 Hague Regulations and 64 of the Geneva Convention VI. This can be rebutted only if the Russian Federation proves that military necessity requires it not to do so. However, under the law of occupation, both Russian and Ukrainian investors will not be protected under Ukraine's BITs. This is because Russian investors fall outside the scope of the Geneva Convention IV and Ukrainian investors fall outside the scope of Ukrainian BITs. This means that the Ukrainian investors, who are claiming damages in the above-mentioned arbitration proceedings could not have relied on the applicability of Ukrainians BITs in accordance with the law of occupation.

6 Conclusion

At least for some investors, the feared legal vacuum has turned into a double protection of investors under Russian and Ukrainian BITs. This article showed that Russia's BITs apply in Crimea by way of extraterritorial application in accordance with the object and purposes of BITs, which is the protection of the rights and interests of natural and legal persons, and in light of the core rationale of the Namibia exception, which requires

---

199   Benvenisti, *supra* note 67, pp. 246-247.

balancing the needs of the ousted sovereign and the needs of the local population. At the same time, Articles 43 of the 1907 Hague Regulations and 64 of the Geneva Convention VI require the occupying power to apply Ukrainian BITs as the law in force of the occupied territory.

Nevertheless, even if investors with investments in Crimea are successful in claiming damages before an international arbitration tribunal, they will most probably face issues of enforcement. Russia is known for its scepticism towards the legitimacy of investor-State arbitration. It is thus not surprising that Russia is not assisting in the pending arbitration proceedings. In Russia's view, in investor-State arbitration, investors always win and States always lose.[200] This also leads to problems as regards to enforcement as the Russian Federation does not waive State immunity even in cases of a purely economic nature.[201]

Moreover, the tension between the law and reality is likely to subsist. Neither the Russian Federation nor the international community supporting Ukraine are likely to step away from their standpoint. Sanctions and counter-sanctions continue to exist. Even though a negotiated solution between Ukraine and the Russian Federation is certainly desirable, such a solution is also not very likely, especially in view of the on-going conflicts in Eastern Ukraine. Nevertheless, as in other occupied territories, such as Northern Cyprus or the occupied territories of Palestine, life in Crimea goes on. This is why it is important that international law provides investors and their investment with effective protection against illegal acts of the occupying power. Anything else would benefit only the party in violation of international law, which would substantially undermine the most precious achievement of international law in the 20th century – the prohibition of the unlawful use of force.

---

200   L. Mälksoo, *Russian Approaches to International Law* (Oxford University Press, Oxford, 2015) p. 129.
201   *Ibid.*, p. 170.

5 The Estrada Doctrine and the English Courts: Determining the Legitimate Government of a State in the Absence of Explicit Recognition of Governments

*Leonor Vulpe Albari**

Abstract

Events such as the civil wars in Libya and in Syria have made urgent the question of what constitutes the legitimate government of a State, and in what circumstances is an authority recognised as the legitimate government of a State. Before the 1980s, most governments formally recognised other governments. Many States now follow the Estrada Doctrine, however; their governments do not explicitly recognise an authority as the government of a State. This practice has left domestic courts that must adjudicate disputes involving foreign governments with the burden of determination. For example, during the Libyan civil war that started in 2011, to adjudicate a dispute concerning Libyan assets held in the UK, English courts had to decide which authority was the legitimate Libyan government. Was it the Gaddafi government or the newly-formed National Transitional Council? This paper elucidates how courts determine the legitimacy of governments. It examines recent cases before the English courts and argues that, for these courts, the most important factor in determining legitimacy is how the British government interacts with authorities claiming to be legitimate governments. The paper concludes that interaction should in fact be the primary consideration of courts.

---

*   LL.M. *cum laude* (Maastricht University), B.Hum. (Carleton University); currently completing a BA of Jurisprudence (Senior Status) at the University Oxford; Visiting Research Fellow at the Department of International and European Law, Maastricht University. The author would like to thank Jure Vidmar, Professor of Public International Law at Maastricht University, for his unending support and guidance in writing this article.

1   Introduction

In the 1980s, many States, including the United Kingdom (UK), the United States (US), and Australia adopted the Estrada Doctrine,[1] according to which foreign governments should not judge (approve or disapprove of) the changes of governments in other States.[2] Indeed, Erika de Wet explains that recognition of governments "may seem outdated" since formally recognising governments has "fallen increasingly out of fashion since the 1980s".[3] Though the manner in which governments recognise foreign governments may have changed, the concept of recognition of governments is not obsolete, neither for governments nor for domestic courts.[4] Furthermore, new State practice, such as the civil wars in Libya and in Syria, has made it necessary to re-evaluate what constitutes the legitimate government authority of a State, and re-examine the circumstances in which an authority is recognised as the legitimate government of a State.

For governments, practice has changed from *explicit* recognition through formal statements, to *implicit* recognition through government-to-government interaction.[5] According to Dapo Akande, not recognising governments, explicitly or implicitly, is an "almost impossible" policy to apply since "States always have to decide on who they will treat

---

1   It has also been adopted by Canada, Belgium, France, and other States (M. N. Shaw, *International Law*, 6th edition, (Cambridge University Press, Cambridge, 2008) pp. 458-459; Oxford Reference, *Estrada Doctrine* (1 January 2009), <www.oxfordreference.com/view/10.1093/oi/authority.20110803095758788>, visited on 1 August 2016).

2   P. C. Jessup, 'The Estrada Doctrine', 25:4 *American Journal of International Law* (1931) pp. 719-720.

3   E. de Wet, 'From Free Town to Cairo via Kiev: The Unpredictable Road of Democratic Legitimacy', *American Journal of International Law Unbound* (2015), <https://www.asil.org/blogs/free-town-cairo-kiev-unpredictable-road-democratic-legitimacy-governmental-recognition>, visited on 28 February 2016; *see also* S. Talmon, 'Recognition of the Libyan National Transitional Council', 15:16 *American Society of International Law* (2011), <www.asil.org/insights/volume/15/issue/16/recognition-libyan-national-transitional-council>, visited on 3 August 2017.

4   Brad R. Roth recognises that recognition of governments has been neglected, but should not be: "[t]his neglect of the legal dimensions of recognition of governments merely demonstrates that renewed consideration of the matter is overdue, for the legal issues involved cannot be side-stepped" (B. R. Roth, *Governmental Illegitimacy in International Law* (Oxford Scholarship Online, March 2012) p. 121).

5   S. Talmon, *Recognition of Governments in International Law: With Particular Reference to Governments in Exile* (Oxford Scholarship Online, January 2010) p. 4.

as the government of another State."⁶ Thus, recognition has continued, but implicitly through interaction. Regarding domestic courts, recognition remains just as relevant as ever. Though courts themselves cannot grant recognition, they must continue to decide which authority is the legitimate government of a foreign State in order to adjudicate many disputes.⁷ English courts, for example, decide who has access to State assets in the UK, which was the issue in *British Arab Commercial Bank plc* v. *The National Transitional Council of the State of Libya* (*British Arab Commercial Bank*) from 2011,⁸ who has control over a State-owned company's bank accounts in the UK,⁹ who enjoys immunities in the UK,¹⁰ who has *locus standi* in English courts,¹¹ and whether acts and orders of an authority should be given effect by English courts.¹²

A formal statement of recognition or non-recognition from a government has "probative value" in continental European courts, but "is conclusive as to the legal status of a foreign authority or entity" in certain courts, and specifically, in English courts.¹³ Further, when it comes to rec-

---

6   D. Akande, 'Which Entity is the Government of Libya and Why does it Matter?' *European Journal of International Law: Talk!* (2011), <www.ejiltalk.org/which-entity-is-the-government-of-libya-and-why-does-it-matter/>, visited on 1 August 2016; *see also* Talmon, *supra* note 5, pp. 6-7; de Wet, *supra* note 3.

7   Roth states: "[d]omestic courts apply domestic law when resolving questions regarding the immunity of foreign sovereigns, the deference accorded acts of state, and the capacity of foreign entities to sue and be sued, although that domestic law may incorporate aspects of international law doctrine" (Roth, *supra* note 4, pp. 153-154). *See also* P. Capps, 'British Policy on the Recognition of Governments', *Public Law* (2014) p. 229.

8   *See, for instance, British Arab Commercial Bank plc* v. *The National Transitional Council of the State of Libya*, 26 August 2011, High Court of Justice Queen's Bench Division Commercial Court, [2011] EWHC 2274 (Comm).

9   *See, for instance, Sierra Leone Telecommunications Co Ltd* v. *Barclays Bank plc*, 6 February 1998, Queen's Bench Division (Commercial Court), [1998] CLC 501.

10 This is also a question of recognition of States. *E.g. The Queen on the Application of HRH Sultan of Pahang* v. *Secretary of State for the Home Department*, 25 May 2011, Court of Appeal (Civil Division), [2011] EWCA Civ 616.

11 *See, for instance, Gur Corporation* v. *Trust Bank of Africa Ltd*, 22 July 1986, Court of Appeal, [1987] QB 599.

12 *See, for instance, Hesperides Hotels Ltd and Another* v. *Aegean Turkish Holidays Ltd and Another*, 23 May 1977, Court of Appeal, [1978] QB 205.

13 A formal statement is also conclusive for American and Canadian courts. *See* S. Talmon, 'Recognition of states and governments in international law', 1:19 *Azerbaijan in the World* (2008), <biweekly.ada.edu.az/vol_1_no_19/Recognition_of_states_and_governments_in_international_law.htm>, visited on 19 August 2016; *Chateau-Gai Wines Ltd* v. *Canada (Attorney General)*, 16 April 1970, Exchequer Court of

ognising governments, English courts should follow the policy of their government: the executive and judiciary should speak with one voice.[14] The question, then, is how have English courts managed to follow the recognition policy of their government, without an explicit statement of recognition or non-recognition as guidance from the government? Have they assumed responsibilities that traditionally fell to government and developed their own criteria for deciding when a government should be recognised? Or, have they scrutinised their government's policy and implicit dealings with foreign authorities in order to know which entity their government recognises as a legitimate government? Or, have they combined both approaches?

This paper examines how English courts have recently approached the problem of having to decide which authority to recognise as the government in a case in the absence of explicit recognition from their government. To begin, the Estrada Doctrine and the shift from explicit to implicit recognition is described. This is followed by an explanation of the principle that, in the UK, the executive and judiciary speak with the same voice when recognition of governments is at issue. Then, a review of English cases illustrates how English courts have approached the problem of implicit recognition. It is argued that interaction or proof of interaction is the most important factor for English courts and that, indeed, interaction *should* be the most important factor since implicit recognition through interaction is how governments are now expressing recognition, and governments are in a better position than are the courts to evaluate other criteria, such as constitutionality and effective control. Finally, it is explained how this English case law informs the general doctrine of recognition of governments.

2 The Estrada Doctrine: Explicit to Implicit Recognition of Governments

The Estrada Doctrine is named after Don Genero Estrada, a former Secretary of Foreign Affairs of Mexico, who stated in 1930 that Mexican diplomats should not expressly recognise governments, as this would in-

---

Canada, CarswellNat 27, para. 28. *See also* A. B. Lyons, 'The Conclusiveness of the Foreign Office Certificate', 23 *British Yearbook of International Law* (1946) p. 240.

14 *See* section 3; *Government of the Republic of Spain* v. *SS "Arantzazu Mendi"*, 23 February 1939, House of Lords, [1939] AC 256, p. 264.

fringe the sovereignty of States.[15] The UK adopted the Estrada Doctrine in 1980, and by the late 1980s many other States had done the same.[16] In 1980, Foreign Secretary Lord Carrington told the House of Lords that the British government would no longer recognise governments, and that the government's "attitude on the question of whether it qualifies to be treated as a Government will be left to be inferred from the nature of the dealings, if any, which we have with it, and in particular on whether we are dealing with it on a normal Government to Government basis."[17]

---

15   Roth explains: "[i]f international law respects sovereignty, one might suppose that the former's jurisdiction does not extend to the method by which domestic regimes come to power, and that such processes, however repugnant to international sensibilities, are exclusively matters of domestic concern" (Roth, *supra* note 4, p. 138). *See also* Jessup, *supra* note 2, pp. 719-720; Oxford Reference, *Estrada Doctrine*, *supra* note 1.

16   J. Vidmar, 'States, Governments, and Collective Recognition', 31 *Chinese (Taiwan) Yearbook of International Law* (2014) p. 151; Shaw, *supra* note 1, pp. 458-459. It is necessary to note, however, that though it is clear that in 1980 the UK decided to no longer explicitly recognise governments, it is not universally accepted that the UK adopted the Estrada Doctrine in particular. Talmon, for example, argues that the UK did not adopt the Estrada Doctrine because "[t]here is no reference to the doctrine ... in the 1980 statements". In addition, the Estrada Doctrine is unclear and "does not address the question how, for the purpose of legal proceedings, the courts may ascertain whether the government of the forum has accepted a regime as a government for the purposes of municipal law" (S. Talmon, 'Recognition of Governments: An Analysis of the New British Policy and Practice', 63:1 *British Yearbook of International Law* (1993) pp. 231, 266). Importantly, though, Talmon agrees that the British government decided to refrain from explicitly recognising governments, and the fact that there was this shift in policy, whether it be called the adoption of the Estrada Doctrine or not, is what is most essential for this paper.

17   Lord Carrington, HL Debs., vol. 408, cols. cc1121-2WA, 28 April 1980, <hansard.millbanksystems.com/written_answers/1980/apr/28/recognition-of-governments-policy-and>, visited on 8 August 2017; *see also* C. Warbrick, 'Recognition of Governments' 56 *The Modern Law Review* (1993) p. 92. There are several practical advantages to adopting the Estrada Doctrine. For example, prematurely recognising an authority as the government of a State can be seen as violating the territorial integrity or political independence of a State, and therefore a breach of international law (Roth, *supra* note 4, p. 138; D. Wippman, 'Military Intervention, Regional Organizations, and Host-State Consent', 7:209 *Duke Journal of Comparative and International Law* (1996), p. 220). To add, recognising a government can be seen as approving that government, and that decision to recognise a certain authority as the government of a State will be subject to public scrutiny. Murphy explains: "[t]he Estrada Doctrine is attractive ... because many States view it as politically difficult to announce publicly, one way or another, whether they 'recognise' a new government, and would prefer simply to open diplomatic channels or otherwise develop relations with the new government without issuing a pronouncement that

Hence, States that have adopted the Estrada Doctrine will avoid using the term recognition and, rather, demonstrate their opinion by dealing with an authority as the government[18] – that is, implicit recognition through interaction.[19]

Even if the practice of making formal statements of recognition has declined, recognition has necessarily persisted, though in a new form. It is very difficult to avoid recognising governments completely. As Hersch Lauterpacht stated as early as 1947, "so long as revolutionary changes within States take place, recognition of governments is a substantial and necessary act". He explained that the Estrada doctrine is "less helpful than may appear at first sight"[20] since it still leaves many questions unanswered. States still need to decide which authority in a foreign State to have diplomatic relations with, or when to sever those relations.[21] According to Stefan Talmon, since the British government adopted the policy of not explicitly recognising governments, "[f]or the purposes of domestic law and the conduct of international relations it is still necessary for the British government to *decide* whether and since when a regime is the government of a State and thus entitles to represent that State in its bilateral relations with the United Kingdom or in legal proceedings in the English courts."[22] In 1965 after the *coup d'état* in the Republic of

---

could be construed as approval of the new government" (Murphy, 'Democratic Legitimacy and the Recognition of States and Governments', 48:3 *The International and Comparative Law Quarterly* (1999) p. 567). *See also* Talmon, *supra* note 5, p. 6.

18   de Wet, *supra* note 3.
19   In 1992, Talmon studied the effects that this 1980 policy had on British foreign relations, as well as on British legal proceedings, but a study of recent cases is needed (Talmon, *supra* note 16). Further, Talmon argues that "it is not the 'phenomenon' of the British government 'recognizing' governments ... but the practice of the Foreign and Commonwealth Office to communicate this decision to the court in terms of 'recognition' which has been abandoned" (Talmon, *supra* note 16, p. 292). This paper argues that, not only has the way in which the government communicates to the court changed, but also English courts now look at interaction or proof of interaction between the British government and the authorities in question in order to determine the legitimate governmental authority of a foreign State.
20   H. Lauterpacht, *Recognition in International Law* (Cambridge University Press, Cambridge, 2012) p. 156.
21   *Ibid.*, pp. 156-157.
22   Talmon, *supra* note 16, p. 238. Talmon also discusses the issue of governments in exile and explains "States still have to decide whether and from which date they regard a certain authority (in exile or *in situ*) as the government of another State ... and if so, to what extent they want to have dealings with it as such" (Talmon, *supra* note 5, pp. 6-7).

the Congo, Henri Rolin, a Belgian statesman,[23] asserted in the Belgian Parliament that, after an unconstitutional change of government, States must decide whether or not they will recognise the new authorities as the legitimate representative of the State.[24] A government must decide who it will deal with as a government[25] for the purposes of concluding treaties or accrediting ambassadors, for example.[26] Thus, recognition of governments, for practical reasons, must, and has, continued implicitly.

Though the Estrada Doctrine has been adopted by many States, and implicit recognition has become the new expression of recognition, explicit recognition still occurs occasionally. On 15 July 2011, thirty-two States, including the UK, France, and the US, explicitly recognised the National Transitional Council (NTC) as the government of Libya through a statement issued during a Libya Contact Group meeting.[27] According to the High Court of England and Wales (High Court of England) in the *British Arab Commercial Bank* case from 26 August 2011, the British government explicitly recognised the NTC a bit later, on 27 July 2011.[28] On this date, Secretary of State for Foreign and Commonwealth Affairs, William Hague, declared: "the United Kingdom recognises and will deal with the National Transitional Council as the sole governmental authority in Libya".[29] Foreign Secretary Hague also wrote in a certificate of recognition that Her Majesty's Government (HMG) recognises the NTC as the government of Libya, and that it does not recognise any other authority (in particular, the Gaddafi regime) as the government in Libya.[30] From this point on, the diplomats from the previously recognised Libyan gov-

---

23 Henri Rolin served as a senator of the Belgian Workers' Party, Minister of Justice, Minister of State, and President of the Senate (J. Salmon, Société française pour le droit international, *Henri Rolin*, <www.sfdi.org/internationalistes/rolin/>, visited on 6 August 2017).
24 Translated and cited in Talmon, *supra* note 5, p. 4.
25 Akande, *supra* note 6.
26 de Wet, *supra* note 3; *see also* Akande, *supra* note 6; Roth, *supra* note 4, p. 123; Murphy, *supra* note 17, p. 545.
27 D. Akande, 'Recognition of Libyan National Transitional Government of Libya', *European Journal of International Law: Talk!* (2011), <www.ejiltalk.org/recognition-of-libyan-national-transitional-council-as-government-of-libya/>, visited on 6 August 2017. As well, in Côte d'Ivoire from 2010 to 2011, and in Honduras in 2009, there were competing authorities claiming to be the government and States expressed their opinions on which entity should be recognised as the legitimate government (Akande, *supra* note 6).
28 *British Arab Commercial Bank* case, *supra* note 8, paras. 2, 6.
29 Cited in *British Arab Commercial Bank* case, *supra* note 8, para. 6.
30 *Ibid.*, para. 23.

ernment were no longer considered the representatives of government, and were instructed to leave the UK.[31]

The Libyan case represents only a brief departure from the Estrada Doctrine, however, and, in general, explicit recognition has given way to implicit recognition through interaction. During the proceedings of *Bouhadi v. Breish* (decision from 17 March 2016), the High Court of England asked the British government whether it recognised the Tobruk government or the Tripoli government as the government of Libya.[32] After the 2014 elections, the Tobruk government was mandated by the House of Representatives, and the Tripoli government was mandated by the General National Congress.[33] On 3 March 2016 the Foreign and Commonwealth Office (FCO) sent a response to the High Court of England explaining that, since 1980, HMG does not recognise governments,[34] and that it has recognised neither the Tobruk nor the Tripoli government.[35] Rather, HMG supports "the efforts of the United Nations and the international community to establish a Government of National Accord".[36] The British government's explicit recognition of the NTC in Libya in 2011, therefore, represents only a momentary departure from the Estrada Doctrine for the UK – one that seems to have been largely ignored by the British government in 2016 when communicating to the High Court of England for *Bouhadi v. Breish*.

---

31 *Ibid.*, para. 6. The Syrian situation does not represent a departure from the Estrada Doctrine because the UK never recognised the National Coalition for Syrian Revolutionary and Opposition Forces (NCS) as the legitimate government of Syria. Rather, the NCS was recognised as the "legitimate representative of the people", which, according to Talmon, was a political rather than legal act (S. Talmon, 'Recognition of Opposition Groups as the Legitimate Representative of a People', 12:2 *Chinese Journal of International Law* (2013) p. 18).

32 *Hassan Bouhadi v. Abdulmagid Breish*, 17 March 2016, High Court of Justice Queen's Bench Division Commercial Court, [2016] EWHC 602 (Comm).

33 *Hassan Bouhadi v. Abdulmagid Breish, Annex: Operative parts of letter of 3 March 2016 from the FCO to the court*, 17 March 2016, High Court of Justice Queen's Bench Division Commercial Court, [2016] EWHC 602 (Comm).

34 *Ibid.*; see also Carrington (HL Debs.), *supra* note 17.

35 *Ibid.*

36 *Ibid.*

3 Recognising Governments with 'One Voice'

English courts have expressed the importance of speaking in the same voice as their government at least since *The Arantzazu Mendi* case of 23 February 1939. This case concerned a ship that had been requisitioned by the Nationalist Government of Spain, and the question was whether this government enjoyed State immunity and could not be impleaded. In this case, Lord Atkin of the House of Lords stated: "Our State cannot speak with two voices on such a matter, the judiciary saying one thing, the executive another. Our sovereign has to decide whom he will recognize as a fellow sovereign in the family of States".[37] In short, when it comes to recognition of States, the government and courts of a State should speak with one voice. The British government had recognised the Government of the Spanish Republic as the *de jure* government of Spain, and the Nationalist Government as having *de facto* control over a large part of Spain.[38] The House of Lords reasoned that there was no difference between recognising a State as *de jure* or *de facto* "for the present purposes", and thus the Nationalist Government was "at the date of the writ a foreign State and could not be impleaded".[39]

The Arantzazu Mendi case and its one voice principle was developed further by the Court of Appeal in *The Sultan of Pahang* from 25 May 2011. The question in the case was whether the immigration control laws of the UK applied to the Sultan of Pahang, or if he benefitted from State immunity, and the immigration laws, therefore, did not apply to him.[40] In a certificate dated 10 November 2008 the British government stated "that

---

37 *The Arantzazu Mendi* case, *supra* note 14, p. 264.
38 Ibid.
39 Ibid., p. 266. It seems that the House of Lords glossed over an important distinction, however. If a State or government is recognised as a *de jure* State or government, it is given a legal status, and courts can accept this status and adjudicate accordingly in a dispute. *De facto* recognition acknowledges that a State or government may be a State or government *in practice*, but not that it is a State or government in law (Talmon, *supra* note 5, p. 68; *see also The Queen on the application of Kibris Türk Hava Yollari CTA Holidays* v. *Secretary of State for Transport*, 28 July 2009, High Court of Justice Queen's Bench Division Administrative Court, [2009] EWHC 1918 (Admin), para. 71). Roth explains: "a Government which is "de jure" derives its authority from sovereignty; a government which is "de facto" derives its authority from the fact that it exerts effective control over the territory in question" (Roth, *supra* note 4, p. 154). The importance of *The Arantzazu Mendi* case, though, is that the English courts ultimately felt that they had not gone against the opinion of the British government.
40 *The Sultan of Pahang* case, *supra* note 10, para. 1.

Pahang is a constituent territory in Malaysia", and "that the Sultan is not the head of State of Malaysia".[41] The certificate was found to be sufficiently clear and unequivocal, and thus conclusive: Pahang is not a sovereign State, and, therefore, the Sultan does not enjoy State immunity.[42]

The Arantzazu Mendi and *The Sultan of Pahang* cases dealt with State immunity, but the one voice principle has also been applied in cases where recognition of governments was at issue. *Somalia* v. *Woodhouse* from 13 March 1992 concerned the proceeds from a cargo of rice that had been paid into a court in the UK. The rice had been destined for the Somali capital, Mogadishu, but could not be delivered because of the fighting in Somalia.[43] The dispute that arose concerned who would have access to the proceeds from the sale of the cargo of rice.[44] In its reasoning, the High Court of England stated that this case did not involve recognition of a State, or any accredited representative of a foreign State; in fact, the UK did not recognise any government or any diplomatic representative from Somalia.[45] If the case did involve recognition of a State or an accredited State representative, the court would have to consider other factors "since it would be contrary to public policy for the court not to recognise as a qualified representative of the head of State of the foreign State the diplomatic representative recognised by Her Majesty's Government." In *Sierra Leone Telecommunications* v. *Barclays Bank* from 6 February 1998, the High Court of England decided that, when it comes to foreign relations, "the Crown in its executive and judicial functions ought to speak with one voice".[46]

More recently, in *British Arab Commercial Bank* from 26 August 2011 the issue concerned the control of the Libyan embassy's account held in the British Arab Commercial Bank in London.[47] The bank asked for a declaration "that it is entitled to act on the instructions of the embassy established by the NTC".[48] In other words, the bank wanted confirmation that the NTC was the legitimate representative of Libya, and thus had a right to establish an embassy in the UK, and control the bank accounts of

---

41 Cited in *The Sultan of Pahang* case, *supra* note 10, para. 8.
42 *The Sultan of Pahang* case, *supra* note 10, paras. 17, 36.
43 *Republic of Somalia* v. *Woodhouse Drake & Carey (Suisse) S.A. and Others*, 13 March 1993, Queen's Bench Division (Commercial Court), [1993] QB 54, p. 54.
44 *Ibid.*; *see also* Warbrick, *supra* note 17, p. 93.
45 *Somalia* v. *Woodhouse*, *supra* note 43, pp. 65-66.
46 *Ibid.*, p. 66.
47 *British Arab Commercial Bank* case, *supra* note 8, para. 1.
48 *Ibid.*, para. 16.

the embassy.[49] The court decided that "the Foreign Secretary's certificate of 24 August 2011 [recognising the NTC as the legitimate government of Libya] is conclusive, because in the field of foreign relations, the Crown in its executive and judicial functions speak with one voice".[50] A reference was made to *The Arantzazu Mendi* and *The Sultan of Pahang* cases.

In *Bouhadi* v. *Breish* from 2016 the issue concerned the appointment of the chairman of the Libyan Investment Authority (LIA), a sovereign wealth fund.[51] The Tobruk government had appointed Hassan Bouhadi, and the Tripoli government had appointed Abdulmagid Breish.[52] In a letter to the High Court of England regarding this case, the FCO explained that HMG does not recognise governments,[53] that it has recognised neither the Tobruk nor the Tripoli government,[54] but that it supports efforts made to establish a Government of National Accord.[55] The court ultimately decided to adjourn the case,[56] as making any declaration in favour of the Tobruk or Tripoli government would "risk cutting across the stated position of HMG [stated in the letter from the FCO]".[57] Thus, in sum, English courts are compelled to follow the opinion of the government.[58]

According to Patrick Capps, the one voice doctrine has been criticised and is judicially controversial "because the Government's power to recognise, when coupled with the "one voice" doctrine, is unconstrained by law".[59] In other words, if the government has the power to confer recognition to governments, and since the court will follow what the government has decided, the government has complete freedom to decide which authority should be recognised as a government.[60] Thus, Capps explains that a second approach has been presented by judges and scholars as an alternative to the one voice doctrine. According to this second approach, the court should not automatically follow the recognition policy of its government, but rather it should look at other evidence, such as the ef-

49   *Ibid.*
50   *Ibid.*, para 25.
51   *Bouhadi* v. *Breish*, *supra* note 32, paras. 4-5.
52   *Ibid.*, paras. 5-8.
53   *Bouhadi* v. *Breish*, Annex, *supra* note 33.
54   *Ibid.*
55   *Ibid.*
56   *Bouhadi* v. *Breish*, *supra* note 32, para. 52.
57   *Ibid.*, para. 49.
58   The one voice principle is also stated in: *Gur Corporation* v. *Trust Bank of Africa*, *supra* note 11, pp. 604, 624-625.
59   Capps, *supra* note 7, p. 231.
60   *Ibid.*

fective control and permanence of an authority.[61] However, even according to this second view, Capps admits that "[t]his said, the court will generally consider the Government to have greater expertise in determining whether an entity can claim governmental status."[62] To add, despite the fact that the one voice doctrine can be subject to criticism, it seems quite accepted by the judiciary and by scholars that it is still the public policy of the UK to avoid having the judiciary and executive speaking in different voices when recognition of governments is at issue. As seen above, in recent cases, the one voice doctrine is still used.[63] In addition, Talmon explains that since the UK stopped explicitly recognising governments, conferring recognition to governments "is still a matter that falls pre-eminently within the Crown's prerogative in foreign affairs".[64]

4   How English Courts Have Dealt with Implicit Recognition

Explicit recognition of governments is very useful for English courts because it allows them to easily adjudicate in accordance with the recognition policy that their government has adopted. In the *British Arab Commercial Bank* case, the High Court of England decided that the NTC was the government of Libya because "the Foreign Secretary's certificate of 24 August 2011 [recognising the NTC] is conclusive".[65] In *Bouhadi* v. *Breish* the High Court of England reasoned that it is "common ground" that when "the British government expressly recognises a new government and certifies as such to the court, this will be binding on the court".[66] In this case, however, unlike the *British Arab Commercial Bank* case, there was no certificate of recognition and the court had to look at other evidence.[67]

Colin Warbrick explains that in the UK before 1980, when governments were expressing recognition explicitly, the status of an authority "was being conclusively determined by the executive certificate".[68] Con-

---

61   Ibid.
62   Ibid.
63   See, for instance, Bouhadi v. Breish, supra note 32.
64   Talmon, *supra* note 16, p. 284.
65   British Arab Commercial Bank case, supra note 8, para. 25.
66   Bouhadi v. Breish, supra note 32, para. 33.
67   For example, the approach from *Somalia* v. *Woodhouse* can be taken. See Bouhadi v. Breish, supra note 32, para. 35.
68   Warbrick, *supra* note 17, p. 94.

stitutionality and effective control of a government were not decisive for courts. Under the new recognition regime (after 1980) the courts have had to adopt a new way to decide which authority in a State is the government.[69] Therefore, the question domestic courts face is the following: now that their governments are not explicitly recognising governments of foreign States and not providing clear guidance, will they examine an authority's constitutionality, its effective control, and other criteria to decide if an authority is a legitimate government? Or, will the courts look for implied recognition from their government's actions?[70]

In *Gur Corporation* v. *Trust Bank of Africa* from 22 July 1986, the question was whether the Republic of Ciskei, declared in 1981 by the South African Parliament to be an independent State, did indeed exist as a separate State with a government and could have *locus standi* in the English courts. The FCO stated in a letter to the court, dated 1 May 1986, that HMG does not recognise governments, and that HMG's attitude "is to be inferred from the nature of its dealings with the regime concerned and in particular whether Her Majesty's Government deals with it on a normal government to government basis."[71] In a second certificate of 16 May 1986 the FCO stated that HMG "does not have any dealings with the 'Government of the Republic of Ciskei' or with 'the Department of Public Works, Republic of Ciskei.'"[72] The High Court of England decided that, since the British government had made representations to the South African Government in relation to certain matters occurring in Ciskei, this clearly implied that the British government considered the government of South Africa as exercising sovereign authority over Ciskei.[73] It was decided that the government of Ciskei, though, had *locus standi* in the English courts, because it was regarded as a "subordinate body set up by the Republic of South Africa to act on its behalf."[74]

69　*Ibid.*
70　Warbrick writes: "[t]he domestic implications of the new policy were not easy to discern. Whether the courts would look for 'implied recognition' from the British government's conduct, whether they would switch their attention from formal status to effectiveness, and what, in either case were the evidential consequences, would become apparent only in practice" (Warbrick, *supra* note 17, p. 92).
71　Cited in *Gur Corporation* v. *Trust Bank of Africa*, *supra* note 11, p. 604.
72　*Ibid.*
73　*Gur Corporation* v. *Trust Bank of Africa, supra* note 11, pp. 624, 626.
74　*Ibid.*, p. 599. It was treated as the German Democratic Republic had been treated in the *Carl Zeiss* case: "a subordinate local government whose acts could be recognized as such" (J. Crawford, *The Creation of States in International Law*, 2nd edition,

In *Somalia* v. *Woodhouse,* the High Court of England stated that before 1980, recognition given by the British government "was the decisive matter and the courts had no role save to inquire of the executive whether or not it had recognised the government in question".[75] Following 1980, the court could no longer rely on its government's explicit recognition to decide whether or not a government is a government.[76] According to the court, it was clear that the British government did not recognise any effective government in Somalia.[77] Nevertheless, the court decided to apply a four factor test in order to determine whether or not a government existed in Somalia.[78] It decided that when an English court needs to decide whether a "government exists as the government of a state" the court must look at "(a) whether it is the constitutional government of the state; (b) the degree, nature and stability of administrative control, if any, that it of itself exercises over the territory of the state; (c) whether Her Majesty's Government has any dealings with it and if so what is the nature of those dealings; and (d) in marginal cases, the extent of international recognition that it has as the government of the state."[79] Ultimately, it was found that there was no government in Somalia, in line with the opinion of the British government.[80]

The *Sierra Leone Telecommunications* v. *Barclays Bank* case concerned Sierratel, a company owned by the government of Sierra Leone, the Kabbah government.[81] Sierratel had an account with Barclays Bank in London which operated under a mandate issued in July 1996.[82] In May 1997, after a *coup d'état* in which military *junta* seized power in Sierra Leone, the UK continued to recognise the Kabbah government, which was democratically elected in February 1996. In December 1997, Barclays Bank received instructions from Freetown, Sierra Leone that new directors had been appointed to Sierratel.[83] The High Court of England held that directors at Sierratel could only be appointed by the government of Sierra Leone, which was not the military *junta,* but the Kabbah government still

---

(Oxford University Press, Oxford, 2006) p. 343; *Carl Zeiss Stiftung* v. *Rayner & Keeler Ltd*, 15 May 1966, House of Lords, [1967] 1 AC 853).
75 *Somalia* v. *Woodhouse, supra* note 43, p. 63.
76 *Ibid.*
77 *Ibid.,* p. 65.
78 *Ibid.,* p. 67.
79 *Ibid.,* p. 68.
80 *Ibid.*
81 *Sierra Leone Telecommunications* v. *Barclays Bank, supra* note 9, p. 501.
82 *Ibid.*
83 *Ibid.*

recognised by the British government.[84] To come to the conclusion that the military *junta* were not the government, the court examined the four factors identified in the *Somalia* v. *Woodhouse*.[85] Interestingly, for the first factor, constitutionality, the court essentially looked at the third factor: statements made by the British government and its dealings with the foreign authority.[86] Additionally, many references to government statements were made where the British government rejected the military coup and requested the constitutional government to be restored.[87] The court's decision not to recognise the military *junta* was, thus, in line with the British government's position.

The dispute of *Kuwait Airways* v. *Iraqi Airways* arose after Iraq invaded Kuwait, dissolved Kuwait Airways, and took possession of ten Kuwaiti aircraft.[88] In the decision from 16 May 2002, the House of Lords, among other issues, decided that Iraq was not the *de facto* government in Kuwait. In this case, there was, again, no certificate of recognition, but in a letter to the House of Lords, the FCO made clear that the British government had "not at any time ... recognised Iraqi occupation or control of Kuwait."[89] According to the House of Lords, this was a "blunt statement" expressing that HMG recognised Kuwait as an independent State, and that it considered the Kuwaiti government as the only *de jure* government.[90] The House of Lords applied the test from *Somalia* v. *Woodhouse*, "the leading decision, following the 1980 decision."[91] It reasoned through all four factors, but when examining the third factor, dealings of the British government, it decided that "an unequivocal position adopted by Her Majesty's Government, even if not formally conclusive, may be compelling, at any rate in the absence of some countervailing and paramount factor."[92] In line with the opinion of the government, the House of Lords

---

84   *Ibid.*
85   *Ibid.*, pp. 506-507.
86   *Ibid.*, p. 509.
87   *Ibid.*, pp. 507-508; *see also* section 5.
88   *Kuwait Airways Corpn* v. *Iraqi Airways Co* (*Nos 4 and 5*), 16 May 2002, House of Lords, [2002] 2 AC 883, paras. 4-5.
89   *Ibid.*, para. 345.
90   *Ibid.*, para. 347.
91   *Ibid.*, para. 351.
92   *Ibid.*, para. 358.

decided that at the time of Resolution 369[93] Iraq was not the *de facto* government of Kuwait.[94]

In *The Queen on the application of Kibris Türk Hava Yollari CTA Holidays v. Secretary of State for Transport* (*Kibris Türk Hava Yollari CTA Holidays*) from 28 July 2009, the question was whether Kibris Türk Hava Yollari (KTHY), an airline company incorporated in Turkey, and its subsidiary, a travel agent company registered in the UK, had the right to receive permits that would allow them to continue to provide flights between Turkey and the UK – flights that would often stop in Ercan, Northern Cyprus.[95] The UK's Secretary of State for Transport declined to grant these permits to KTHY in February 2007.[96] In November 1983, Turkish Cypriot authorities in Northern Cyprus declared the Turkish Republic of Northern Cyprus (TRNC) to be an independent State.[97] In its decision, the High Court of England stated that since 1980 the British government no longer recognises governments,[98] but it examined statements made by the British government regarding the TRNC and Cyprus and concluded that, since 1983, the UK has continued to recognise Cyprus as a State and its government, and has not said or done anything to demonstrate that it has recognised explicitly or implicitly the TRNC as a State, or its government.[99] The court decided that the Secretary of State for Transport's refusal to grant the permits to KTHY was lawful because granting permits would attribute validity to acts of the TRNC's government (which the court cannot do because the TRNC is not recognised), and because granting the permits would constitute recognition of the TRNC (which the British government does not wish to recognise).[100] To add, the court decided that the UK was under a duty not to recognise the TRNC, and granting the permits would

---

93   The Iraqi Resolution 369 "had the purported effect of dissolving KAC [Kuwait Airways Corpn] and transferring its assets, including the ten aircraft, to IAC [Iraqi Airways Company]" (*Kuwait Airways* v. *Iraqi Airways* (*Nos 4 and 5*), *supra* note 88, para. 7).
94   *Kuwait Airways* v. *Iraqi Airways* (*Nos 4 and 5*), *supra* note 88, para. 360.
95   *Kibris Türk Hava Yollari CTA Holidays* case, *supra* note 39, paras. 1-7.
96   *Ibid.*, para. 7.
97   *Ibid.*
98   *Ibid.*, para. 68.
99   *Ibid.*, para. 75.
100   *Ibid.*, paras. 85, 90.

breach this duty.[101] This decision was appealed, but the appeal was dismissed in 2010.[102]

In *British Arab Commercial Bank* from 2011, there was a certificate from the British government recognising the NTC, but there was no certificate regarding the Libyan embassy and its *Chargé d'Affaires*, Mahmud Nacua, stating whether or not it constituted the accredited diplomatic mission of Libya to the UK, and he one of its representatives. However, according to the High Court of England, this question was "unambiguously addressed" in the letters from the FCO to the Bank.[103] In these letters it is clear that the British government considered Nacua as the accredited representative of Libya in the UK.[104] Thus, in line with the government's position, the court accepted that Nacua was on an accredited diplomatic mission. In all these cases, the courts speak with one voice with the British government.

According to the High Court of England in *Bouhadi v. Breish* from 2016, in the absence of a certificate of recognition, the *Somalia v. Woodhouse* approach should be taken.[105] In the end though, in *Bouhadi v. Breish* the court did not examine the four factors from *Somalia v. Woodhouse*, but rather relied on a letter sent by the FCO to the court to come to its conclusion. The FCO stated that HMG recognised neither the authority who chose Bouhadi, nor the one who chose Breish as the government of Libya.[106] Wary of contradicting the British government by favouring either the Tobruk or Tripoli government, the court adjourned the case.[107]

It is important to note that in some of these cases it is difficult to separate recognition of States and recognition of governments, even though

---

101 *Ibid.*, para. 90.
102 *The Queen (on the application of Kibris Türk Hava Yollari, CTA Holidays Limited)* v. *Secretary of State for Transport* v. *The Republic of Cyprus*, 12 October 2010, Court of Appeal (Civil Division), [2010] EWCA Civ 1093.
103 *British Arab Commercial Bank* case, *supra* note 8, para. 26.
104 *Ibid.*
105 *Bouhadi v. Breish*, *supra* note 32, para. 35.
106 See section 3.
107 The High Court of England decided: "the declarations which the court is invited to make would risk cutting across the stated position of HMG. The court is invited to declare that one or other party is chairman of the LIA, but as stated in the letter of 3 March 2016, the government's policy in accordance with the position currently taken by the international community is to place the chairmanship within the sphere of the Government of National Accord. Applying the above case law, public policy points against the court imposing a different solution, particularly on such a sensitive matter" (*Bouhadi v. Breish*, *supra* note 32, para. 49).

they are two different concepts.¹⁰⁸ For example, in *Gur Corporation* v. *Trust Bank of Africa* the issue concerned Ciskei, a non-recognised quasi-independent homeland of South Africa. It is not clear if the question in the case was whether Ciskei was recognised as an independent State, or as a government, or whether it was a combination of both. Ultimately, Ciskei was not recognised as an independent State nor as a government of a State, but as a subordinate body within South Africa.¹⁰⁹ Though in theory recognition of States and governments are distinct concepts, in practice the two may overlap.

5 Interaction or Proof of Interaction is the Most Important Factor for English Courts

Warbrick explains that the test in *Somalia* v. *Woodhouse* allows the court to approach a government recognition question differently "in relation to the purpose for which the question is being asked."¹¹⁰ However, a review of the cases suggests that in every instance it is the third factor, interaction, which is most important. Even if English courts look at many factors (constitutionality, effective control, international recognition, as well as interaction), what seems to carry the most weight is the British government's interaction with the authority or proof of this interaction expressed in statements made by the British government to the court.

Before the four factor test of *Somalia* v. *Woodhouse*, in *Gur Corporation* v. *Trust Bank of Africa* the court recognised the importance of inter-

---

108 Recognition of States is often discussed in combination with recognition of governments, but the recognition of States occurs only once, and is a completely different legal act. States have rights and obligations under international law, whereas governments are the apparatus of the State that "assert rights, incur obligations, exercise powers, and confer immunities on behalf of states" (B. R. Roth, 'Whither Democratic Legitimism?: Contextualizing Recent Developments in the Recognition and Non-recognition of Governments', *American Journal of International Law Unbound* (2015), <www.asil.org/blogs/whither-democratic-legitimism-contextualizing-recent-developments-recognition-and-non> visited on 7 August 2017).

109 *Gur Corporation* v. *Trust Bank of Africa, supra* note 11, p. 599.

110 For example, Warbrick argues that if an authority's ability to exercise a State's rights is in question (for example, whether the authority has standing to sue in court as a government), the court must focus its attention on the political status of the authority. If the validity of acts and decrees is in question, the court must focus its attention on the "administrative effectiveness" of the authority (Warbrick, *supra* note 17, p. 96).

action. Since the British government had made representations to the South African Government in relation to certain matters occurring in Ciskei, it was clear that the British government considered the government of South Africa as exercising sovereign authority over Ciskei.[111] In other words, it was inferred from the British government's conduct and interaction with South Africa that South Africa was still the government in Ciskei and a decision was made accordingly.

In *Somalia v. Woodhouse* it seems that the implied recognition approach was rejected,[112] but it is argued that, on closer examination, this approach was only rejected partially. When the UK declared that it would no longer recognise governments, Foreign Secretary Lord Carrington told the House of Lords that the government's "attitude ... will be left to be inferred from the nature of the dealings, if any, which we may have with it".[113] In *Somalia v. Woodhouse* the High Court of England decided that "the phrase "left to be inferred" is designed to fulfil a need for information in an international or political, not a judicial, context."[114] This decision is in fact only a partial rejection of the implied recognition approach.

First, according to the court the inferred recognition approach may be impractical because the absence of dealings between the British government and an authority cannot be conclusive.[115] This does not mean that the court rejects the possibility that the *existence* of interaction can demonstrate recognition; it only states that the absence of interaction cannot be used to demonstrate conclusively that there is no recognition. Second, the court reasoned that when the British government deals with a foreign authority as a government "on a normal government to government basis ... it is unlikely in the extreme that the inference that the foreign government is the government of that state will be capable of being rebutted".[116] Policy considerations, that the judicial and executive arms should speak with the same voice, would be "paramount".[117] In this case, though, the court states: "[b]ut now that the question has ceased to be one of recognition, the theoretical possibility of rebuttal must exist."[118] Thus, the court recognises that implicit recognition through normal government

---

111   *Gur Corporation v. Trust Bank of Africa, supra* note 11, pp. 624, 626.
112   In particular, Warbrick argues this (Warbrick, *supra* note 17, p. 94).
113   Carrington (HL Debs.), *supra* note 17.
114   *Somalia v. Woodhouse, supra* note 43, p. 63.
115   *Ibid.*
116   *Ibid.*, p. 65.
117   *Ibid.*, p. 66.
118   *Ibid.*

to government interaction can be almost decisive. In this case, though, it is not decisive because the government is not recognising any entity at all. The court has to decide whether a government even exists, which can then be recognised. Third, interaction is included as one of the four factors that must be examined when determining whether a government exists, acknowledging that interaction can demonstrate recognition to a certain extent.

Even if the implied recognition through interaction approach was rejected in *Somalia* v. *Woodhouse*, it continued to play an important role in cases that followed it. In *Sierra Leone Telecommunications* v. *Barclays Bank*, the four factor test was applied, but the emphasis was put on government statements. To decide whether the government was constitutional, the High Court of England referenced: a statement from Tony Lloyd, Minister of State at the FCO, made on 27 June 1997, calling the overthrow of the government in Sierra Leone illegal and requesting the constitutional order to be restored;[119] an FCO letter to Stephenson Hardwood (who instructed Timothy Saloman, for the plaintiff) from 28 November 1997 condemning the *coup* and "looking forward to the restoration of the constitutional order";[120] an FCO letter from 13 January 1998 to Professor Foray, Sierra Leone High Commissioner, which included a written answer to the House of Lords stating the British government's position *vis-à-vis* Sierra Leone.[121] Clearly, the court did not look itself at the situation in Sierra Leone and decide if the military *junta* was constitutional; it looked for the answer from the British government. For the second factor, degree of administrative control, the court evaluated the situation in Sierra Leone. The court used evidence from the Sierra Leone High Commissioner and affidavits.[122] For the third factor, dealings of the British government, the court made a reference to the section in the judgment that discusses constitutionality. The statements that discuss constitutionality also make it clear that the British government is not dealing with the military *junta* as a legitimate government. This demonstrates that, for the first and third factors, the court was essentially looking at interaction and proof of interaction expressed through different statements. Finally, the fourth factor, international recognition, is not exam-

---

119 *Sierra Leone Telecommunications* v. *Barclays Bank, supra* note 9, p. 507.
120 *Ibid.*
121 *Ibid.*, p. 508.
122 *Ibid.*

ined in this case. Thus, interaction seems to have played a primary role in the reasoning of the court for this case.

In *Kuwait Airways* v. *Iraqi Airways*, there was a blunt statement by the British government not recognising the Iraqi occupation of Kuwait, and the court made a decision in accordance with this position. It also stated that an unequivocal position may not be "formally conclusive", but may be "compelling".[123] In *Kibris Türk Hava Yollari CTA Holidays*, the court concluded that the British government did not in any way recognise the TRNC as a State, or its government, and only recognised Cyprus as a State and its elected government.[124] It examined statements made by the British government that demonstrated this. For example, the court cited Mr. Anthony Smith, Director for European Political Affairs at the FCO, who declared: "The UK view is that the Head of State duly elected by the Greek Cypriot community in accordance with the Constitution has remained in office and it therefore continues to recognise the existing State of the Republic of Cyprus."[125] The British government only recognises Cyprus as a State and its government – not the TRNC. In accordance with this position, the court found that it was lawful for the Secretary of State for Transport to refuse to grant permits to KTHY that would allow it to operate flights between the UK and Turkey. Granting the permits would demonstrate recognition of the TRNC, which would go against the policy of the British government, and would also be a breach of the UK's duty not to recognise the TRNC.[126] It is interesting to note that in both the *Kibris Türk Hava Yollari CTA Holidays* and *Kuwait Airways* v. *Iraqi Airways* cases, it is in fact the explicit *non*-recognition of an authority that underlines which authority *is* recognised by the British government.

In *British Arab Commercial Bank*, the letters from the FCO to the Bank were clear enough to demonstrate that the British government recognised Nacua as the Libyan *Chargé d'Affaires ad interim*. In the letters from 8 and 12 August 2011 the FCO explains: "The UK recognises and is now dealing with the National Transitional Council (NTC) ... On 4 August 2011 the Government accepted the nomination of Mr Mahmud Nacua as the Libyan Chargé d'Affaires ad interim, and will accredit him accordingly".[127]

---

123   *Kuwait Airways* v. *Iraqi Airways* (*Nos 4 and 5*), *supra* note 88, para. 358.
124   *Kibris Türk Hava Yollari CTA Holidays* case, *supra* note 39, para. 90.
125   Cited in *Kibris Türk Hava Yollari CTA Holidays* case, *supra* note 39, para. 27.
126   *Kibris Türk Hava Yollari CTA Holidays* case, *supra* note 39, para. 90.
127   *British Arab Commercial Bank* case, *supra* note 8, para. 26.

Capps claims that when the British government still explicitly recognised foreign governments, there existed two models: the immune field model (which essentially is the one voice doctrine: the executive recognises governments, and the judiciary speaks in the same voice) and the judicial competence model. According to the judicial competence model, the court has the competence to decide which authority is the government of a foreign State. It can ask the government for information regarding the authorities in foreign States in order to make that decision, but it is not obliged to follow the opinion of the government.[128] Capps argues that in the *British Arab Commercial Bank* case, a combination of both the immune field model (one voice doctrine) and the judicial competence model was used since the court looked at facts, such as HMG's statements regarding the authorities in Libya, but recognised that if the British government had formally recognised an authority as the government, this would be paramount and the court would not make a decision contrary to the government's position.[129] It is argued that the fact that the court looked at statements that were made by the British government concerning the authorities in Libya in *British Arab Commercial Bank* does not demonstrate that the court found itself competent to decide what authority in Libya was the government, as Capps presents. Rather, examining these statements was merely the way in which the court tried to determine which authority the British government had recognised as the government of Libya, in order to make a decision according to the government's position.

In *Bouhadi* v. *Breish,* the court did not even go through the four factors of *Somalia* v. *Woodhouse* and relied only on the FCO letter to the court that gave good guidance on the government's position. The FCO letter states: "HMG's highest priority is to support the efforts of the United Nations and the international community to establish a Government of National Accord".[130] The letter explains that the Libyan Political Agreement (LPA) was signed in December 2015, and that Fayez Serraj was named in this agreement "as Head of the Presidency Council, which is the body recognised in the LPA that is authorised to exercise the executive authority of the Libyan Government."[131] Interestingly, the letter discusses the British government's interaction with Serraj: "HMG has had ongoing deal-

---

128 Capps, *supra* note 7, p. 236.
129 *Ibid.*, p. 241.
130 *Bouhadi* v. *Breish, Annex, supra* note 33.
131 *Ibid.*

ings with Mr Serraj and other members of the Presidency Council in this capacity since the adoption of the LPA."[132] The court adjourned the case because declaring Bouhadi or Breish as chairman of the LIA would have cut across the position of the British government that recognised neither the Tobruk nor the Tripoli government, but rather supported a Government of National Accord.[133] Proof of interaction, provided in the letter to the court, seems to be the primary source of information that the court used to determine the government's position.

Lastly, though *Ting Lei Miao* v. *Chen Li Hung* is a case from Hong Kong, many significant references were made to English cases, and to the UK's policy of not recognising governments. Also, the dispute arose, and the first decision was given before Hong Kong was handed over from the UK to the People's Republic of China on 1 July 1997. In the decision from 27 June 1997 the High Court of Hong Kong decided that the British government had not recognised the Taiwanese authorities as a *de facto* or *de jure* government and that the Taiwanese bankruptcy order should not be given effect.[134] In the decisions from 2 June 1998, and 27 January 2000, the Hong Kong Court of Appeal, and then the Court of Final Appeal disagreed with the High Court and decided that the Taiwanese bankruptcy order *should* be given effect in Hong Kong, but that this did not mean that Taiwan was recognised as an independent State or as having a *de jure* or *de facto* government.[135] In the last two decisions, due to the handover of Hong Kong to the People's Republic of China, it was not necessary to decide whether or not the British government had recognised Taiwan as a State or government[136] but, significantly, it was nonetheless decided that Taiwan was not recognised as a State or government, in line with the positions of the government of the People's Republic of China and the UK.

In *Ting Lei Miao* v. *Chen Li Hung* from 27 June 1997 specifically, the High Court of Hong Kong made important references to interaction. According to the court, the British government no longer recognises govern-

---

132 Ibid.
133 Ibid.
134 *Ting Lei Miao* v. *Chen Li Hung & Another*, 27 June 1997, High Court, [1997] HKLRD 841, pp. 850, 856.
135 *Ting Lei Miao* v. *Chen Li Hung & Others*, 25-27 February and 2 July 1998, Court of Appeal, [1999] 1 HKLRD 123, pp. 135, 137-138; *Chen Li Hung & Others* v. *Ting Lei Miao & Others*, 27 January 2000, Court of Final Appeal [2000] 1 HKLRD 252, pp. 253, 266-267.
136 *Ting Lei Miao* v. *Chen Li Hung* (1998), *supra* note 135, p. 128; *Chen Li Hung* v. *Ting Lei Miao*, *supra* note 135.

ments, but the FCO would provide the court with information on "what dealings, if any, it [the executive] had with the new regime and the nature of such dealings".[137] For each case, the court would then infer from this information whether a foreign government's acts or orders should have effect.[138] The court decided that the British government did not recognise the Taiwanese authorities as a *de facto* or *de jure* government, and, significantly, that "[t]here were no official dealings between the United Kingdom Government and the authorities in Taiwan on a government to government basis."[139] Indeed, the FCO certificate cited in the case answers only two questions: what government is recognised as the *de facto* or *de jure* government in Taiwan by HMG; and *what dealings* HMG has with any regime in Taiwan.[140]

An exception to the rule that interaction or proof of interaction is the most important factor for English courts when deciding which authority is the government of a State can be found in *Secretary of State for the Home Department* v. *CC and another* from 19 October 2012. Two British citizens were arrested and detained in Somaliland and on returning to the UK they were subject to control orders and Terrorism Prevention and Investigation Measures (TPIMs). In this case heard by the Administrative Court, these control orders and TPIMs were under statutory review.

Lord Justice Lloyd Jones made important comments on recognition of governments when deciding on the status of the authority claiming to be the government of Somaliland.[141] He recognised that since 1980 the British government no longer recognises governments,[142] but stated that the government "has in the present case assisted the court by providing in its letter of 16 July 2012 information about the nature of the dealings Her Majesty's Government has with Somaliland."[143] According to Lord Justice Lloyd Jones, this letter is not binding on the court but is "impor-

---

137 *Ting Lei Miao* v. *Chen Li Hung* (1997), *supra* note 134, p. 842.
138 The High Court of Hong Kong decided: "[i]t was then left to the courts in receipt of a certificate issued by the Foreign and Commonwealth Office to infer in individual cases and for the purposes of those cases whether the acts or steps in question which had been taken by the foreign government concerned should be given effect to" (*Ting Lei Miao* v. *Chen Li Hung* (1997), *supra* note 134, p. 842).
139 *Ting Lei Miao* v. *Chen Li Hung* (1997), *supra* note 134, p. 842.
140 *Ibid.*, p. 849.
141 *Secretary of State for the Home Department* v. *CC and another*, 19 October 2012, Queen's Bench Division Administrative Court, [2012] EWHC 2837 (Admin), para. 120.
142 *Ibid.*, para. 121.
143 *Ibid.*, para. 123.

tant evidence".[144] He referenced the *Somalia* case and decided that it was necessary to look at the four factors established in *Somalia* in order to decide on the status of the authority in Somaliland.[145] Using the evidence contained in the FCO letter, Lord Justice Lloyd Jones concluded that the *de facto* government in Somaliland was the Somaliland administration, not the Transitional Federal Government (TGF).[146] Indeed, according to the FCO letter (as cited by the court), "HMG does acknowledge that the Somaliland administration has effective control, and exercises de facto administrative authority, over all the territory of Somaliland, except parts of the border regions of Sool and Sanaag"[147] and "in practice, given the ongoing instability in south central Somalia, the authority of the Transitional Federal Government does not currently extend to Somaliland".[148] Thus, in this case, Lord Justice Lloyd Jones truly examined the four factors established in the *Somalia* case, especially the effective control factor, and made a decision accordingly. The dealings between HMG and the Somaliland administration were just one factor among others that were examined in the decision.[149]

However, importantly Lord Justice Lloyd Jones did not decide whether the Somaliland administration was the *de jure* government of Somaliland, but rather only decided that the "Somaliland administration is performing the functions of a government within that part of Somaliland".[150] If the court had decided which authority was the *de jure* government of Somaliland, and not only what authority was performing, in practice, the functions of a government, perhaps interaction between HMG and that authority would have been more significant.

5.1 Recognising Acts or Orders of a Foreign Authority Does Not Necessarily Constitute Recognition of a Government

Interaction is the most important factor, it seems, except when domestic courts need to decide if acts or orders by an authority are valid.[151] Warbrick explains that when this is at issue, more attention should be paid to the administrative effectiveness of the government (second factor in

---

144 *Ibid.*
145 *Ibid.*, para. 122.
146 *Ibid.*, para. 131.
147 *Ibid.*, para. 124.
148 *Ibid.*, para. 126.
149 *Ibid.*, para. 129.
150 *Ibid.*
151 Warbrick, *supra* note 17, p. 96.

Somalia v. *Woodhouse* test).[152] However, this does not contradict the argument that interaction is the most important factor when courts have to deal with recognition of governments, since recognising certain acts and orders of an authority is not equivalent to recognising a government as being legitimate. A court can accept an act or order as being valid, without recognising the authority.

In its Advisory Opinion, *Legal Consequences for States of the Continued Presence of South Africa in Namibia (South West Africa) notwithstanding Security Council Resolution 276* from 1971, the ICJ decided that official acts performed by the South African government in Namibia were "illegal and invalid" but that "this invalidity cannot be extended to those acts, such as, for instance, the registration of births, deaths and marriages, the effects of which can be ignored only to the detriment of the inhabitants of the Territory."[153] In *Hesperides Hotels* v. *Aegean Turkish Holidays* from 23 May 1977, which dealt with the seizure of hotels in North Cyprus, Lord Denning of the Court of Appeal decided: "I would unhesitatingly hold that the courts of this country can recognise the laws or acts of a body which is in effective control of a territory even though it has not been recognised by Her Majesty's Government de jure or de facto".[154] Acts and orders can be given effect, however, as long as this does not go against public policy considerations.[155] In *Kibris Türk Hava Yollari CTA Holidays* from 2009, the court decided that it is "obliged to refuse to give effect to the validity of acts carried out in a territory which is unrecognised unless the acts in question can properly be regarded as regulating the day to day affairs of the people within the territory in question and can properly be regarded as essentially private in character."[156]

Therefore, recognising certain acts or orders as having effect does not necessarily constitute recognising the issuing authority as a government. Even if effectiveness is a more important factor when deciding whether to give effect to acts or orders, this does not contradict the statement that interaction is ultimately the most important factor when recognis-

---

152   *Ibid.*
153   *Legal Consequences for States of the Continued Presence of South Africa in Namibia (South West Africa) notwithstanding Security Council Resolution 276 (1970)*, 21 June 1971, ICJ, Advisory Opinion, para. 125, <www.icj-cij.org/files/case-related/53/053-19710621-ADV-01-00-EN.pdf>, visited on 8 August 2017.
154   *Hesperides Hotels* v. *Aegean Turkish Holidays*, *supra* note 12, p. 218.
155   *Ibid.*
156   *Kibris Türk Hava Yollari CTA Holidays* case, *supra* note 39, para. 90.

ing governments, since recognition of acts and orders, and recognition of governments are two separate issues.

6 Interaction Should be the Most Important Factor for English Courts

Interaction seems to be the primary consideration for English courts, and it is argued that it *should* be the primary consideration for two reasons. First, the government and domestic courts should speak with the same voice concerning recognition of governments,[157] and the practice of implicit recognition through interaction has now replaced the formal act of explicit recognition. Thus, examining interaction and proof of interaction is the best way for the court to determine the voice of the government and make a decision accordingly. Second, governments are in a better position than are the courts to evaluate constitutionality and effective control in order to grant recognition; if possible, English courts should leave such evaluations to governments.

Governments continue to express recognition, but they are doing so implicitly.[158] Talmon writes: "the policy of recognizing States, not governments, is only abolishing (or playing down) formal public statements on the recognition of governments but not the concept of recognition of governments as such."[159] For example, when a government is replaced by another authority through a *coup d'état*, States do not need to explicitly recognise the new government; they can implicitly recognise it by having diplomatic relations with it.[160] Jure Vidmar explains that in situations where there are competing authorities in a State, "actions of states imply their views with regard to the problem of which government is considered to be the legitimate representative of a certain state".[161] De Wet writes that formal statements are less common, but States still rec-

---

157   *See* section 3.
158   Indeed, this is possible because implicit recognition can produce the same legal effects as explicit recognition (*see* section 7).
159   Talmon, *supra* note 5, p. 7. As well, Talmon writes: "[r]ecognition is a unilateral act performed by the recognizing State's government. It may be express or implicit. The act of recognition does not necessarily require the use of the terms recognition or recognize. Recognition is more than a word. A State may simply say that it acknowledges, regards, considers, deals with, or treats a group in a certain capacity, in order to convey its recognition" (Talmon, *supra* note 3).
160   Talmon, *supra* note 5, p. 8.
161   Vidmar, *supra* note 16, p. 152.

ognise a government implicitly "by dealing with them as such."[162] The International Law Commission (ILC), in its *Sixth Report on unilateral acts of States*, explains that recognition of governments "can be performed either explicitly or implicitly",[163] and that "various forms of conduct or acts" can express recognition.[164] Hence, English courts should examine the British government's statements and interaction (its implicit recognition) in order to determine whom it recognises. Examining this interaction is the best way that the court can discern the government's position, and then make a decision in line with this position.

If a court were to look at whether or not a government is constitutional, and whether or not it has effective control, it would be deciding which authority in a foreign State is the government, and essentially making a judgment that has always been in the hands of governments. Courts should be wary of assuming a responsibility which has important legal and political consequences, and for which governments are best prepared. Lauterpacht explained in 1947 that there are "weighty objections" to giving international courts the power to grant *State* recognition.[165] He explains: "there is substance in the view that it is undesirable to burden the court with a task whose implications and potential consequences are of capital political significance."[166] The same can be said about giving domestic courts the power to recognise *governments*: it may be undesirable to give them a task that has such great political consequences.[167] When a government is recognised, it is given the right to assert a State's rights and fulfil its obligations.[168]

As well, according to Talmon, if courts were to apply the criteria from the *Somalia* case in order to determine which authority was the government of a State, this would create "legal uncertainty and indeterminacy".[169] In cases where it is not clear whether or not a government is constitutional,

---

162 de Wet, *supra* note 3.
163 V. R. Cedeño, *Sixth Report on unilateral acts of States, by Victor Rodríguez Cedeño, Special Rapporteur*, (Document A/CN.4/534) para. 25.
164 *Ibid.*, para. 26.
165 Lauterpacht, *supra* note 20.
166 *Ibid.*
167 Indeed, Talmon writes: "in cases where the courts are uncertain as to the status of a foreign regime it has been a long-standing rule of English public law that the proper source of information as to a regime's status is Her Majesty's Government and that the courts are bound to act on the information given to them through the competent Secretary of State" (Talmon, *supra* note 16, p. 278).
168 *See* section 7.
169 Talmon, *supra* note 16, p. 285.

Talmon argues the authority may be regarded as constitutional by some courts and not by others.[170] Further, " 'degree' and 'stability' of administrative control ... are relative concepts which are often influenced by subjective, especially political, considerations or approval and disapproval or the regime in question".[171] Thus, leaving recognition of governments exclusively up to the courts would create uncertainty in the law, and, since recognition has such great political consequences, political uncertainty as well.

The English courts have acknowledged that recognition of governments should be a task fulfilled by the government executive. In *Gur Corporation* v. *Trust Bank of Africa*, the Court of Appeal reasoned that the executive and judicial arms of the government should speak with one voice, "and that recognition of a foreign state or government is a matter of foreign policy on which the executive is in a markedly superior position to form a judgment".[172] In *Sierra Leone Telecommunications* v. *Barclays Bank* the High Court of England agreed and decided that the government is indeed in a "markedly superior position" to grant recognition to a government or State.[173] In *Ting Lei Miao* v. *Chen Li Hung* from 1997, the High Court of Hong Kong decided that "[i]t was not the function of the court to declare or rule that a particular foreign government was recognised as a de jure or de facto government of the place. The court should not attempt to receive evidence or embark on an inquiry for such a purpose".[174] If it did, it would "run the risk of descending, unnecessarily and undesirably, into the political arena".[175]

In sum, in the absence of explicit guidance from their governments, courts may consider constitutionality or effective control if they need to determine the legitimacy of a government, but they should avoid this, and, indeed, they often can. The court's primary consideration should be their government's interaction or proof of interaction; in most cases these provide a reliable indication of their government's position consid-

---

170 *Ibid.*
171 *Ibid.*
172 *Gur Corporation* v. *Trust Bank of Africa, supra* note 11, pp. 604, 616, 625.
173 *Sierra Leone Telecommunications* v. *Barclays Bank, supra* note 9, p. 506; *see also Gur Corporation* v. *Trust Bank of Africa, supra* note 11, pp. 604, 616, 625; *Kuwait Airways* v. *Iraqi Airways (Nos 4 and 5), supra* note 88, para. 350.
174 *Ting Lei Miao* v. *Chen Li Hung* (1997), *supra* note 134, p. 842.
175 *Ibid.*, p. 849. Rather, the court decided that it should look at the certificate given from the FCO, because though it may not present a conclusive conclusion, it presents conclusive facts that must then be used by the court (*Ting Lei Miao* v. *Chen Li Hung* (1997), *supra* note 134, p. 842).

ering an authority's claim to be the legitimate government of a State. The court can then follow the government's position. If courts were to start evaluating the legitimacy of governments themselves, and making decisions with such great political consequences, they may well be venturing outside the law and into the realm of politics.

7 The Problem of Implicit Recognition for English Courts

Though English courts should be looking primarily at interaction or proof of interaction in order to determine the opinion of their government and then make a decision accordingly, this approach is not without its difficulties. Recognising a certain authority as the *de jure* government of a State creates a new legal situation. For instance, when recognition is given, the recognised government gains *locus standi* as the government of the State in the courts of the States that have recognised it.[176] Further, for the exceptional situation of intervention by invitation, only a recognised *de jure* government will have the right to request military intervention on its territory from other States.[177] Recent events in Syria, for example, have renewed the debates on who in a civil war has the legal authority to request civil intervention, or even if such requests are legal during a civil war.

Implicit recognition through interaction can produce the same legal effects as explicit recognition through a formal statement. Talmon explains that, by interacting with an authority as a government, having diplomatic relations with it, giving it access to assets in the UK, and giving it *locus standi* in the English courts, for example, the British government will have recognised a government,[178] and thus, produced a new legal situation – one that would have also been created through explicit recognition.

---

176 A recognised *de jure* government can negotiate and conclude treaties; it has accredited ambassadors; it has the right to send representatives to international organizations; it has the right to manage the State's natural resources, and assets at home and abroad; it can have official (and diplomatic) relations with other States whose governments have recognised it; and the head of State and the State's ministers will enjoy immunity when travelling to other States whose governments have recognised it (de Wet, *supra* note 3; Talmon, *supra* note 3).
177 de Wet, *supra* note 3.
178 Talmon, *supra* note 5, p. 7.

However, implicit recognition through interaction *can* create a new legal situation, but it does not always, which is indeed one of the reasons it poses such a problem for English courts. First, interaction will not constitute recognition when it is accompanied by a statement declaring that it does not. After the *coup* in the Gambia on 23 July 1994, the British government sent an envoy to meet with the *junta*. Sources from the FCO clarified that this meeting with the *junta* did not "imply recognition of the new government".[179] To add, in 1989 Minister of State for Foreign and Commonwealth Affairs William Waldegrave declared that interactions with any party in Cambodia should not be taken as HMG's recognition of any of these parties as the legitimate government of that State. He stated: "neither our recognition of the reality of the situation, nor any other action of ours implies recognition of the coalition Government of Democratic Kampuchea or any other party as the legitimate Government in Cambodia."[180]

Second, and more importantly, sometimes interaction occurs merely because States should cooperate not to impede the normal business of everyday life,[181] or to look after its interests. For instance, Serbia meets with the authorities of Kosovo to address security problems, but maintains that it does not recognise Kosovo as a State.[182] Serbia claims that it is dealing, not with the government of an independent State, but with the leaders of the Provisional Institutions of Self-Government of Kosovo (PISG) established under the UN Resolution 1244, whereas Kosovo believes the PISG to be obsolete.[183] Having only implicit recognition (expressed through interaction) as guidance from the government can be problematic for English courts because it is not clear how much interaction or what types of interaction will constitute recognition. Though

---

179 I. Black, 'British envoy meets Gambian coup leaders as Commonwealth faces latest threat to democracy', *The Guardian*, 26 July 1994, p. 11; cited in Talmon, *supra* note 5, footnote 18; *see also* T. Baldry, HC Debs., vol. 248, cols. 1027-8W, 1 November 1994, <hansard.millbanksystems.com/written_answers/1994/nov/01/the-gambia#column_1028w>, visited on 8 August 2017.

180 W. Waldegrave, HC Debs., vol. 160, col. 46, 13 November 1989, <hansard.millbanksystems.com/commons/1989/nov/13/cambodia#column_46>, visited on 8 August 2017; Talmon, *supra* note 5, footnote 18.

181 *See Namibia* Advisory Opinion, *supra* note 153, para. 125.

182 J. Ker-Lindsay, 'Engagement without recognition: the limits of diplomatic interaction with contested states', 91:2 *International Affairs* (2015) p. 278.

183 *Ibid.* It is also accepted "that meeting with officials of a contested state, no matter how senior, in the framework of a peace process does not amount to recognition" (*Ibid.*, p. 276).

looking primarily at interaction is the most reasonable approach in the absence of explicit recognition, it leaves courts with the difficult task of drawing the line between what is merely interaction, and what is interaction that implies recognition.

8 Concluding Remarks: What Does All This Mean for the General Doctrine of Recognition of Governments?

When recognition of governments is at issue, English courts must speak in the same voice as their government, but since 1980, they have had to do this without explicit recognition from the British government as guidance. An analysis of recent cases suggests that, when recognition of governments is at issue, English courts will focus primarily on interaction or proof of interaction to determine the position of their government and make a decision in accordance with this position.[184] Even in *Somalia v. Woodhouse*, this implied recognition approach was only partially rejected, and the High Court of England admitted that when the British government deals with a foreign authority as a government it is "unlikely in the extreme" that the conclusion that this authority is the government will be rebutted.[185]

The implications of this recent practice in the English courts for other domestic courts, and for the doctrine of recognition of governments in general is manifold. First, the problem that the English courts face is important not only in other jurisdictions, such as the US and Canada where a formal statement is conclusive,[186] but also in jurisdictions where a formal statement has only probative value. Though a formal statement has only probative value in European jurisdictions,[187] for example, this does not mean that the absence of a formal statement will not be felt. Thus,

---

[184] For example, in *Sierra Leone Telecommunications* v. *Barclays Bank* the government did not recognise the military *junta*, and neither did the High Court of England. The court mostly looked at the British government's statements regarding Sierra Leone. In *Bouhadi* v. *Breish* the government did not recognise the Tobruk or Tripoli authorities, and the High Court of England decided that neither authority was the government (*Sierra Leone Telecommunications* v. *Barclays Bank*, *supra* note 9; *Bouhadi* v. *Breish*, *supra* note 32).

[185] *Somalia* v. *Woodhouse*, *supra* note 43, p. 65.

[186] Talmon, *supra* note 13; *Chateau-Gai Wines Ltd* v. *Canada*, *supra* note 13, para. 28.

[187] Talmon, *supra* note 13.

the problem discussed in this paper has relevance for many domestic courts in many jurisdictions.

Second, examining English case law has illustrated how recognition of governments has evolved from explicit to implicit recognition, and how the focus on this concept has, or at least should, shift from determining *what criteria* are met for recognition to be given, to determining *at what point* recognition is in fact given. For example, several scholars, including de Wet, Vidmar, and Akande, explain that the starting point,[188] or the "crucial yardstick",[189] for recognising *de jure* governments is effective control over territory;[190] when this criterion is met, recognition will often be implied. However, now that recognition is no longer explicit, the question which seems to be most pressing, at least for domestic courts, is not in what circumstances recognition is given, but when exactly recognition is given. In short, what government statement, what interaction, and how much interaction will constitute recognition?[191]

Indeed, this analysis of case law shows that more attention should be paid to interaction as the expression of implicit recognition. In the cases cited, the position of the government was quite clear. For example, in *Bouhadi* v. *Breish* the FCO had written to the court and stated that it recognised neither the Tobruk nor the Tripoli government.[192] In *Kuwait Airways* v. *Iraqi Airways*, the British government had clearly not recognised the Iraqi occupation and control of Kuwait.[193] However, the government's position may not always be so clear, and not all interaction constitutes recognition. Implicit recognition through interaction *can,* but does not always, produce the same legal effects as explicit recognition.[194] Since interaction, as argued, has such an important role to play for, at least, English domestic courts, more attention should be paid to how much interaction, and what types of interaction constitute recognition.

Third, the idea behind the Estrada Doctrine is that States should avoid meddling in the internal affairs of other States and infringing on their

---

188 de Wet, *supra* note 3.
189 J. Vidmar, 'Democratic Legitimacy Between Port-au-Prince and Cairo: A Reply to Erika de Wet', *American Journal of International Law Unbound* (2015), <www.asil.org/blogs/democratic-legitimacy-between-port-au-prince-and-cairo-reply-erika-de-wet>, visited on 8 August 2017.
190 *Ibid.*; Akande, *supra* note 27; de Wet, *supra* note 3.
191 According to Talmon, there are different types of dealings, and the court now has the task of interpreting those dealings (Talmon, *supra* note 16, pp. 266-67).
192 *Bouhadi* v. *Breish, Annex, supra* note 33.
193 *Kuwait Airways* v. *Iraqi Airways (Nos 4 and 5)*, *supra* note 88, para. 345.
194 *See* section 7.

sovereignty.[195] However, it is questionable whether States that have adopted this doctrine have in fact stopped interfering in the internal affairs of other States, since they still recognise authorities, though implicitly. In fact, the switch from explicit to implicit recognition just passes on the burden of officially deciding which authority is the legitimate government of a State to courts, who cannot avoid this when a dispute concerning recognition arises.

Fourth, recognition of governments has always been weighted with political and legal considerations, and continues to be so weighted, despite the shift from explicit to implicit recognition. Recognition is a political act[196] governed by some international legal rules[197] which creates a new legal situation. Since domestic courts, the judicial rather than the executive arm of the State, are now making decisions on recognition without explicit guidance of their governments, it would appear that this act has become increasingly legal and less political. However, since, ultimately the courts will follow the recognition policy of their governments, and simply determine this policy by looking primarily at interaction, the decision is still made by the government and the court will still follow. Thus, recognition remains a political act, and perhaps even more so than before, when governments practiced explicit recognition.

Fifth, an examination of English case law and the dynamic between the English courts and the British government suggests that recognition of governments has, not only remained political, but has shifted even further from law into politics.[198] According to Vidmar, the fact that recognition of governments is "not a one-time act" opens the door to more political influence.[199] Since governments have adopted the Estrada Doctrine and the practice of implicit recognition, it appears that the act has become even more flexible; courts decide recognition on a case-by-case basis and now governments can do the same. Though they no longer make formal statements, the British government continues to inform the court of its position and of its dealings with certain authorities at the time of

---

195 Jessup, *supra* note 2, pp. 719-720; *see* section 2.
196 Vidmar, *supra* note 16, p. 136.
197 For example, recognising a government prematurely may constitute an internationally wrongful act that will give rise to State responsibility (Talmon, *supra* note 13).
198 Talmon writes: "[s]ome have argued that the new policy was undesirable because it was likely to lead to the overt politicization of the judiciary" (Talmon, *supra* note 16, p. 232).
199 Vidmar, *supra* note 16, p. 151.

the case.[200] Since the British government no longer explicitly recognises governments, it can decide its position and express this position when a dispute arises. If its position and interaction shifts, the government can simply express this new position to the court if another dispute concerning that authority arises. Indeed, the government may be less constrained to change its position when it has expressed this position not in a formal certificate of recognition, but only in reference to a specific issue at a specific time before the courts.

To conclude, the difficulties that were created when governments began adopting the Estrada Doctrine will not be easily resolved. As a start, it may be useful to acknowledge that implicit recognition may not be recognition at all. When explicit recognition is given, there is a legal act of recognition: the government issues a formal statement recognising an authority, and this creates certain legal consequences.[201] Implicit recognition, on the other hand, is implied through government policy and interaction. It can create the same legal situation as explicit recognition, but does so by very different means. Thus, explicit recognition can be described as recognition, but implicit recognition, expressed in all its forms of interaction, may be better considered as a form of acceptance.

---

200 For example, the FCO letter in *Bouhadi* v. *Breish* represents an example where the British government informed the court of its position towards the authorities in Libya (*Bouhadi* v. *Breish, Annex, supra* note 33).

201 A. Schuit, 'Recognition of Governments in International Law and the Recent Conflict in Libya', 14 *International Community Law Review* (2012) p. 383; Vidmar, *supra* note 16, p. 137.